Betty Crocker's
CAKE and
FROSTING MIX
COOKBOOK

Illustrated by Alice Golden

GOLDEN PRESS NEW YORK

FIRST EDITION

FIRST PRINTING

Dear Friend,

In the past, making a cake was a great deal of work. Consider, for example, the 18th century recipe for "Nun's Cake," which called for creaming butter, eggs and sugar for two arm-aching hours. Or recall colonial days, when American homemakers developed the rich Pound Cake; it was made with one pound each of sugar, butter and flour—and a half a day's work.

Frostings were equally time-consuming and tedious to prepare. Here is a 1774 recipe: "...24 eggs to be beaten well with a whisk for two or three hours, then spread on a cake with a thin, broad board or a bunch of feathers."

However, in the 1940's "came the revolution"—the appearance of cake and frosting mixes. Ease and convenience are now the hallmarks of cake-making, and the woman of today can be a mix-minded artist.

Because every artist must know the basics, this book begins with the mix fundamentals. Then—on to the creative secrets, with shortcut ways to showy masterpieces. Next the recipes, easy to follow, with many additions, variations and decorating ideas, so you can suit the cake to the occasion.

With this book in hand, you can stretch your imagination—experiment with the new and improvise with the old. Mixes, a boon to the busy and vital woman of today, put the artistry of cake and frosting making within everyone's reach. So, to express the artist in you—say it with cake.

Cordially,

Betty Crocker

P.S. All the recipes in this book have been tested for you in our kitchens at General Mills and by homemakers across the country according to our policy.

Contents

CAKES LIKE MAMA MADE

Buttermilk Chocolate Cake. Good as Grandma's! Big, oven-fresh squares of cake that melt in the mouth are made from our German Chocolate Cake Mix; you add old-fashioned buttermilk and top with rich Coconut-Pecan Frosting. See page 36.

Cake and Frosting Previe

SNACKING WITH SWEETS

Dessert Sandwiches. It's a sandwich...it's a cake ...it's a perfect after-school snack! Made from two slices of cake with a favorite frosting spread between. Cut into thirds for dainty tidbits, pack in a lunch box or serve with mix-and-match frostings at an informal party. See page 57.

HAPPY BIRTHDAY, DEAR EVERYBODY

Balloon Cake. Gay as carnival days, this cake for a favorite birthday child flies a festive cluster of pastel candy mint "balloons" on licorice strings. See page 58.

WHEN COMPANY COMES

Caramel-Nut Cake Ring. This golden, nut-rich caramel coffee cake is made with ease from our Yellow Cake Mix. You can expect it to cause delighted approval at your next coffee party. See page 78.

CALENDAR CAKES

Della Robbia Cake. Our beauteous Christmas cake, wreathed in marzipan, was inspired by the work of the 15th century Florentine sculptor whose name it bears. See page 108.

ONCE IN A BLUE MOON

Twin Heart Bridal Shower Cake. This romantic cake gives a message as tender as its feathery white texture. Make it for a wedding, a bridal shower or an anniversary party. See page 118.

CAKES FOR THE CONNOISSEUR

Gâteau Parisienne. A cake for sophisticates—tall, delicate angel food with subtly flavored crème de cacao whipped cream frosting and a beautiful garnish of frosted green grapes. See page 128.

On the Cover

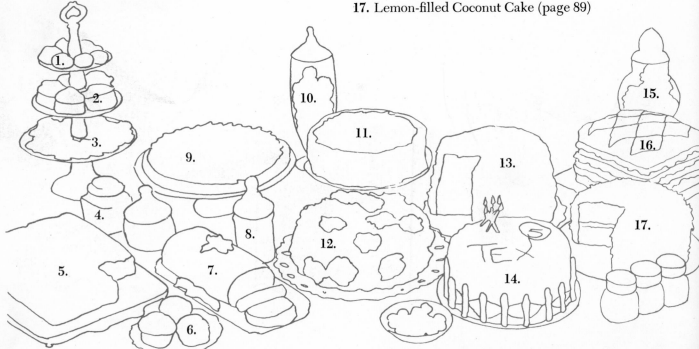

CAKE MIX BASICS

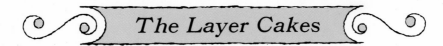

The Layer Cakes

The One Important Rule

Read the directions on the package carefully each time you prepare a cake mix. Directions may change as research works to produce ever finer ingredients.

Do's and Don'ts

Do use the pan sizes recommended on the package.

Do grease pans generously and dust with flour to prevent cake from sticking. See page 8.

Do time your beating exactly, using a clock or a timer. Overbeating can break down cake structure, causing lower volume.

Do heat your oven to the correct temperature.

Don't add to or subtract from the number of eggs called for. Too many eggs toughen the cake; too few make it crumbly.

Don't substitute milk for water. Dried milk is already in the mix.

A Few Hints to Start

To measure water: Use liquid measuring cup to prevent spilling. With measuring line at eye level, pour liquid into cup.

To mix batter: First, moisten ingredients by blending at low speed on standard or portable mixer. Continue beating according to package directions, using a rubber scraper to push batter from sides and bottom of bowl.

If mixing by hand, beat 150 strokes for each minute of mixing time specified. You can stop and rest when your arm gets tired; just be sure to keep track of the number of strokes.

Pan Pointers

Directions usually call for two layer pans, each of which is 1½ inches deep and 8 or 9 inches in diameter— or one oblong pan, 13x9x2 inches. Pans should be measured across the top, from inside edge to inside edge.

Many pans have the size marked on the back; with these, you can see at a glance if you have the right size pan.

The one in the middle is your cake, naturally! The one at the top was baked in a pan that was too small and the batter ran over. The cake at the bottom was baked in a pan that was too large. It is pale, flat on top and has low volume. But the cake in the middle is just right. It has a gently rounded top and a light golden brown crust, indicating that it was baked in the correct size pan.

9"x9"x2"
TOO SMALL

13"x9"x2"
CORRECT

If directions call for an oblong pan, 13x9x2 inches, use it. An 8- or 9-inch square pan will be too small. If there is too much batter in a pan, it may run over or the cake may fall. If this happens, the texture will be compact and heavy.

The material of the pan is also important. This cake was baked in a shiny metal pan, which reflects heat away from the cake and gives the tender, light brown crust you want. Here half the cake has been turned upside down so you can see that both top and bottom are baked to just the right degree of brownness.

Don't use enamel or dark metal pans! If they are used, too much heat is absorbed and the cake will be too brown and crusty.

If you don't have shiny metal pans, you can bake a cake in a heat-proof glass pan. Just lower the oven temperature 25 degrees; use the same baking time given in the recipe.

Pan Preparation

To prepare pans, grease bottoms and sides generously with solid shortening (*not* butter, margarine or oil), using at least ½ tablespoon for each layer pan. Use a narrow paintbrush, pastry brush or waxed paper to spread it evenly.

Dust each greased pan with about ½ tablespoon flour, until well coated on bottom and sides. Remove any excess flour by inverting pan and tapping gently.

For teflon-lined pans, follow manufacturer's instructions.

Betty Crocker Note: If you prefer, pans can be greased and lined with commercial paper liners or waxed paper cut to fit the bottoms of pans. There are also special pans with detachable bottoms for easy removal of cake. Like regular pans, these should be greased and floured well.

Cake Baking Clues

Pour batter into prepared layer pans or oblong pan. Divide the batter evenly between layer pans.

Place pans on middle rack at least 1 inch from sides of oven. Pans should not touch. This permits proper circulation of heat, necessary for the layers to bake evenly.

After cake has baked the minimum time, touch center lightly. If no imprint remains, cake is done. Or insert wooden pick in center. If it comes out clean, cake is done.

When you bake a cake, remember:
If you use a temperature lower than that called for in the recipe, your cake will probably be pale, and have a pitted surface, heavy coarse texture, low volume and a flat top.

Baking at a temperature that is too high may well result in a cake with dark crust, cracks and a hump in the center and an uneven texture.

Cooling and Removing

Allow layers to cool 10 minutes on wire racks before removing from pans. If cakes are left in pans too long, they become soggy and difficult to remove.

Now—to remove cake easily from the pan, place a towel over a second cooling rack. Place the covered rack over the top of the cake. Invert the cake and racks together to transfer the cake to the covered rack. (The towel prevents the wire bars from breaking the crust or leaving imprints on top of the cake.)

Carefully lift the pan from the cake.

A warm tender cake may crack if it rests on its rounded top surface. To prevent this, place another wire rack over the bottom of the cake. Hold both racks . . .

. . . and turn right side up. Remove second layer in same manner. Notice that it takes 3 cooling racks to remove 2 layers from pans. Allow layers to cool completely on racks.

Cupcake Clues

Cupcakes have nicely rounded tops and hold their shape best when baked in paper-lined muffin pans. (You don't have to grease or wash pans, either.) Fill muffin cups half full. Bake according to directions.

Baking in Different Pan Sizes

Odd-shaped Pans (for lamb, bell, star, heart and Christmas tree cakes): To measure capacity of an odd-shaped pan, fill pan with water. Measure the water. Use half that amount of cake mix batter. Bake until wooden pick inserted in center comes out clean. Use any remaining batter for cupcakes; bake as directed on package.

Loaf Pans: Follow package directions except—use 2 tablespoons less water. Bake in two greased and floured shiny loaf pans, 9x5x3 inches, for *35 to 40 minutes.*

Miniature Loaf Pans: Grease and flour six miniature loaf pans, 4½x2¾ x1¼ inches, and one layer pan, 8 or 9x1½ inches. Follow package directions for preparing batter. Using about half the batter, fill each miniature loaf pan half full. Pour remaining half of batter into prepared layer pan. Bake small loaves *20 to 25 minutes,* layer *25 to 35 minutes.*

Jelly Roll Pan (sheet pan): Follow package directions except — spread batter in greased and floured jelly roll pan, 15½x10½x1 inch. Bake *25 to 30 minutes.* Cool in pan. Frost and cut into squares to serve. Or, invert cake while still warm onto serving platter or tray. *Makes about 35 two-inch squares.*

Square Pans: Follow package directions except — bake cake in two greased and floured square layer pans, 8x8x2 inches, for *30 to 35 minutes,* or 9x9x2 inches, for *25 to 30 minutes.*

Good Mixer's Guide to Improvising with a Layer Cake Mix

	Follow package directions except—	White	Yellow	Devils Food / Dark Chocolate Fudge / German Chocolate / Milk Chocolate	Honey Spice / Spice 'n Apple	Lemon Velvet
Cherry-Nut	Fold ½ cup finely chopped nuts and ½ cup finely chopped maraschino cherries, well drained, into batter.	*	*	*		*
Maple-Nut	Add 2 teaspoons maple flavoring before mixing. Fold ½ cup finely chopped nuts into batter.	*	*			
Mocha	Stir 2 tablespoons instant coffee into dry mix.	*	*	*	*	
Chocolate-Spice	Add 2 teaspoons cinnamon, ½ teaspoon nutmeg and ½ teaspoon ground cloves before mixing cake.			*		
Nutmeg-Mace	Add ½ teaspoon mace and ½ teaspoon nutmeg before mixing cake.		*	*		
Chipped Chocolate	Fold 2 squares (2 ounces) shaved sweet, semisweet or unsweetened chocolate (about ½ cup) into batter.	*	*	*		
Toasted Coconut	Fold 1 to 1½ cups flaked coconut, toasted, into batter.	*	*	*		*
Orange	Fold 2 tablespoons grated orange peel into batter.	*	*	*	*	*
Chocolate-Mint	Fold ¼ teaspoon peppermint extract into batter.			*		
Mint	Add ¼ teaspoon peppermint extract before mixing cake. Tint, if desired, with red or green food coloring.	*				

Why Isn't My Cake Perfect?

1 **What causes heaviness,** **low volume** **or a rubbery layer** **in a cake?**	• It could be that you either under or overbeat the batter. • You might have used too much water. Be sure to use the exact amount of water called for, no more. See package directions for each flavor. • Maybe your oven was too cool. Be sure your oven controls are accurate; you can have the local utility company check your oven. If this service is not available or is too costly, check it yourself with a reliable oven thermometer. • You didn't "doctor up" the cake mix by adding oil, did you? Our cake mixes contain just the right amount of each ingredient to make a perfect cake. Adding extra oil may upset the delicate balance of the mix formula and cause a failure. For the same reason we do not recommend substituting fruit juice or carbonated beverages for liquid.
2 **Why is my cake dry** **or crumbly** **or both?**	• You may have undermeasured the liquid. Be sure to use the exact amount of water called for, no less. • The oven may have been too hot. Be sure your oven controls are accurate. • You could have overbaked your cake. Most package directions give a range of time. Check when the minimum time has elapsed. • You didn't, did you, use milk in place of water? Our cake mixes contain dry milk solids. Adding milk can make the cake dry and coarse. • Did you skimp or add to the number of eggs?
3 **Why is my cake** **coarse-textured—or,** **why does it have** **holes and tunnels?**	• Underbeating will cause the coarse texture. Beat the *full* time given on the package. See page 7. • Again, the oven temperature could have been too high.
4 **Why did my cake fall?**	• You underbaked it. • The oven temperature wasn't correct. • The pan was too small. Remember, you must use pan sizes recommended. • You couldn't resist—you tested too soon for doneness. Allow the minimum baking time to elapse before opening the oven door. • Something moved or jarred the cake before it was baked.

Why Isn't My Cake Perfect?

5 **What causes** **a wrinkled top** **and extreme shrinkage?**	• Usually too much water. • Or it could be you overmixed. Watch mixing time carefully. Beat cake batter as directed on package. Overmixing actually breaks down the cake structure, causing low volume and extreme shrinkage during the cooling of the cake. • Underbaking also can make your cake fall and look shriveled. • Again, did you add oil to the cake mix?
6 **What causes a cake** **to be humped or peaked** **in the center?**	• The oven temperature may have been too high. • Maybe the pan was too small.
7 **Why does a cake** **have a sticky top?**	• Maybe because of humidity. In humid weather, crusts collect moisture from the air and become sticky. This is especially likely to happen if the cakes are high in sugar content, as these cakes are. • You may have stored the cake while it was still warm. Always allow it to cool thoroughly first. • Perhaps your cake was underbaked, or the oven temperature was too low. • Overmeasurement of liquid could be your problem.
8 **What causes** **a cake to stick** **to the pan?**	• Not greasing the pan enough. • Leaving the cake in the pan too long.
9 **What causes a cake** **to break apart?**	• Cooling it wrong side up. Our tender cakes are even more delicate hot out of the oven. When you turn the cake out on a rack, put another rack on top and quickly reverse the cake so it cools right side up. This will keep it from breaking or cracking.

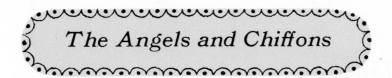

The Angels and Chiffons

The One Important Rule

Same rule, different cakes. *Read the directions on the package carefully each time you prepare a cake mix. Directions may change as research works to produce finer ingredients every year.*

Do's and Don'ts

Do be sure all utensils are free of grease—it could prevent egg whites from beating up as they should. (Avoid plastic bowls; some are porous and may retain an oil film.)

Do use the pan size suggested in the directions. 10x4 inches is standard size. This type of cake is usually baked in a tube pan, which permits heat to come up through the center of the cake, baking it more quickly.

Do heat your oven to the correct temperature.

Do follow the baking time specified. Place pan on the lowest rack of your oven so heat will circulate around the top of the cake.

Don't grease the pan. The batter must cling to the sides if the cake is to rise to full height.

Turn baked cake upside down immediately and support tube on funnel or bottle until completely cool—at least two hours. This prevents the cake from shrinking or falling. Remember, it is very delicate, especially while hot.

Cooling and Removing

Hold a spatula or table knife firmly against the pan, and with short up and down strokes loosen cake from sides and tube.

Next, turn the pan over and hit its edge sharply on the table. Then let the cake slip out and place it on a serving plate.

If you have a teflon-lined pan, be sure to follow the manufacturer's instructions for removing the cake.

Baking an Angel in Loaf Pans

Prepare cake mix as directed on package. Pour batter into two ungreased loaf pans, 9x5x3 inches. Bake *40 to 45 minutes*. To cool, invert immediately after removing from oven. Snap spring-type clothespins on corner of pan for "legs." Or rest edges of pan on two other inverted pans. (See picture for cooling chiffon cakes.)

Baking Chiffon in Other Pans

Chiffon cakes are wonderfully versatile and can be baked in many shapes and sizes.

Pan Size, Temperature and Timing

Oblong pan, 13x9x2 inches
350° for 45 to 55 minutes

Two square pans, 9x9x2 inches
350° for 35 to 45 minutes

Two loaf pans, 9x5x3 inches
350° for 45 to 55 minutes

Two jelly roll pans, 15½x10½x1 inch
350° for 25 to 30 minutes

Muffin cups*
400° for 15 to 20 minutes

*Use paper liners in muffin cups; fill each ⅞ full (about ¼ cup of batter). *Makes about 4 dozen cupcakes.*

Cooling: Snap spring-type clothespins on corners of pan for "legs." Or rest edges of pan on two other inverted pans.

Good Mixer's Guide to Improvising with an Angel Food Mix

Follow directions on package except—

Almond: Add 1½ teaspoons almond extract during last ½ minute of mixing.

Cherry-Nut: After mixing, fold in ½ cup finely chopped maraschino cherries, well drained, and ½ cup finely chopped nuts.

Pastel: Add a few drops red or green food coloring to batter during last ½ minute of mixing.

Rainbow: Divide batter in half. Delicately tint one portion with red or green food coloring. Alternately drop white and colored batters by large spoonfuls into pan.

Pink Peppermint: During last ½ minute of mixing, add ¼ teaspoon peppermint extract. Pour half the batter into pan. Add 3 to 4 drops red food coloring to batter remaining in bowl. Fold in. Pour into pan; marble pink and white batters slightly.

Peppermint Stick: Just before pouring into pan, sprinkle about 4 drops *each* red and green food coloring over batter. Fold in with a few strokes, marbling batter.

Spice: During last ½ minute of mixing, add 1 teaspoon pumpkin pie spice.

My Angel's No Angel! Please Tell Me Why

1 **Why was my angel food cake low in volume?**	● You probably underbeat it. Time the beating carefully and beat according to package directions. Batter should be thick and hold soft peaks. The length of time needed may vary with the type and condition of the mixer. ● Or maybe you greased the pan! *Never* grease angel food pans. The cake must cling to the sides as it rises, and hang from the pan as it cools. If your pan has been used for other bakings, wash it in hot sudsy water.
2 **Why did my angel fall?**	● Maybe you didn't invert the pan immediately after baking. ● Or you may have removed the cake from the pan before it was cool.
3 **Why did my angel food cake fall out of the pan?**	● Perhaps you didn't bake it long enough. Don't open the oven door until the minimum time is up! ● Greasing the pan could do it, as mentioned above. ● You might not have cooled it properly. ● What about the oven temperature—were you precise?
4 **Why did my angel food cake run over?**	● Probably because you didn't use the pan size called for on the package.

Where Did I Go Wrong with My Chiffon?

1 **Why was my chiffon cake low in volume?**	● Maybe you underbeat the egg whites. ● Maybe you overfolded. ● The wrong oven temperature will do it—either too high or too low. ● Could you have removed the cake from the pan before it was cool?
2 **Why did my chiffon cake fall out of the pan?**	● You underbaked it. ● The oven temperature was too low. ● You *greased* the pan? That's the reason.
3 **Why did my chiffon cake have a rubbery layer?**	● You underbeat the egg whites. ● Or you underfolded them. ● You overfolded them.

How to Store, Freeze and Thaw

To Store Mixes

Store in a cool, dry place. Cake mixes will keep in unopened packages up to a year, under normal storage conditions. They contain no ingredients that will deteriorate within that time.

To Store Cakes
(until serving time)

Frosted cakes: Cakes with creamy-type frosting should be kept under a cake safe, a large inverted bowl, or loosely covered with foil, plastic wrap or waxed paper. Cakes with fluffy-type frosting are best served the first day; if necessary to store overnight, use a cake safe or inverted bowl and slip a knife under the edge so container is not completely air-tight.

Cakes with whipped cream or cream fillings should be kept in the refrigerator.

Unfrosted cakes: Allow cakes to cool thoroughly before storing. Cakes covered before they are cool become sticky on top.

To Freeze Cakes

Frosted cakes: Creamy-type frostings freeze best. Fluffy-type frostings freeze well but are difficult to wrap because they stick to the wrapper. To avoid some of the sticking, freeze frosted cakes before wrapping. Or insert wooden picks around the top of cakes to hold wrapping away from the frostings. Wrap in moisture-proof material such as plastic wrap or aluminum foil. To prevent crushing, place frosted cakes or cupcakes in sturdy box and overwrap. Do not store frosted cakes longer than 2 to 3 months. Individual slices can be cut, as needed, for lunch boxes or meals for two—no need to thaw the entire cake.

It is best not to freeze cakes with custard or fruit fillings, for they can make cakes soggy during thawing. Cakes filled with whipped cream can be frozen satisfactorily, following the method described for frosted cakes. However, do not freeze for more than 3 months.

Freezing cake batter is not recommended, because some of the rising capacity may be lost during freezing and thawing. (Bake it instead, and invite the neighbors for coffee and cake—or freeze baked cake for later use.)

Unfrosted cakes: All types of unfrosted cakes and cupcakes can be frozen. Allow cakes to cool thoroughly before packaging. Place baked layers on rounds of cardboard, then overwrap.

Properly wrapped unfrosted cakes remain in top condition for 4 to 6 months.

To Thaw Cakes

Let stand, still wrapped or covered, at room temperature (do not thaw in the oven) for the following length of time:

Frosted cakes: about 2 hours.

Unfrosted layers: about 1 hour.

Cakes with whipped cream: 3 to 4 hours, in refrigerator.

Cupcakes: about 30 minutes.

Individual cake slices: about 5 minutes.

To Bake in Quantity

Make 2 or more of any recipe in this book to serve a crowd. However, we recommend that you prepare only one package of cake or frosting mix at a time.

Yardstick for Yields

Size and Kind	Servings
8-inch layer cake	10 to 14
9-inch layer cake	12 to 16
13x9x2-inch oblong cake	12 to 15
8- or 9-inch square cake	9
angel or chiffon cake	12 to 16

FROSTING MIX BASICS-TO-ARTISTICS

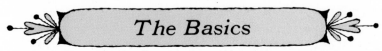
The Basics

Creamy-type frosting mix: Follow the package directions, measuring the water and butter carefully. Then beat until mixture is smooth, glossy and thick enough to spread. If frosting is too thick, add a few more drops hot water. Frost cake immediately for best results.

Ready-to-spread frosting: Open the can and away you go! There's absolutely no preparation with this creamy-type frosting. Just spread with a flourish.

Betty Crocker Note: Each of these convenience frostings will frost two 8- or 9-inch cake layers, a 13x9x2-inch oblong cake, an angel food or a chiffon cake.

Fluffy-type frosting mix: Again, follow the package directions, measuring the water carefully. Be sure beaters and bowl are free from grease so frosting will beat up properly. (Avoid plastic bowls; some are porous and may retain an oil film.) Add *boiling* water (as directions indicate) to insure high, fluffy frosting. Frost cake immediately because frosting sets quickly. Fluffy-type frostings are best served the day they are made.

How to Frost a Two-layer Cake

1. Cool layers thoroughly on cake rack; brush off loose crumbs.

3. Place second layer right side up on filling. First frost sides of cake with a very light coat to seal in crumbs.

5. Spread frosting over the top just to built-up edge. Make attractive swirls or leave smooth for decorating.

2. Place one layer upside down on flat plate. Spread ¼ of frosting almost to outer edge with spatula (choose a metal spatula with a flexible blade; a stiff blade may dig into the cake).

4. Spread more frosting on the sides, using upward strokes. (Bringing the frosting up high on the sides of the cake will result in a nicely shaped frosted cake.)

Tip for the perfectionist: Place your unfrosted cake on four strips of waxed paper, arranged on a cake plate as shown. When cake is frosted, pull out the strips and you'll have a clean plate!

Frosting an Oblong

Place oblong cake, right side up, on an oblong plate or tray to frost sides as well as top. Or leave the cake in the pan and frost only the top (ideal if you're going to take it on a trip).

Frosting Cupcakes Quickly

Twirl the top of each little cake—lightly—in a bowl of fluffy-type frosting. It's the easiest way to achieve pretty frosting peaks. And, look, no extra utensils!

How to "Dress" an Angel or Chiffon

Angels or chiffons can be frosted or they can be glazed with a coat of thin icing. First, cool cake thoroughly, remove from pan and place top side down on a serving plate. Then brush away crumbs and proceed as you would for frosting a two-layer cake.

To frost: Prepare one package of frosting mix. Frost sides of cake first with a very light coat to seal in crumbs. Add more frosting to the sides with up-and-down strokes or swirls. Spread frosting over the top of cake in swirls.

To glaze: Using one of the recipes below, pour and spread glaze over the entire top of cake and allow it to drizzle down the sides. Glaze will set within 30 minutes.

CREAMY ORANGE GLAZE

Beat 1 package (3 ounces) cream cheese at medium speed on mixer until softened. Combine with 2 tablespoons orange juice. Measure half a package Betty Crocker Creamy White Frosting Mix (about 1¾ cups dry mix); blend with cheese mixture. Beat until smooth. Stir in 1 to 2 tablespoons grated orange peel. Pour and spread glaze over top of cake and allow it to drizzle down sides. Refrigerate.

ALMOND GLAZE

Combine ⅓ cup heated milk, 1 tablespoon corn syrup, ¾ teaspoon almond extract and 1 package Betty Crocker Creamy White Frosting Mix (dry mix) in small mixing bowl; beat smooth. If thick, add 1 to 2 tablespoons milk. Pour and spread glaze slowly over top and sides of cake. Sprinkle top with chopped toasted almonds. Glaze will set within ½ hour. Store any leftover glaze in refrigerator.

CREAMY WHITE GLAZE

Measure 1¾ cups Betty Crocker Creamy White Frosting Mix (dry mix) into small bowl; blend in 2 to 3 tablespoons hot water and 1 tablespoon light corn syrup. Beat until smooth. Add 1 to 2 teaspoons more water, if necessary.

Orange: Follow recipe (above) except—substitute orange juice for hot water and add 1 teaspoon grated orange peel.

Coffee: Follow recipe (above) except—add 1 teaspoon instant coffee.

Chocolate: Follow recipe (left) except—use our Chocolate Fudge Frosting Mix.

Mocha: Follow recipe (left) except—use our Chocolate Fudge Frosting Mix and add 2 teaspoons instant coffee.

Lemon: Follow recipe (left) except—use our Lemon Velvet Frosting Mix.

Confetti: Follow recipe (left) except—use our Creamy White Frosting Mix; add ½ teaspoon almond extract and 2 to 3 drops food coloring (red, green or yellow) to match one of the colors in our Confetti Angel Food Cake.

How to Handle the Additions

Melting chocolate: Place chocolate in top of double boiler or small bowl. Set in or over hot (not boiling) water until it melts. Remove chocolate with rubber scraper.

Cutting dates or marshmallows: Use kitchen scissors. Dip scissors in hot water occasionally to prevent them from sticking.

Tinting coconut: Place 1 cup coconut in jar or plastic bag. Mix 1 to 2 drops food coloring with 1 teaspoon water. Add to coconut. Screw on lid or fold over top of bag and shake until coconut is uniformly colored.

Or add about 1 teaspoon colored decorators' sugar to coconut and shake as directed above.

Toasting coconut: Place coconut on a baking sheet. Toast in 350° oven until golden brown, 8 to 10 minutes, stirring frequently. Watch carefully.

Chopping nuts: Chop with long straight knife. Hold point against cutting board and chop through nuts, swinging handle around in quarter circle. Chop coarsely or finely as recipe directs.

Grating peel: Rub washed fruit in short strokes across small area of grater. Grate only outermost colored part of peel.

Spicy coconut: Blend ½ teaspoon cinnamon with ½ teaspoon water. Add coconut and stir until coconut is completely coated with spice mixture. (Perfect for spice layer cake or cupcakes.)

How to Split Cakes for Filling

If recipe calls for split layers, try either of the following methods for slicing layers in half. For best results, be sure cake is completely cool.

4-LAYER CAKES   **3-LAYER ANGEL OR CHIFFON**

Wooden pick markers: Mark middle points on sides of layer with wooden picks. Using picks as guide, cut through the layer with long, thin sharp knife.

Thread trick: Split layer by pulling a piece of heavy sewing thread horizontally, back and forth, through the layer.

Measure cake with ruler and mark into 3 even widths with wooden picks. With wooden picks as guide and using serrated knife, cut with light, sawing motion. (Use same technique for splitting into 4 layers.)

Improvising with a Frosting Mix

EASY VARIATIONS WITH CREAMY WHITE FROSTING MIX

Follow package directions except—

Mocha: Before mixing, add 1½ teaspoons instant coffee.

Mocha-Ginger: Before mixing, add 1½ teaspoons instant coffee. After mixing, fold in 2 tablespoons finely chopped crystallized ginger.

Spice: Before mixing, add ½ teaspoon cinnamon, ¼ teaspoon nutmeg and ¼ teaspoon ground cloves.

Raspberry or Strawberry: Substitute crushed fresh or frozen fruit for water.

Lemon, Orange or Lime: Substitute fruit juice for water.

Raisin-Nut: After mixing, fold in ½ cup chopped raisins and ½ cup chopped nuts.

Raisin-Rum: After mixing, fold in 1 to 1½ teaspoons rum flavoring and ½ cup chopped golden raisins.

Peppermint: After mixing, fold in ½ teaspoon peppermint extract and 3 to 4 drops green food coloring.

Banana-Nut: Blend butter, ⅓ cup mashed banana and ½ teaspoon lemon juice thoroughly into frosting mix with fork. Omit water. Sprinkle cake with chopped nuts.

Maple-Nut: After mixing, fold in ½ teaspoon maple flavoring and ½ cup chopped pecans.

Creamy Cheese: Substitute 1 package (8 ounces) cream cheese, softened and creamed with 1 tablespoon milk, for the butter and hot water.

EASY VARIATIONS WITH CHOCOLATE FUDGE OR DARK CHOCOLATE FUDGE FROSTING MIX

Follow package directions except—

Mocha: Before mixing, add 2 teaspoons instant coffee.

Peppermint Fudge: After mixing, add ¼ to ½ teaspoon peppermint extract.

Rocky Road: After mixing, add 12 marshmallows, finely cut up, or 1 cup miniature marshmallows and ½ cup chopped peanuts.

EASY VARIATIONS
WITH FLUFFY WHITE FROSTING MIX

Follow package directions except—

Mocha: Before mixing, add 2 teaspoons instant coffee.

Nutmeg: Before mixing, add ½ teaspoon nutmeg.

Cinnamon: Before mixing, add 1 teaspoon cinnamon.

Clove: Before mixing, add ¼ teaspoon ground cloves.

Three-Spice: Before mixing, add ½ teaspoon cinnamon, ¼ teaspoon nutmeg and ¼ teaspoon ground cloves.

Banana: Before mixing, add ¼ cup mashed bananas.

Cherry-Nut: After mixing, fold in ⅓ cup chopped well-drained maraschino cherries and ½ cup chopped nuts.

Orange-Coconut: After mixing, fold in 1 tablespoon grated orange peel and ½ cup flaked coconut.

Orange-Raisin: After mixing, fold in ½ cup chopped nuts, 1½ cups raisins and 2 tablespoons coarsely grated orange peel.

Maple-Nut: After mixing, fold in ½ teaspoon maple flavoring and ½ cup chopped pecans.

Peppermint: After mixing, fold in ¼ teaspoon peppermint extract. Red or green food coloring may be added, if desired.

Almond: After mixing, fold in ½ teaspoon almond extract.

Chocolate Chip: After mixing, fold in ½ cup semisweet chocolate pieces.

Nut: After mixing, fold in ½ cup chopped nuts.

Jelly: Beat ½ cup jelly with fork until syrupy. Fold into 1 cup of frosting. Use between layers and on top of cake. Frost sides with remaining frosting.

Gingersnap: Into ⅓ of frosting fold ½ cup gingersnap crumbs. Use for filling. Frost sides and top with remaining frosting. Sprinkle top of cake with more gingersnap crumbs, if desired.

Getting Fancy

Spiral Frosting: Frost cake with any flavor Betty Crocker Creamy-type Frosting Mix prepared as directed on package. Hold spatula at the center of frosted cake; gradually draw the spatula toward you, turning the cake as you do so.

Scalloped Frosting: Frost cake with any flavor Betty Crocker Creamy-type Frosting Mix prepared as directed on package. Press the tip of an inverted teaspoon into frosted cake. Repeat in rows across the cake to complete the design.

Hobnail Design Frosting: Frost cake with Betty Crocker Creamy-type Frosting Mix prepared as directed on package. Pile it very thickly on the top. Then, press down with bowl of spoon, swirl slightly and draw up sharply. Repeat all over cake.

Carnival Frosting: Frost cake with Betty Crocker Fluffy White Frosting Mix prepared as directed on package. Mark top and sides into 8 equal wedges and panels. Sprinkle confetti candy over alternate wedges and press onto alternate side panels.

Allegretti Design: Over hot water melt 1 square (1 ounce) unsweetened chocolate with ¼ teaspoon shortening. Using a teaspoon, drizzle chocolate around top edge of frosted cake, letting chocolate run down sides in uneven lines.

Jelly Swirl Frosting: Frost cake with Betty Crocker Fluffy White Frosting Mix prepared as directed on package. Then swirl your favorite jelly or jam through the frosting, using a spoon or spatula.

Sculpture with Frosting

Shadow Frosting: Frost an oblong cake with Betty Crocker Fluffy White Frosting Mix prepared as directed on package. Over hot water melt 1 square (1 ounce) unsweetened chocolate with ¼ teaspoon shortening. Using teaspoon, drip or pour melted chocolate in parallel lines, about 1½ inches apart, on top of frosted cake. Immediately draw knife or spatula back and forth across chocolate for feathery effect.

Chocolate Swirl Frosting: Frost cake with Betty Crocker Fluffy White Frosting Mix prepared as directed on package. Drizzle 1 square (1 ounce) semisweet chocolate, melted, in swirls over top of frosting.

Dahlia Dream Cake and how to make it: Frost your favorite layer cake with Betty Crocker Fluffy White Frosting Mix prepared as directed on package. Reserve 1 cup frosting and tint yellow. Drop 10 mounds of frosting around center of cake. Draw out with spoon to make petal shapes. Add 10 smaller mounds for second layer of petals, pulling tips up with back of spoon. Pull frosting up to shape center; decorate with silver dragées.

Frosting Designs

Choose the trimming you like best. Almost anything goes: chopped nuts, flaked or shredded coconut, crushed candies . . . popcorn, Daisy°s, Trix cereal . . . or the specially prepared frosting trims like nonpareils, candy sprinkles, silver dragées. Then create your own designs on creamy- or fluffy-type frosting by one of these freehand methods:

1. Draw a design on frosted cake or use cookie cutter dipped in food coloring and pressed into frosting. Fill in design with crushed candies or chopped nuts.
2. Press trim onto the side of frosted cake, using the palm of your hand. To catch spills, place strips of waxed paper on cake plate before cake is frosted (see page 17).
3. Scatter trim over frosted cake in spirals, diagonal stripes, pinwheel design or around the edge for a border.
4. Sprinkle trim over the top of frosted cake for a solid effect or abstract design.
5. For initials or lettering, use silver dragées, semisweet chocolate pieces or red cinnamon candies.

Garnishes for Frostings

Cherry or Kumquat Flowers: Snip well-drained maraschino cherries or fresh or preserved kumquats into 4 or 6 sections, cutting about ¾ of the way down. Spread sections apart gently to resemble petals. Arrange on cake. At side of each flower, place leaves cut from green maraschino cherries or gumdrops.

To flame, soak sugar cubes in lemon extract just before serving. Place a cube in the center of each cherry or kumquat. Ignite cubes with match at serving time.

Brazil Nut Curls: In small saucepan, heat about 1 cup water to boiling. Place about 10 shelled Brazil nuts in water. Remove pan from heat; let stand 5 minutes. Remove one nut at a time and quickly slice lengthwise (with vegetable parer), cutting off paper thin curls of nutmeat. Repeat. Use to trim frosted cake.

Brazil Nut Flowers: Using Brazil Nut Curls (above) for petals, place around candied cherries.

Frosted Grapes: Dip small clusters of green grapes in slightly beaten egg white and then in granulated sugar. Dry on rack.

Chocolate Leaves: Wash and dry about 2 dozen leaves of varying sizes and shapes. Melt 2 squares (2 ounces) semisweet chocolate or ½ cup semisweet chocolate pieces with 1 teaspoon butter. Paint chocolate on backs of leaves about ⅛ inch thick and just to the edges. Chill until firm. Peel off leaves; trim cake with hardened chocolate leaves.

Chocolate Curls: With a vegetable parer or thin, sharp knife, slice across bar of sweet milk chocolate with long, thin strokes. Semisweet or unsweetened chocolate can be used, but curls will be much smaller.

GUMDROP ROSES

For each rose, roll out 3 or 4 large gumdrops on well-sugared board into ovals about ⅛ inch thick. Sprinkle sugar over gumdrops, too, to prevent rolling pin from sticking. Cut ovals in half crosswise for petals.

Roll one half-oval tightly to form the center of the rose. Place additional half-ovals around center, overlapping slightly, and press together at the base. Trim base.

Cut leaf shapes from rolled green gumdrops.

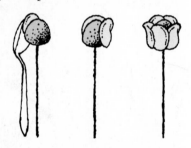

GUMDROP FLOWERS

Make these easy flowers with Decorator Icing (this page) or use Betty Crocker Creamy White Frosting Mix prepared as directed on package and tinted as desired (½ cup makes 5 or 6 flowers).

Put a medium-sized gumdrop on a wooden pick. Fill the tip end of a teaspoon with frosting; level it off along edge of bowl. Draw the spoon down over the gumdrop, making a petal. (Icing must be stiff so shape of flowers holds up.)

Turning the gumdrop, keep adding petals—2 or 3 rows depending on size of gumdrop and shape of spoon.

DECORATOR ICING

One package of frosting mix makes enough to frost and decorate your cake.

Prepare Betty Crocker Fluffy White Frosting Mix as directed on package. Reserve 1 cup. Use remainder to frost an 8-inch layer cake or a 13x 9x2-inch cake. To the 1 cup reserved frosting add 1 to 1½ cups sifted confectioners' sugar, adding a little at a time until frosting is stiff enough to hold its shape. If too thin, blend in more confectioners' sugar. If too thick, blend in a drop or two of water.

Divide and tint with a few drops food coloring. Use in decorating cone for writing, lattice work, borders and simple flowers.

Betty Crocker Note: If recipe calls for 1½ cups reserved frosting, follow directions above except—add 1½ to 2 cups sifted confectioners' sugar.

HOW TO USE A DECORATING CONE

1. With one finger, fit tip tightly into cone. Fill about half full. Fold top as shown to keep icing in.

2. Hold with one hand near top of cone. Use other hand to guide tip. For most work, hold cone at 45° angle.

3. For drop flowers and rosettes, hold cone straight up and down. Press out icing, twist cone and release.
Try a few practice strokes on the back of an inverted cake pan or on waxed paper.

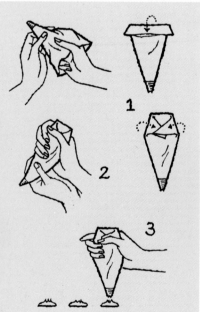

TO MAKE THROW-AWAY CONES

Cut a 15-inch square of parchment or heavy paper into two triangles. Or fold a 12-inch square of waxed paper to form triangle.

Grasping edges with thumb and forefinger, twist to form cone with point at center of longest side (A).

Fold down top edges and fasten cone with transparent tape. Snip off small opening at pointed end (A) for writing and outlining. For leaf designs, cut an inverted V from tip of cone. For shells, cut a series of tiny V's at tip. Metal tips may also be purchased and inserted if desired.

OR make an envelope cone: Place about ⅓ cup Decorator Icing (left) in an envelope; fold sides to make cone. Cut off a tiny corner of envelope to make tip. Refill cone as needed.

FOUR BASIC DECORATING TIPS

TO MAKE ROSES

Use petal tip and flower nail. Hold cone with narrow opening of tip up. Turning flower nail counter-clockwise slowly, press out frosting in tiny circle to form center of rose.

Writing tip is used for writing, numbers, lattice work and delicate tracery.

Petal tip creates petals for roses and other flowers. Also used for ribbons and borders.

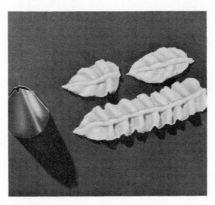

To form first petal, make standing half circle to one side of center. Add 2 more petals, forming triangle. Add petals, overlapping.

Star tip is used to pipe small borders, make simple flowers, rosettes and fancy letters.

Leaf tip makes leaves, long petals, dainty borders and designs.

Remove rose from nail with kitchen shears. Cut almost through base of rose and place on cake. Then cut completely through; ease rose off.

TO MAKE
LILY OF THE VALLEY

Using writing tip, draw a stem line on cake. Then make a double row of dots, one on each side of the stem, pressing in and pulling out to make the little bell effect of the flowers. With leaf tip, make long leaves, crossing them at base.

Betty Crocker Note: To handle roses easily, attach a 2-inch square of waxed paper to flower nail with a dab of frosting. When each rose is completed, remove waxed paper with rose from nail and place on rack until set. Carefully remove from waxed paper with spatula and place in desired position on cake.

Cutting Directions

Use a thin sharp knife or a serrated knife. Insert the point of knife into the cake, keeping the point down and handle up. Slice, pulling the knife toward you. If frosting sticks, dip knife in hot water, or wipe with damp paper towel after cutting each slice.

To cut angels or chiffons, use a light, sawing motion. Or an electric knife does the trick beautifully!

To Cut Layer Cakes for More and Daintier Slices

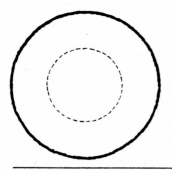

Halfway to the center, cut cake in a circle. Cut pieces from outer circle; then from inner circle. *Makes 28 pieces.*

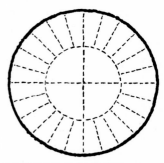

—————————————— OR ——————————————

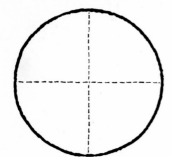

Cut cake into 4 quarters. Then cut each quarter into slices. The pieces closest to the middle of cake can be cut in half. *Makes 28 pieces.*

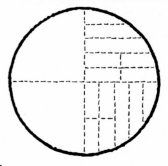

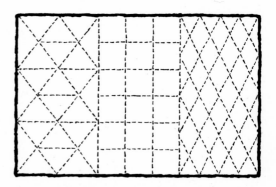

To Cut Oblong Cake for Parties

Cut 13x9x2-inch cake lengthwise into thirds. Then cut diagonally to make diamonds and triangles.

To Cut Sheet Cake for Parties

Cut 15½x10½x1-inch cake into thirds; then cut into diamonds, squares and triangles as shown.

I Have a Frosting Problem!

CREAMY-TYPE

1 **Why is my frosting too thin?**	● Maybe you overmeasured the water. You may be able to thicken frosting by placing bowl in a pan of ice water and beating a little longer. If still too thin, gradually beat in a small amount of confectioners' sugar.
2 **Why is my frosting too thick?**	● Could be you undermeasured the water. Add a few more drops, a little at a time. ● Did you forget to add the butter? ● An interruption—and you had to let it stand too long before frosting the cake. Solution: add a few more drops of water and beat a little longer.

FLUFFY-TYPE

1 **Why didn't my frosting beat up?**	● There was grease on the utensils, perhaps. Be sure all traces of butter, shortening or oil have been removed by washing in hot, soapy water. ● Did you by chance add the flavorings or food coloring at the beginning of the mixing process? These, as well as nuts or coconut, should be added *after* the mixing. ● The bowl may have been too large. A small deep bowl is best. ● Perhaps you used a plastic bowl. It can retain an oil film, remember?
2 **Why was my frosting sticky?**	● You may not have measured the water accurately. ● Are you sure the water was boiling? ● It's possible the humidity was too high. ● Maybe you didn't beat long enough.
3 **Why was my frosting rubbery?**	● Improper storage. Think back, did you slip a knife under the cake safe? ● Consider the humidity—was it extremely *low* that day? ● Overbeating could be the reason. ● Undermeasurement of liquid. That's a familiar failing; use your liquid measuring cup—at eye level, remember.
4 **Why did my frosting seem to disappear, or soak into the cake— or disintegrate the next day?**	● Perhaps you underbeat. ● Could be you frosted the cake before it was thoroughly cooled. ● Improper storage might be the problem (see page 16). ● High humidity, a factor which can result from climate or geographic location. ● Length of storage time. Because fluffy-type frostings are best served the day they are made, enjoy them fresh and you'll have no worries.

CAKES LIKE MAMA MADE

Mama could generate more excitement with her homemade cakes than a parade down Main Street. She did things the hard way, but she did them well. So with nostalgia—and also a sigh of relief—we now re-create those old-fashioned cakes with modern-day mixes. Some are served warm from the oven or broiler—for example, the upside-down or toasted-topping cakes. Some are the traveling kind, such as the frosted oblongs. Others are richer, heavier cakes, so popular with men—the spice and apple cakes and those with fruit fillings. And still another group recalls yesterday's occasional shortcut treatments with sauces, ice cream and jellies. You'll recognize many of the names from the past, but the methods are all up-to-date American.

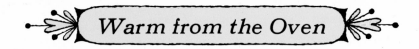

Warm from the Oven

BROILED BANANA CRUNCH CAKE

Forget about bananas having to be eaten fast! This cake won't be around that long.

1 package Betty Crocker Yellow Cake Mix
⅓ cup soft butter or margarine
⅔ cup brown sugar (packed)
¼ cup light cream
1 cup flaked coconut
2 or 3 bananas, peeled

Heat oven to 350°. Prepare cake mix as directed on package. Pour half the batter (about 2½ cups) into greased and floured square pan, 9x9x2 inches. Bake *25 to 30 minutes,* or until cake springs back when touched lightly in center.

Mix butter, brown sugar, cream and coconut. Cut bananas in half crosswise, then slice into lengthwise strips. Arrange in single layer on top of cake. Cover bananas evenly with brown sugar mixture. Broil 3 inches from heat 2 to 3 minutes, or until golden brown and bubbly. Serve warm.

Bake remaining batter in greased and floured 8- or 9-inch round layer pan as directed on package.

BROILED HONEY-COCONUT CAKE

Bake Betty Crocker Honey Spice Cake Mix in oblong pan, 13x9x2 inches, as directed on package. As soon as cake is removed from oven, drizzle ½ cup honey over top and sprinkle with 1 cup flaked coconut; broil a few minutes to toast coconut. Serve warm.

BROILED PINEAPPLE-COCONUT CAKE

1 package Betty Crocker Yellow Cake Mix
1 cup brown sugar (packed)
1 can (8¾ ounces) crushed pineapple, well drained
¼ cup soft butter or margarine
½ cup chopped nuts
½ cup flaked coconut

Bake cake in oblong pan, 13x9x2 inches, as directed on package. Mix brown sugar, pineapple and butter; spread on warm cake. Sprinkle nuts and coconut over top. Broil 3 inches from heat 2 to 3 minutes, or until golden brown and bubbly.

For a Smaller Cake: Follow recipe (above) except—bake cake in layers as directed on package. Use half of topping ingredients for one layer. (Freeze second layer for later use.) *9 servings.*

Also good made with our Tropical Mist, Honey Spice or Butter Brickle Cake Mixes.

Reheating a Broiled Cake?

It's a snap! Just cover with aluminum foil and heat in 350° oven about 10 minutes.

BROILED PRALINE CAKE

Time to rediscover how good a broiled frosting can be. Caramelly, coconutty, crunchy—and warm. Pictured below.

1 package Betty Crocker Yellow Cake Mix
1 package Betty Crocker Golden Caramel Frosting Mix
3 tablespoons soft butter or margarine
3 tablespoons hot water
1 tablespoon light corn syrup
1 cup flaked coconut
½ cup chopped nuts

Bake cake in oblong pan, 13x9x2 inches, as directed on package. In bowl, combine frosting mix, butter, water and corn syrup thoroughly. Stir in coconut and nuts. While cake is still warm, spread topping over it. Broil 3 inches from heat 2 to 3 minutes, or until brown and bubbly. Serve warm with whipped cream, if desired.

Broiled Chocolate-Coconut Cake: Follow recipe (above) except—use Devils Food, Dark Chocolate Fudge, White or Yellow Cake Mix and Chocolate Fudge Frosting Mix.

Broiled Lemon-Coconut Cake: Follow recipe (above) except—use Lemon Velvet, White or Yellow Cake Mix and Lemon Velvet Frosting Mix.

BROILED COCONUT CRUNCH TOPPING

Good on any flavor Betty Crocker Layer Cake Mix.

⅓ cup soft butter or margarine
⅔ cup brown sugar (packed)
¼ cup light cream
1 cup shredded coconut or crushed Wheaties
½ cup chopped nuts

Mix all ingredients. Spread over top of warm 13x9x2-inch oblong cake. Broil 3 inches from heat 2 to 3 minutes, or until golden brown and bubbly.

For 8- or 9-inch square cake: Use 3 tablespoons butter or margarine, ⅓ cup brown sugar (packed), 2 tablespoons cream, ½ cup coconut or Wheaties and ¼ cup chopped nuts.

For Picture-pretty Results

For company or for the family, you'll want your right-from-the-broiler cake to be perfect. Just follow these simple rules:

● Watch closely. Don't let topping burn!

● For neat and easy serving, let cake stand a few minutes before cutting. If necessary, use kitchen shears to help you through the topping.

● Are you an advance-planner? Bake cake ahead of time; put topping on just before broiling.

BROILED CINNAMON CRUNCH TOPPING

Try on any flavor Betty Crocker Layer Cake Mix.

¾ cup brown sugar (packed)
1 tablespoon cinnamon
⅓ cup Gold Medal Flour (regular or Wondra)
¼ cup soft butter or margarine
1 cup chopped nuts
¼ cup milk or light cream

Mix all ingredients. Spread over top of warm 13x9x2-inch oblong cake. Broil 3 inches from heat 2 to 3 minutes, or until golden brown and bubbly.

TOASTED FLUFF TOPPINGS

How do you like your Toasted Fluff Topping? A little spice is nice . . . or sprinkle with nuts, candies or coconut. Serve while the oven-warmth lingers.

Prepare Betty Crocker Fluffy White Frosting Mix as directed on package. Spread on top of cooled cake. Heat oven to 500°. Just before serving, place frosted cake in oven 3 to 5 minutes, or until lightly browned. Serve immediately. *Makes enough for one 13x9x2-inch oblong or two 8- or 9-inch layers.*

Toasted Nut Fluff: Sprinkle ½ cup chopped nuts over frosted cake before browning.

Chocolate Chip Fluff: Sprinkle semisweet chocolate pieces over frosted cake before browning.

Toasty Clove Fluff: Add ¼ teaspoon ground cloves to dry frosting mix.

Toasty Nutmeg Fluff: Add ½ teaspoon nutmeg to dry frosting mix.

Toasty Cinnamon Fluff: Add 1 teaspoon cinnamon to dry frosting mix.

Toasty Three-Spice Fluff: Add ½ teaspoon cinnamon and ¼ teaspoon *each* nutmeg and ground cloves to dry frosting mix.

Toasted Coconut Fluff: Sprinkle flaked coconut over frosted cake before browning.

Toasted Cherry Fluff: Use Betty Crocker Cherry Fluff Frosting Mix.

Betty Crocker Note: If you use topping for layers, you can frost them individually and then toast; *or,* fill and frost in the usual way, then toast.

TOASTED MARSHMALLOW CAKE

1 package any chocolate flavor Betty Crocker Cake Mix
8 marshmallows
⅓ cup brown sugar (packed)
⅓ cup chopped nuts

Heat oven to 350°. Prepare cake mix as directed on package. Pour half the batter (about 2½ cups) into greased and floured square pan, 9x9x2 inches. Cut marshmallows in half crosswise and arrange in rows over batter in pan. Mix brown sugar and nuts; sprinkle over top.

Bake *25 to 35 minutes*, or until wooden pick inserted in center comes out clean. (If marshmallows are turning too brown, cover cake with aluminum foil.) Serve warm.

Bake remaining batter in greased and floured 8- or 9-inch round layer pan as directed on package.

For a Larger Cake: Follow recipe (above) except—pour all of batter into greased and floured oblong pan, 13x9x2 inches. Use 12 marshmallows, ½ cup brown sugar (packed) and ½ cup chopped nuts. Bake *40 to 45 minutes.*

CRANBERRY-ORANGE UPSIDE-DOWN CAKE

¼ cup butter or margarine
½ cup brown sugar (packed)
¼ cup chopped walnuts
1 jar (14 ounces) cranberry-orange relish or 1 package (10½ ounces) frozen cranberry-orange relish or 1 cup Cranberry-Orange Relish (below)
1 package Betty Crocker Yellow Cake Mix

Heat oven to 350°. Melt butter over low heat in square pan, 9x9x2 inches, or round layer pan, 9x1½ inches. Sprinkle brown sugar and walnuts evenly over butter. Spoon relish over sugar mixture. Prepare cake mix as directed on package. Pour half the batter (about 2½ cups) evenly over cranberry mixture in pan.

Bake *35 to 45 minutes*, or until wooden pick inserted in center comes out clean. Invert at once on serving plate. Leave pan over cake a few minutes. Serve warm or cold with whipped cream. *9 servings.*

Bake remaining batter in greased and floured 8- or 9-inch round layer pan as directed on package.

Cranberry-Orange Relish: Put through food chopper 2 cups cranberries, peel and pulp of 1 small orange. Mix in 1 cup sugar; let stand several hours. Refrigerate leftover relish.

For a Larger Cake: Follow recipe (above) except—use ⅓ cup butter or margarine and ½ cup walnuts in oblong pan, 13x9x2 inches. Pour all of batter over fruit. (Cranberry mixture will be in a thinner layer.) Bake *40 to 45 minutes.*

PINEAPPLE UPSIDE-DOWN CAKE

¼ cup butter or margarine
½ cup brown sugar (packed)
1 can (8½ ounces) pineapple slices, drained°
Maraschino cherries and pecan halves, if desired
1 package Betty Crocker Yellow Cake Mix

Heat oven to 350°. Melt butter over low heat in square pan, 8x8x2 inches or 9x9x2 inches, or round layer pan, 9x1½ inches. Sprinkle brown sugar evenly over butter. Arrange pineapple slices over sugar mixture. Decorate with cherries and pecans. Prepare cake mix as directed on package. Pour half the batter (about 2½ cups) evenly over fruit in pan.

Bake *35 to 45 minutes*, or until wooden pick inserted in center comes out clean. Invert at once on serving plate. Leave pan over cake a few minutes. Serve warm, plain or with whipped cream. *9 servings*.

Bake remaining batter in greased and floured 8- or 9-inch round layer pan as directed on package.

°*1 can (13½ ounces) crushed pineapple, drained, or 1 can (13½ ounces) pineapple tidbits, drained, may be substituted for pineapple slices.*

For a Larger Cake: Follow recipe (left) except—use ½ cup butter or margarine, 1 cup brown sugar (packed) and 8 to 10 drained pineapple slices (1 pound 14 ounce-can) in oblong pan, 13x9x2 inches. Pour all of batter over fruit. Bake *45 to 55 minutes*.

Checkerboard Upside-down Cake: Follow recipe (left) except—substitute about 12 dried apricots, cooked and drained, and about 12 pitted cooked prunes for the pineapple. Arrange alternately over sugar mixture.

Apricot or Peach Upside-down Cake: Follow recipe (left) except—substitute 1 can (1 pound 4 ounces) canned apricot halves, well drained, or 1 can (1 pound 4 ounces) peach slices, well drained, for the pineapple.

Cinnamon Apple Upside-down Cake: Follow recipe (left) except—substitute 1 jar (14 ounces) cinnamon apple rings, drained, for the pineapple slices. Cut apple rings in half and arrange in parallel rows over sugar mixture.

For variety in upside-down cakes try our Honey Spice, Tropical Mist, Butter Brickle or Lemon Velvet Cake Mix.

CHEERY CHERRY CRUNCH

Who says Mama had a prerogative to warm and crunchy fruit desserts! Look what you can do with cake mixes and pie fillings right from the packages. After one taste, your friends will want the recipe. Pictured below.

½ cup butter or margarine
1 package Betty Crocker Yellow Cake Mix
2 cans (1 pound 5 ounces each) cherry pie filling
½ cup chopped walnuts

Heat oven to 350°. Cut butter into cake mix (dry mix) until mixture resembles coarse cornmeal. Reserve 1 cup mixture. Pat remaining mixture lightly into ungreased oblong pan, 13x9x2 inches, building up ½-inch edge. Spread pie filling over cake mixture to within ½ inch of pan edge. Mix walnuts and the 1 cup reserved mixture; sprinkle over top.

Bake *45 to 50 minutes.* Serve warm with whipped cream or ice cream. *12 to 15 servings.*

Betty Crocker Note: For a crisper, thinner dessert, use 1 can cherry pie filling; bake *35 to 40 minutes.*

For a Smaller Cake: Follow recipe (above) except—use ½ package cake mix (dry mix), ¼ cup butter or margarine, ¼ cup chopped nuts and 1 can (1 pound 5 ounces) cherry pie filling. Bake in square pan, 8x8x2 inches or 9x9x2 inches, *35 to 40 minutes.*

For variety, try these combinations:

Devils Food Cake Mix and apricot pie filling
Lemon Velvet Cake Mix and peach pie filling
White Cake Mix and blueberry pie filling
Honey Spice Cake Mix or Spice 'n Apple Cake
Mix and apple pie filling

CHERRY TOP-OVER CAKE

Heat oven to 350°. Pour contents of 1 can (1 pound 5 ounces) cherry pie filling into ungreased square pan, 9x9x2 inches. Heat in oven about 5 minutes. Prepare Betty Crocker White Cake Mix as directed on package. Pour half the batter (about 2½ cups) evenly over cherries in pan.

Bake *40 to 50 minutes,* or until wooden pick inserted in center comes out clean. While warm, cut into squares and turn upside down onto dessert dishes. Top with ice cream or whipped cream. *9 servings.*

Bake remaining batter in greased and floured 8- or 9-inch round layer pan as directed on package.

MINCEMEAT UPSIDE-DOWN CAKE

1 tablespoon butter or margarine
1½ cups prepared mincemeat
½ cup chopped nuts
1 package Betty Crocker Yellow Cake Mix

Heat oven to 350°. Melt butter over low heat in square pan, 9x9x2 inches. Spread mincemeat and nuts over butter. Prepare cake mix as directed on package. Pour half the batter (about 2½ cups) evenly over mincemeat in pan.

Bake *35 to 45 minutes,* or until wooden pick inserted in center comes out clean. Invert at once on serving plate. Leave pan over cake a few minutes. Serve warm or chilled, topped with whipped cream or Hard Sauce (page 105). *9 servings.*

Bake remaining batter in greased and floured 8- or 9-inch round layer pan as directed on package.

GRAPEFRUIT UPSIDE-DOWN CAKE

Refreshing, tangy grapefruit for an upside-down cake! And then you double the fruity flavor with orange topping.

⅓ cup butter or margarine
½ cup brown sugar (packed)
¼ teaspoon cinnamon
Dash nutmeg
1 can (1 pound) grapefruit sections (15 to 20)
8 to 10 maraschino cherries, halved
1 package Betty Crocker Yellow Cake Mix
Orange Cream Fluff (below)

Heat oven to 350°. Melt butter in square pan, 9x9x2 inches. Mix brown sugar, cinnamon and nutmeg; sprinkle evenly over butter. Arrange grapefruit sections and cherry halves in attractive pattern on butter-sugar mixture. Prepare cake mix as directed on package. Pour half the batter (about 2½ cups) evenly over fruit in pan.

Bake *35 to 45 minutes,* or until wooden pick inserted in center comes out clean. Invert at once on serving plate. Leave pan over cake a few minutes. Serve warm with Orange Cream Fluff. *9 servings.*

Use remaining batter to bake cupcakes (about 18) as directed on package.

Orange Cream Fluff:

1 package (about 3½ ounces) vanilla pudding and pie filling
1 cup orange juice
2 tablespoons lemon juice
1 cup whipping cream, whipped

Combine pudding (dry mix) and fruit juices in saucepan. Cook over medium heat, stirring constantly, until mixture comes to a full boil. Cool; fold in whipped cream. Refrigerate until serving time.

STRAWBERRY-RHUBARB UPSIDE-DOWN CAKE

1 cup cut-up rhubarb (1-inch pieces)
1 cup cut-up strawberries
¼ cup sugar
1 package Betty Crocker Yellow Cake Mix

Heat oven to 350°. Arrange fruit in greased square pan, 8x8x2 inches. Sprinkle with sugar. Prepare cake mix as directed on package. Pour half the batter (about 2½ cups) evenly over fruit in pan.

Bake *35 to 45 minutes.* Cut into squares and serve warm from the pan; top with whipped cream. *9 servings.*

Bake remaining batter in greased and floured 8- or 9-inch round layer pan as directed on package.

BANANA DEVILS FOOD UPSIDE-DOWN CAKE

¼ cup butter or margarine
½ cup brown sugar (packed)
2 or 3 medium bananas, peeled and cut into ½-inch slices
1 package Betty Crocker Devils Food Cake Mix
Eggnog Sauce (below) or whipped cream

Heat oven to 350°. Melt butter over low heat in square pan, 8x8x2 inches or 9x9x2 inches, or round layer pan, 9x1½ inches. Sprinkle brown sugar evenly over butter. Arrange banana slices in rows over sugar mixture. Prepare cake mix as directed on package. Pour half the batter (about 2½ cups) evenly over bananas in pan.

Bake *35 to 45 minutes,* or until wooden pick inserted in center comes out clean. Invert at once on serving plate. Leave pan over cake a few minutes. Serve warm with Eggnog Sauce or whipped cream. *9 servings.*

Bake remaining batter in greased and floured 8- or 9-inch round layer pan as directed on package.

Eggnog Sauce:

2 egg yolks
½ cup confectioners' sugar
1 to 2 tablespoons rum or sherry flavoring
½ cup whipping cream, whipped stiff

Beat egg yolks until thick and lemon colored. Beat in confectioners' sugar and flavoring. Fold in whipped cream. Refrigerate until serving time.

> **Also good with** our Yellow, Honey Spice or Tropical Mist Cake Mixes.

BLUEBERRY CAKE COBBLER

Heat oven to 350°. Prepare Betty Crocker Yellow Cake Mix as directed on package. Pour half the batter (about 2½ cups) into greased and floured square pan, 9x9x2 inches. Pour 1 can (1 pound 5 ounces) blueberry pie filling evenly over cake batter.

Bake *40 to 45 minutes,* or until wooden pick inserted in center comes out clean. While warm, cut into squares and turn upside down onto dessert dishes. Top with whipped cream. *9 servings.*

Bake remaining batter in greased and floured 8- or 9-inch round layer pan as directed on package.

CRUNCHY-NUT MARBLE CAKE

Heat oven to 350°. Spread 1 cup chopped nuts in greased and floured oblong pan, 13x9x2 inches. Prepare Betty Crocker Marble Cake Mix as directed on package. Spoon batter into pan and marble. Bake *40 to 45 minutes.* Cool.

Cut into 3-inch squares. Split each to make two layers. Serve with nut side on top. Fill with slightly softened vanilla ice cream; top with Chocolate Sauce (page 55). *12 servings.*

PINEAPPLE DELIGHT

Heat oven to 350°. Spread Betty Crocker Yellow Cake Mix (dry mix) evenly in greased oblong pan, 13x9x2 inches. Spoon 1 can (1 pound 4 ounces) crushed pineapple, undrained, (2½ cups) evenly over dry mix. Prick with fork about a dozen times (this will allow juice to flow through to bottom of pan and bring some dry cake mix to the surface). Sprinkle with ½ cup slivered almonds.

Bake *40 to 45 minutes,* or until edge is golden brown. Cut into squares and serve warm or cold topped with whipped cream or ice cream. *12 to 15 servings.*

SPICY APPLE CASSEROLES

Modern-day imitation of the cobbler, baked and served in individual baking dishes.

1 can (1 pound 5 ounces) apple pie filling
¼ cup water
1 teaspoon lemon juice
½ teaspoon cinnamon
1 package Betty Crocker Honey Spice Cake Mix

Heat oven to 350°. In saucepan, heat pie filling, water, lemon juice and cinnamon, stirring occasionally. Prepare cake mix as directed on package. Arrange 6 ungreased baking dishes (about 1-cup size) on baking sheet. Pour ⅓ cup apple filling mixture into each; top each with ¼ cup batter.

Bake *25 to 30 minutes.* Serve in baking dishes topped with whipped cream, ice cream or Hard Sauce (page 105). *6 servings.*

Pour remaining batter into greased and floured square pan, 9x9x2 inches. Bake *25 to 30 minutes.*

Betty Crocker Note: If individual baking dishes are not available, spread hot apple filling in ungreased square pan, 9x9x2 inches. Pour half the batter (about 2½ cups) evenly over filling. Bake *35 to 40 minutes,* or until wooden pick inserted in center comes out clean.

 *Cakes that Carry Well*

ROCKY ROAD CAKE

A smooth traveler even on a rocky road. This cake borrows its name from the marshmallows and almonds in the frosting, reminiscent of rocky road ice cream.

1 package any chocolate flavor Betty Crocker Cake Mix
1 package Betty Crocker Chocolate Fudge Frosting Mix
½ cup chopped toasted almonds
1 cup miniature marshmallows

Bake cake in oblong pan, 13x9x2 inches, as directed on package. Cool. Prepare frosting mix as directed on package. Stir in almonds and marshmallows. If too stiff to spread, add a few drops water. Spread on cake.

MAPLE SYRUP CAKE

Delicious warm or cold.

1 package Betty Crocker Yellow Cake Mix
⅓ cup sugar
1 teaspoon cinnamon
1 cup maple syrup
½ cup chopped nuts

Bake cake in oblong pan, 13x9x2 inches, as directed on package. Cool 5 minutes; score into large diamond shapes. Mix sugar and cinnamon; sprinkle on top of cake. Heat syrup slightly; pour over cake. Sprinkle nuts over top. Let stand a few minutes; serve from pan.

LEMON MALLOW CAKE

Bake Betty Crocker Lemon Velvet Cake Mix in oblong pan, 13x9x2 inches, as directed on package. Cool. Cover top with Lemon Filling (page 89) or use 1 package (about 3½ ounces) lemon pudding and pie filling cooked as directed and cooled. Frost with Betty Crocker Fluffy White Frosting Mix prepared as directed on package.

ORANGE DEVILS FOOD CAKE

Prepare Betty Crocker Devils Food Cake Mix as directed on package except—add 2 tablespoons grated orange peel to batter. Pour batter into greased and floured oblong pan, 13x9x2 inches. Bake as directed. Cool.

Prepare Betty Crocker Fluffy White Frosting Mix as directed on package. Frost cake. Sprinkle 1 tablespoon grated orange peel over top.

PINEAPPLE-GLAZED CAKE

Bake Betty Crocker Yellow Cake Mix in oblong pan, 13x9x2 inches, as directed on package. In small saucepan, heat to boiling 1 can (13½ ounces) crushed pineapple, undrained, with ½ cup brown sugar (packed). With point of sharp knife, mark hot cake into 1-inch squares, cutting ½ inch deep. Spoon hot pineapple mixture over hot cake. Cool. Serve from pan.

TRIPLE FUDGE CAKE

For those who like their chocolate desserts really fudgy! Chocolate cake mix combined with chocolate pudding, self-frosted with chocolate chips and nuts. Unique texture, delicious taste. Pictured below.

1 package (about 4 ounces) chocolate pudding and pie filling
1 package Betty Crocker Devils Food Cake Mix
½ cup semisweet chocolate pieces
½ cup chopped nuts

Heat oven to 350°. In large saucepan, cook chocolate pudding as directed on package. Blend cake mix (dry mix) thoroughly into hot pudding by hand or electric mixer, 1 to 2 minutes. Pour into greased and floured oblong pan, 13x9x2 inches. Sprinkle top of batter with chocolate pieces and nuts. Bake *30 to 35 minutes.* Serve warm or cold with whipped cream, if desired.

Betty Crocker Note: For variety, try this recipe with any of our other chocolate flavor cake mixes.

BUTTERMILK CHOCOLATE CAKE

Pictured on page 4.

Prepare Betty Crocker German Chocolate Cake Mix as directed on package except—use 1 cup buttermilk, ⅓ cup water, 2 eggs and 3 tablespoons soft butter. Pour batter into greased and floured oblong pan, 13x9x2 inches. Bake as directed. Cool.

Prepare Betty Crocker Coconut-Pecan Frosting Mix as directed on package. Spread on cake.

MOCHA MARBLE CAKE

Prepare Betty Crocker Marble Cake Mix as directed on package except—use cold brewed coffee instead of water or add 1 tablespoon instant coffee before mixing. Pour batter into greased and floured oblong pan, 13x9x2 inches. Bake as directed. Cool.

Prepare Betty Crocker Fluffy White Frosting Mix as directed on package except—substitute hot brewed coffee for the boiling water or blend 2 teaspoons instant coffee into dry mix. Fold in ½ cup miniature chocolate pieces or ½ cup shaved semisweet or unsweetened chocolate after beating, if desired. Frost cake.

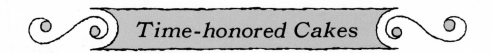

Time-honored Cakes

JOHNNY APPLESEED CAKE

1 package Betty Crocker Honey Spice Cake Mix
1 can (1 pound) applesauce (1¾ cups)
2 eggs
Browned Butter Frosting, Applesauce Whipped Cream Topping (below) or Fluffy Apple Butter Frosting (page 39)

Heat oven to 350°. Combine cake mix (dry mix), applesauce and eggs in large mixer bowl. Blend ½ minute low speed on mixer, scraping sides and bottom of bowl constantly. Beat 4 minutes medium speed, scraping bowl often. Pour batter into greased and floured oblong pan, 13x9x2 inches.

Bake *40 to 45 minutes*, or until wooden pick inserted in center comes out clean. Cool. Frost with one of frostings or serve with topping.

Browned Butter Frosting: Prepare Betty Crocker Creamy White Frosting Mix as directed on package except—lightly brown the butter over low heat before adding to the frosting mix.

Applesauce Whipped Cream Topping:

1 cup whipping cream
¼ cup confectioners' sugar
1 cup applesauce
½ teaspoon nutmeg, if desired

Whip cream and confectioners' sugar until stiff. Fold in applesauce and nutmeg. Chill. *Makes about 3 cups.*

PILGRIM PUMPKIN CAKE*

1 package Betty Crocker Honey Spice Cake Mix
1 can (1 pound) solid pack pumpkin (2 cups)
2 teaspoons soda
2 eggs
⅓ cup water
Penuche Cream Topping (below)

Heat oven to 350°. In large mixer bowl combine all ingredients except Penuche Cream Topping. Beat 30 seconds low speed on mixer; beat 4 minutes medium speed. Pour batter into greased and floured oblong pan, 13x9x2 inches.

Bake *45 to 50 minutes*. Serve warm with Penuche Cream Topping. Sprinkle with chopped pecans, if desired.

Penuche Cream Topping: Beat 1 cup whipping cream, ¼ cup brown sugar (packed), 1 teaspoon vanilla and ½ to 1 teaspoon rum flavoring until stiff.

Pumpkin-Nut Cake: Fold ½ cup chopped walnuts or pecans into batter before pouring into pan.

Pumpkin-Raisin Cake: Fold ½ cup raisins into batter before pouring into pan.

**We do not recommend this recipe for high altitude areas.*

CAROLINA LEMON POUND CAKE

Pictured below.

Heat oven to 350°. Grease and flour a tube pan, 10x4 inches, bundt pan, or 2-quart anodized aluminum mold.* Prepare Betty Crocker Lemon Velvet Cake Mix as directed on package except—use 2 tablespoons less water. Add ½ cup finely chopped nuts, if desired. Pour batter into prepared pan. Bake *45 to 55 minutes* or until wooden pick inserted in center comes out clean. Cool 10 minutes; remove from pan. Dust with confectioners' sugar, glaze with Lemon Glaze (page 19) or serve with ice cream and fresh or frozen (thawed) fruit.

Chocolate Chip Pound Cake: Follow recipe (above) except—use our White Cake Mix and egg whites instead of whole eggs. After mixing, fold in ½ cup chopped chocolate pieces.

Betty Crocker Note: To keep cake moist, store in plastic wrap or freeze and use as needed.

**Do not bake in 2-quart mold if you live in a high altitude area.*

GOLD COAST BANANA CAKE

This one's banana inside and out; they're added to both the cake and frosting.

Heat oven to 350°. Prepare Betty Crocker Yellow Cake Mix as directed on package except—stir ⅛ teaspoon soda into mix before adding liquid and eggs; use ¼ cup less water and add 1 cup mashed bananas (2 to 3 medium). Fold ½ cup finely chopped nuts into batter. Pour batter into greased and floured oblong pan, 13x9x2 inches, or two round layer pans, 8 or 9x1½ inches.

Bake oblong *40 to 45 minutes*, layers *30 to 40 minutes*, or until wooden pick inserted in center comes out clean. Cool. Fill and frost with sweetened whipped cream and sliced bananas or with Banana-Nut Frosting (page 20).

Honey Spice-Banana Cake*: Follow recipe (above) except—use our Honey Spice Cake Mix.

Banana-Nut Loaf: Follow recipe (above) except—pour batter into two greased and floured shiny loaf pans, 9x5x3 inches. Bake *45 to 50 minutes*, or until wooden pick inserted in center comes out clean.

**We do not recommend this recipe for high altitude areas.*

COUNTRY LOAF CAKE

More ways to double your pleasure; turn out two loaf cakes from one mix. With your choice of batter extras, fruit glazes or frosting mix tricks.

Heat oven to 350° (325° for glass pans). Prepare any flavor Betty Crocker Layer Cake Mix as directed on package except—use 2 tablespoons less water. Pour batter into two greased and floured shiny loaf pans, 9x5x3 inches.

Bake 35 *to* 40 *minutes,* or until wooden pick inserted in center comes out clean. Cool. If desired, dust with confectioners' sugar.

Almond Loaf Cake: Follow recipe (above) using our White Cake Mix except—add ½ teaspoon almond extract to batter. Before baking, sprinkle ½ cup slivered almonds over batter.

Anise Loaf Cake: Follow recipe (above) using our White Cake Mix except—add 1 tablespoon crushed anise seed before adding liquid.

Glazed Nut Loaf: Follow recipe (above) except—fold ½ cup finely chopped nuts into batter. While still warm, spread Creamy White Glaze (page 19) on top, letting it drizzle down sides. Decorate top with candied cherries and nuts.

Fruit Shortcakes: Serve slices of loaf cake with sweetened whipped cream or ice cream and fresh, frozen (thawed) or canned fruit.

Singed Slices: Cut loaf cake in ½-inch slices. Brush sides with melted butter or margarine. Broil 4 inches from heat about 1 minute on each side, until golden brown. Top with jelly, marmalade or confectioners' sugar, or serve with a fruit sauce.

Toasted Cake Sundaes: Toast ½-inch slices of loaf cake. Top with ice cream and your favorite dessert sauce. Serve immediately, while cake is warm.

Country Ribbon Loaf: Follow recipe (left) using Betty Crocker Yellow Cake Mix.

Place cake loaves in freezer overnight. Cut each frozen loaf lengthwise into 5 layers. Reassemble each loaf, filling layers and frosting sides and tops with Betty Crocker Chocolate Satin ready-to-spread Frosting. One can will fill and frost one loaf.

Lemon Loaf: Follow recipe (left) using our Lemon Velvet Cake Mix. Cool cake 10 minutes; remove from pan. Prick several times on top with a fork. Pour Orange-Lemon Glaze (below), a little at a time, over the top.

Orange-Lemon Glaze:

1¼ cups confectioners' sugar
2 tablespoons orange juice
1 teaspoon lemon juice
1 tablespoon grated orange peel
1 teaspoon grated lemon peel

Blend all ingredients.

Orange Loaf: Follow recipe (left) using our Yellow Cake Mix. Cool cake 10 minutes; remove from pan. Prick several times on top with a fork. Pour Orange Glaze (below), a little at a time, over the top.

Orange Glaze:

Blend 1 cup confectioners' sugar, ½ cup orange juice and ½ teaspoon grated orange peel.

COLONIAL JELLY ROLL

Heat oven to 350°. Prepare Betty Crocker Lemon Chiffon Cake Mix as directed on package. Pour into two shiny ungreased jelly roll pans, 15½x10½x1 inch, spreading gently to all sides. (Or use one jelly roll pan and one shiny ungreased loaf pan, 9x5x3 inches.) Bake roll(s) *20 to 25 minutes, loaf 45 to 55 minutes.*

Invert loaf to cool. When sheet cake has cooled about 10 minutes, loosen sides and ease from pan onto towel generously dusted with confectioners' sugar. Trim off edges, if they are stiff. Roll up and cool on wire rack.

Unroll cake, remove towel and spread with softened (not syrupy) jelly or jam. Roll again. If desired, sprinkle with confectioners' sugar. Cut into 1-inch slices. *Each roll serves 10 to 12.*

Orange Roll: Follow recipe (above) except—spread with Orange Filling (page 88).

Strawberry Cream Roll (Pictured on cover): Follow recipe (above) except—whip ½ cup whipping cream with 2 tablespoons confectioners' sugar. Spread on roll. Sprinkle with 2 cups sliced fresh strawberries. Reroll and chill 1 hour or until ready to serve. Sprinkle with confectioners' sugar before serving.

Lemon Cream Roll: Follow recipe (above) except— spread roll with Lemon Cream Filling: Add 1 package Betty Crocker Lemon Velvet Frosting Mix (dry mix) to 1½ cups whipping cream and chill 1 hour; beat just until stiff. Spread filling to within 1 inch of edges. (There is enough filling for two rolls.) Reroll and chill 1 hour or until ready to serve. To serve, cut into 1-inch slices and top with whole cranberry sauce, fresh or frozen (thawed) raspberries or strawberries.

Betty Crocker Note: If you prefer, cake may be baked in two loaf pans, 9x5x3 inches. Split each loaf, making two layers. Fill and frost each loaf with Lemon Cream Filling. Chill. Serve as above.

MOCHA SPICE CAKE

1 package Betty Crocker Honey Spice Cake Mix
1 package Betty Crocker Creamy White Frosting Mix
2 teaspoons instant coffee
¼ cup chopped raisins
¼ cup chopped nuts

Bake cake in two round layer pans, 8 or 9x1½ inches, as directed on package. Prepare frosting mix as directed on package except—dissolve coffee in the hot water before adding to the dry mix. To 1 cup of the mocha frosting add raisins and nuts. Fill layers and frost top of cake with raisin-nut frosting. Frost sides of cake with remaining mocha frosting.

Betty Crocker Note: If raisin-nut frosting is too stiff to spread, add a few drops water.

SPICY APPLE BUTTER CAKE

Bake Betty Crocker Honey Spice Cake Mix in two round layer pans, 8 or 9x1½ inches, as directed on package. Fill with Apple Butter Filling (below) and frost with Fluffy Apple Butter Frosting (below).

Apple Butter Filling:
½ cup sugar
3 tablespoons cornstarch
¾ cup water
½ cup apple butter
½ cup chopped nuts
¼ teaspoon grated lemon peel

Mix sugar and cornstarch in saucepan. Slowly stir in water. Add apple butter and stir. Cook, stirring constantly, until mixture thickens and boils. Boil and stir 1 minute. Stir in nuts and lemon peel. Cool.

Fluffy Apple Butter Frosting: Prepare Betty Crocker Fluffy White Frosting Mix as directed on package except—fold in ½ cup apple butter.

CHARLESTON APRICOT-FILLED CAKE

1 package Betty Crocker White Cake Mix
1 jar (4½ ounces) apricot baby food
½ cup apricot jam
1 package Betty Crocker Fluffy White Frosting Mix

Bake cake in two round layer pans, 8 or 9x1½ inches, as directed on package. Cool. Split to make 4 layers (page 20). Mix baby food and jam; use ⅓ cup mixture between each layer. Prepare frosting mix as directed on package. Frost sides and top of cake.

CALIFORNIA PRUNE-FILLED CAKE

Prepare Betty Crocker Honey Spice Cake Mix as directed on package except—use ½ cup prune juice for part of the liquid. Pour batter into two greased and floured round layer pans, 8 or 9x1½ inches. Bake as directed. Cool.

Prepare Betty Crocker Fluffy White Frosting Mix as directed on package except—use ½ cup boiling prune juice instead of water. Add ½ cup finely chopped cooked or canned prunes, well drained, and 1 teaspoon grated lemon peel to ¾ cup frosting; use as filling for cake. Frost sides and top of cake with remaining frosting. Sprinkle top with chopped walnuts.

BANANA CREAM CAKE

Bake Betty Crocker Yellow Cake Mix in two round layer pans, 8 or 9x1½ inches, as directed on package. Cool. Put layers together with sweetened whipped cream and sliced bananas. Top with more whipped cream and sliced bananas. Chill.

HONEY SPICE CAKE WITH TAWNY CIDER FILLING

Bake Betty Crocker Honey Spice Cake Mix in two round layer pans, 8 or 9x1½ inches, as directed on package. Cool. Fill layers with Tawny Cider Filling (below) and frost cake with Betty Crocker Fluffy White Frosting Mix prepared as directed on package.

Tawny Cider Filling:
½ cup sugar
3 tablespoons cornstarch
¼ teaspoon salt
1 cup cider
2 tablespoons lemon juice
2 tablespoons butter or margarine

Combine sugar, cornstarch and salt in saucepan. Slowly stir in cider. Cook, stirring constantly, until mixture thickens and boils. Boil and stir 1 minute. Remove from heat; stir in lemon juice and butter. Cool.

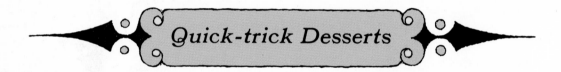

Quick-trick Desserts

LEMON-ORANGE CAKE

1 package Betty Crocker Lemon Velvet Cake Mix
1 can (6 ounces) frozen orange juice concentrate
2 tablespoons soft butter or margarine
½ cup sifted confectioners' sugar

Bake cake in two round layer pans, 8 or 9x1½ inches, as directed on package. Cool. Split to make 4 layers (page 20). Thaw orange juice concentrate; reserve 1 tablespoon for glaze. Fill layers with remaining orange juice, using 3 tablespoons between each layer. Mix the reserved 1 tablespoon concentrate with butter and confectioners' sugar. Spread on top of cake. Chill.

JELLY FIESTA CAKE

Bake Betty Crocker White Cake Mix in oblong pan, 13x9x2 inches, as directed on package. Cool. Whip ½ to ¾ cup of your favorite jelly with a fork until syrupy. Frost top of cake with jelly. Sprinkle thickly with flaked coconut.

ORANGE-HONEY SPICE CAKE

Bake Betty Crocker Honey Spice Cake Mix in oblong pan, 13x9x2 inches, as directed on package. Mix ¼ cup frozen orange juice concentrate (thawed) and ⅓ cup honey. Pour over hot cake. Serve warm.

JELLY RIBBON CAKE

Bake Betty Crocker Yellow Cake Mix in two round layer pans, 8 or 9x1½ inches, as directed on package. Cool. Split to make 4 layers (page 20). With fork, soften 1½ cups tart jelly or jam (such as orange marmalade, red currant, blackberry or strawberry). A different flavor jam or jelly may be used between each layer. Use about ½ cup between each layer. Sift confectioners' sugar over top of cake.

FRUIT "SHORT" CAKE

Bake Betty Crocker Yellow Cake Mix in two round layer pans, 8 or 9x1½ inches, as directed on package. Cool.

Split one layer to make two layers. Spoon about 1½ cups fruit* between layers. Whip ½ cup whipping cream with 2 tablespoons confectioners' sugar until stiff; use to top cake. Serve immediately or refrigerate until serving time. *6 servings.*

Use remaining layer as desired.

You may use fresh (sweetened), frozen (thawed) or canned fruit. (Be sure it is well drained.) Good choices: berries, peaches or bananas.

Other delicious toppings for cake squares will be found on page 94.

CAKE AND ICE CREAM PIE

Pictured at right.

Bake Betty Crocker Devils Food Cake Mix in two round layer pans, 8 or 9x1½ inches, as directed on package. Cool. Spoon 1 pint vanilla ice cream over one cake layer. Top with Chocolate Sauce (page 55) and whipped cream, if desired. Sprinkle with chopped maraschino cherries or nuts. Serve immediately. *6 to 8 servings.*

Freeze second layer for later use.

GERMAN CHOCOLATE SQUARES WITH CARAMEL SAUCE

Heat oven to 350°. Prepare Betty Crocker German Chocolate Cake Mix as directed on package except—after beating, fold in ½ cup finely chopped maraschino cherries and the coconut-pecan mixture from Betty Crocker Coconut-Pecan Frosting Mix. Pour batter into greased and floured oblong pan, 13x9x2 inches.

Bake *35 to 40 minutes.* Cool. Cut into squares and top with hot Caramel Sauce (below).

Caramel Sauce:

Frosting mix from Betty Crocker Coconut-Pecan Frosting Mix
2 tablespoons light corn syrup
3 tablespoons butter or margarine
⅔ cup milk

Combine frosting mix (dry mix), corn syrup and butter in top of double boiler. Add milk gradually. Heat over rapidly boiling water 5 minutes, stirring occasionally. Remove from heat. Store leftover sauce in refrigerator. *Makes 2 cups.*

CHOCOLATE MALT TORTE

Heat oven to 350°. Prepare Betty Crocker Chocolate Malt Cake Mix as directed on package. Pour batter into a greased and floured jelly roll pan, 15½x10½x1 inch. Bake *25 to 30 minutes.* Cool.

Cut cake into three pieces, each 10x5 inches. Cook 1 package (about 3½ ounces) vanilla pudding and pie filling as directed on package except—add 1 teaspoon unflavored gelatin before cooking. Cool. Use to fill cake. Frost with Betty Crocker Chocolate Malt Frosting Mix prepared as directed on package.

PEACH-CARAMEL SHORTCAKE

Bake Betty Crocker Yellow Cake Mix in oblong pan, 13x9x2 inches, as directed on package. Cool. Cut into squares. Split each square; spoon fresh or frozen (thawed) sliced peaches between layers and over top. Top with warm Golden Caramel Sauce (page 56) and sweetened whipped cream, if desired.

BUTTER RUM CAKE SUNDAES

Bake Betty Crocker Spice 'n Apple Cake Mix in oblong pan, 13x9x2 inches, as directed on package. Cool. Cut into squares. Place a slice or scoop of vanilla ice cream on each square and top with Butter Rum Sauce (below).

Butter Rum Sauce:

½ cup butter*
1 package Betty Crocker Creamy White Frosting Mix
2 tablespoons light corn syrup
⅔ cup milk
1 teaspoon rum flavoring
½ cup chopped nuts, if desired

Brown butter in saucepan over medium heat. (Heat until it becomes foamy and turns golden brown, but do not burn.) Cool. Blend in frosting mix (dry mix) and corn syrup. Stir in milk gradually. Heat over rapidly boiling water 5 minutes, stirring occasionally. Remove from heat and cool slightly. Add rum flavoring and nuts. Serve warm. Store leftover sauce covered in refrigerator. *Makes 2 cups.*

*If desired, use only ¼ cup butter.

CAKE SQUARES WITH HOT FRUIT SAUCE

Bake your favorite flavor Betty Crocker Layer Cake Mix in oblong pan, 13x9x2 inches, as directed on package. Cool. Cut into squares.

Heat fruit pie filling such as peach, blueberry or cherry. Spoon hot fruit sauce over cake squares. Top with whipped cream, if desired.

RAINBOW FRUIT SAUCE

Try this on squares of Betty Crocker Yellow, Butter Brickle or Honey Spice Cake Mix.

2 to 4 tablespoons brown sugar
1 tablespoon cornstarch
1 can (1 pound 13 ounces) fruit cocktail, drained (reserve syrup)
1½ tablespoons lemon juice

Mix brown sugar and cornstarch in saucepan. Slowly stir in syrup from fruit cocktail. Cook, stirring constantly, until mixture thickens and boils. Boil and stir 1 minute. Remove from heat; stir in lemon juice and drained fruit. Serve sauce warm or cool. *Makes 2 cups.*

PINK CIDER SAUCE

Use this to top warm cake squares made from our Honey Spice Cake Mix.

½ cup sugar
2 tablespoons cornstarch
¼ teaspoon salt
2 cups cider
2 tablespoons lemon juice
Few drops red food coloring
2 tablespoons butter or margarine

Combine sugar, cornstarch and salt in saucepan. Slowly stir in cider. Cook, stirring constantly, until mixture thickens and boils. Boil and stir 1 minute. Remove from heat; stir in lemon juice, food coloring and butter. *Makes 2 cups.*

ROCKY ROAD SAUCE

Use to top warm squares of any chocolate flavor Betty Crocker Cake Mix.

1 package Betty Crocker Chocolate Fudge Frosting Mix
2 tablespoons light corn syrup
3 tablespoons butter or margarine
⅔ cup milk
1 cup miniature marshmallows
½ cup diced roasted almonds
1 teaspoon vanilla

Combine frosting mix (dry mix), corn syrup and butter in top of double boiler. Gradually stir in milk. Cook over rapidly boiling water 5 minutes, stirring occasionally. Remove from heat and cool. Add marshmallows, almonds and vanilla. Store leftover sauce in covered container in refrigerator. *Makes 2 cups.*

PRUNE MALLOW TOPPING

Serve over warm Honey Spice cake squares.

¾ cup uncooked prunes
16 marshmallows (¼ pound)
1 cup whipping cream, whipped
⅓ cup chopped nuts

Cook prunes until tender. (Use enough water to make at least ½ cup juice.) When cool, pit and cut prunes to make ½ cup. In saucepan, stir ½ cup prune juice and marshmallows over direct heat just until marshmallows melt. Remove from heat. Cool; chill just until partially set. Fold in whipped cream, prunes and nuts. Chill thoroughly or pour into freezer trays and freeze until firm. *Makes 3 cups.*

Betty Crocker Note: If marshmallow mixture should get too firm to fold into whipped cream, beat with rotary beater.

CANDY BAR TOPPING

Spoon over cake squares or wedges made from any of our chocolate flavor cake mixes.

1 cup whipping cream
1 tablespoon confectioners' sugar
2 bars (1 ounce each) milk chocolate-nut candy

Whip cream with confectioners' sugar. Cut candy bars in slivers. Fold into whipped cream. *Makes enough for 6 to 8 servings.*

PINEAPPLE CREAM TOPPING

Serve over our Honey Spice, Lemon Velvet, Butter Brickle or Lemon Chiffon cake squares.

Combine 1 package (about 3½ ounces) vanilla instant pudding (dry mix) and 1 can (8¾ ounces) crushed pineapple, with syrup. Fold into 1 cup whipping cream, whipped. Chill. *Makes 3 cups.*

HONEY-GINGER CREAM TOPPING

Serve over our Honey Spice cake squares.

Whip 1 cup whipping cream, gradually adding 2 tablespoons honey and ¼ teaspoon ginger. *Makes 2 cups.*

SNACKING WITH SWEETS

Hooray for snacks, the all-American excuse to pause for a bite to eat—midmorning, midafternoon, midnight, mid-anything. And another cheer for finger foods, a deservedly popular snack form: cookies, candies and cupcakes. Casual, easy to eat and run with and energizing—as snacks should be.

The following recipes are versatile, too—they suit snacktime, of course, but they're also perfect as gifts and can easily be used for mealtime desserts or company refreshments. Best of all, these treats say with love how nice it is to have a family around the house.

Cookies

SPICY LEMON-DATE BARS

Pictured above.

1 package Betty Crocker Honey Spice Cake Mix
¼ cup water
2 eggs
¼ cup soft butter or margarine
¼ cup brown sugar (packed)
1½ cups chopped dates
½ cup chopped nuts
Lemon Glaze (below)

Heat oven to 375°. Combine half the cake mix (dry mix), the water, eggs, butter and brown sugar in mixing bowl; mix thoroughly. Blend in remaining cake mix. Stir in dates and nuts. Spread in greased and floured jelly roll pan, 15½x10½x1 inch.

Bake *20 to 25 minutes.* While warm, spread with Lemon Glaze. Cut into bars, 3x1½ inches. *Makes about 30.*

Lemon Glaze: Beat 1 cup confectioners' sugar, ½ teaspoon grated lemon peel, 1 teaspoon lemon juice and 2 tablespoons milk until smooth.

CREAM CHEESE COOKIES

Pictured below.

¼ cup butter or margarine
1 package (8 ounces) cream cheese
1 egg yolk
¼ teaspoon vanilla
1 package Betty Crocker Yellow Cake Mix

Cream butter and cheese. Blend in egg yolk and vanilla. Add cake mix (dry mix), ⅓ at a time; mix well. If mixer is used, add last part of cake mix by hand. Chill dough 30 minutes.

Heat oven to 375°. Finish cookies in one of the ways given below. *Makes 6 to 8 dozen.*

1. Use cookie press to shape cookies on ungreased baking sheet. Bake *6 to 9 minutes,* or until delicately browned. Cool cookies before removing from baking sheet.
2. Drop by scant teaspoonfuls onto ungreased baking sheet. Bake *8 to 10 minutes,* or until delicately browned. Cool cookies before removing from baking sheet.

Betty Crocker Note: ½ cup flaked coconut or chopped nuts may be added to dough for drop cookies.

CHOCOLATE CHIP COCONUT CHEWS

Pictured below, left.

Heat oven to 325°. Prepare Betty Crocker Fluffy White Frosting Mix as directed on package. Place 1 package (8 ounces) shredded coconut and 1 package (6 ounces) semisweet chocolate pieces in a large bowl. Stir in frosting with a fork. With two forks, drop lightly in small mounds (each about tablespoon-size) onto lightly greased baking sheet. Bake *17 to 20 minutes. Makes about 3½ dozen.*

Betty Crocker Note: Allow to cool a minute or two before removing from baking sheet. Store lightly covered (*not* in airtight container).

CHERRY FUDGE BARS

Pictured above, right.

1 package (about 4 ounces) chocolate pudding and pie filling
1 package any chocolate flavor Betty Crocker Cake Mix
1 cup maraschino cherries, chopped
1 cup chopped nuts
1 package (6 ounces) semisweet chocolate pieces (1 cup)

Heat oven to 350°. In large saucepan, cook pudding as directed on package. Blend cake mix (dry mix) thoroughly into hot pudding by hand or with electric mixer, 1 to 2 minutes. Add cherries. Pour into greased and floured jelly roll pan, 15½x10½x1 inch. Sprinkle with nuts and chocolate pieces.

Bake *25 to 30 minutes.* Cool and cut into bars. *Makes 40.*

For dessert, cut into 24 squares and serve warm topped with whipped cream.

FUDGE CRINKLES

Pictured above and below, left.

2 eggs
⅔ cup shortening
1 package any chocolate flavor Betty Crocker Cake Mix
1 package any chocolate flavor Betty Crocker Frosting Mix

Heat oven to 375°. Blend eggs and shortening in mixer bowl. Add about half of the cake mix (dry mix). Beat medium speed on mixer until light and fluffy. Add remaining cake mix. Blend on low speed, scraping bowl often.

Form into 1-inch balls; place on ungreased baking sheet. Bake *10 to 12 minutes.* Cookies will rise, then settle, but will be soft in center when done. Allow to cool on baking sheet 1 to 2 minutes before removing.

Prepare frosting mix as directed on package. Frost cookies. Decorate with chopped nuts, red cinnamon candies or colored nonpareils, if desired. Or make "sandwich" cookies by putting two cookies together with frosting as filling. *Makes 4 dozen single cookies or 2 dozen "sandwiches."*

Chocolate Snappers (Pictured below, right): Make dough for Fudge Crinkles (above). For each "snapper," place three pecan halves (with ends touching in center) on greased baking sheet. Form dough into 1-inch balls and place in center of each group of nuts. Bake *8 to 10 minutes at 375°.* Cool slightly before removing from baking sheet. Cool thoroughly on wire rack. Frost each cookie with Betty Crocker Chocolate Satin ready-to-spread Frosting.

Cookie Jar Crinkles

To Make:	Follow recipe (left) except— use one of these Betty Crocker Cake Mix flavors	Vary by adding 1 cup of any of the following to the dough							Try frosted with one of the following Betty Crocker Frosting Mixes prepared as directed on the package or Betty Crocker Satin ready-to-spread Frosting
		Chopped Nuts	Raisins	Chopped Dates	Semisweet Chocolate Pieces	Flaked Coconut	Cut-up Candied Cherries or Candied Fruit	Cut-up Gumdrops	
Golden Crinkles	**Yellow**	*	*	*	*	*	*	*	**Lemon Velvet or Chocolate Fudge Frosting Mix**
Spice Crinkles	**Honey Spice or Spice 'n Apple**	*	*	*	*	*	*	*	**Golden Caramel Frosting Mix**
Lemon Crinkles	**Lemon Velvet**	*	*	*		*	*	*	**Lemon Velvet Frosting Mix**
Caramel Crinkles	**Butter Brickle**	*	*	*	*	*	*	*	**Butter Brickle Frosting Mix**
Cherry Fudge Crinkles	**Cherry Fudge**	*	*		*	*	*		**Cherry Fudge Frosting Mix**
Chocolate Malt Crinkles	**Chocolate Malt**	*	*		*	*	*		**Chocolate Malt Frosting Mix**
German Chocolate Crinkles	**German Chocolate**	*	*		*	*	*		**Coconut-Pecan Frosting Mix**

CHOCOLATE-NUT BARS

Pictured below, left.

1 package Betty Crocker Devils Food Cake Mix
¼ cup water
2 eggs
¼ cup soft butter or margarine
¼ cup brown sugar (packed)
1 cup chopped pecans
1 package Betty Crocker Chocolate Fudge Frosting Mix

Heat oven to 375°. Combine half the cake mix (dry mix), the water, eggs, butter and brown sugar in mixing bowl; mix thoroughly. Blend in remaining cake mix. Stir in nuts. Spread in greased and floured jelly roll pan, 15½x10½x1 inch.

Bake *20 to 25 minutes.* Cool. Spread with frosting mix prepared as directed on package. Cut into bars, 3x 1½ inches. *Makes about 30.*

Chocolate-Mocha Bars: Bake Chocolate-Nut Bars (above). Frost with Creamy Mocha Frosting: Prepare Betty Crocker Creamy White Frosting Mix as directed on package except—stir in 1½ teaspoons instant coffee before mixing.

Chocolate-Mint Bars: Bake Chocolate-Nut Bars (above). Frost with Creamy Mint Frosting: Prepare Betty Crocker Creamy White Frosting Mix as directed on package except—add ½ teaspoon peppermint extract and 3 to 4 drops red or green food coloring.

COCONUT-APRICOT BARS

Pictured above.

1 package Betty Crocker Lemon Velvet Cake Mix
¼ cup water
2 eggs
¼ cup soft butter or margarine
¼ cup brown sugar (packed)
1 cup flaked coconut
1 cup chopped dried apricots
Lemon Glaze (page 43)

Heat oven to 375°. Combine half the cake mix (dry mix), the water, eggs, butter and brown sugar in mixing bowl; mix thoroughly. Blend in remaining cake mix. Stir in coconut and apricots. Spread in greased and floured jelly roll pan, 15½x10½x1 inch.

Bake *20 to 25 minutes.* While warm, spread with Lemon Glaze. Cut into bars, 3x1½ inches. *Makes about 30.*

PEANUT BUTTER COOKIES

Pictured at left.

1 cup crunchy peanut butter
⅓ cup water
2 eggs
1 package Betty Crocker Yellow Cake Mix

Heat oven to 375°. In large mixing bowl beat peanut butter, water, eggs and about half of the cake mix (dry mix) until smooth and well blended. Add remaining cake mix; blend thoroughly, using hands if necessary. Drop dough by teaspoonfuls, 3 inches apart, onto ungreased baking sheet. Press down center of each cookie with floured thumb, fork or tip of spoon. Bake *about 10 minutes,* or until golden brown. Allow cookies to cool 1 to 2 minutes on baking sheet. Remove to rack and cool thoroughly. *Makes 4 dozen.*

Peanut Butter and Jelly Cookies: At serving time, place about ½ teaspoon red jelly in thumbprint of each cookie.

PEANUT BARS

Prepare Betty Crocker Lemon Chiffon Cake Mix as directed on package; bake in two ungreased square pans, 9x9x2 inches, for *35 to 45 minutes*. Invert to cool. Remove from pans.

Cut into 2¼x1-inch bars. Frost sides and tops with Betty Crocker Vanilla Satin ready-to-spread Frosting; roll immediately in chopped, salted peanuts (13½-ounce can). *Each square makes 36 bars.*

Toasted Coconut Bars: Follow recipe (above) except—roll frosted bars in toasted coconut.

Coconut Squares: Follow recipe (above) except—cut cake into 1½-inch squares. Roll frosted squares in shredded coconut. *Makes 36 squares.*

Bittersweets: Follow recipe (above) except—cut cake into 1½-inch squares. Roll frosted squares in 1 square (1 ounce) unsweetened or semisweet chocolate, grated. *Makes 36 squares.*

Cinnamon Bars: Follow recipe (above) except—roll frosted bars in mixture of 1 teaspoon cinnamon and ½ cup sugar.

Other cookie or bar recipes you will enjoy are Toasted Trio Cake (page 86), Date Meringue Bars (page 86), Chocolate Meltaways (page 86) and Butter Mix Cookies (page 108).

OATMEAL SPICE COOKIES

Pictured above.

1 package Betty Crocker Honey Spice Cake Mix
⅔ cup shortening
2 eggs
1 cup oats
¼ cup water
1 cup chopped dates
½ cup chopped nuts

Heat oven to 375°. Combine half the cake mix (dry mix), the shortening and eggs in mixing bowl; mix thoroughly. Blend in remaining cake mix (dry mix), the oats and water. Stir in dates and nuts. Drop dough by teaspoonfuls, about 2 inches apart, onto ungreased baking sheet. Bake *10 to 12 minutes. Makes about 5 dozen.*

Banana Oatmeal Cookies: Follow recipe (above) except—add 1 cup mashed bananas to shortening mixture.

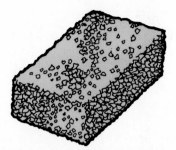

PARTY MERINGUE KISSES

Pictured below.

Heat oven to 275°. In small mixer bowl, blend Betty Crocker Fluffy White Frosting Mix (dry mix), ⅓ cup confectioners' sugar and ⅓ cup cold water until frosting and sugar are dissolved. Beat 3 to 5 minutes high speed on mixer, scraping bowl occasionally, until mixture is thick and holds very stiff peaks. Drop rounded teaspoonfuls, 1 inch apart, onto baking sheet covered with aluminum foil or brown paper.

Bake *45 minutes.* Turn off oven and leave kisses in 45 minutes longer to dry out completely. *Makes about 3½ dozen.*

Cherry-Nut Kisses: Follow recipe (above) except—fold ⅓ cup chopped nuts and ¼ cup chopped candied cherries into mixture after beating.

Chocolate Chip Kisses: Follow recipe (above) except—fold 1 cup semisweet chocolate pieces into mixture after beating.

Coconut Kisses: Follow recipe (above) except—fold 1½ cups flaked coconut into mixture after beating.

Betty Crocker Note: Variations will make *4½ to 5 dozen* and will have slightly cracked tops. Drop about 30 kisses onto each of two baking sheets.

CHOCOLATE CHIP-NUT BARS

1 package Betty Crocker Yellow Cake Mix
¼ cup water
2 eggs
¼ cup soft butter or margarine
¼ cup brown sugar (packed)
1 package (12 ounces) semisweet chocolate pieces
½ cup chopped nuts

Heat oven to 375°. Combine half the cake mix (dry mix), the water, eggs, butter and brown sugar in mixing bowl; mix thoroughly. Blend in remaining cake mix. Stir in chocolate pieces and nuts. Spread in greased and floured jelly roll pan, 15½x10½x1 inch.

Bake *20 to 25 minutes.* Cool. Cut into bars, 3x1½ inches. *Makes about 30.*

Chocolate-topped Peanut Bars: Follow recipe (above) except—substitute 1½ cups chopped salted peanuts for the chocolate pieces and nuts. Frost with our Chocolate Satin ready-to-spread Frosting.

Jeweled Bars: Follow recipe (left) except—omit chocolate pieces and nuts. Fold in 1½ cups miniature gumdrops, halved. Cool. Sprinkle with confectioners' sugar.

Apricot-Cherry Bars: Follow recipe (left) except—substitute ½ cup chopped maraschino cherries and 1 cup chopped dried apricots for the chocolate pieces and nuts. While warm, spread with Orange Glaze: Blend 1 cup confectioners' sugar, 1 teaspoon grated orange peel and 2 tablespoons orange juice until smooth.

Candies

CHOCOLATE FUDGE

2 tablespoons butter or margarine
3 tablespoons water
1 package Betty Crocker Chocolate Fudge Frosting Mix
½ cup chopped nuts

Melt butter with water in top of double boiler. Blend in frosting mix (dry mix) until smooth. Heat over rapidly boiling water 5 minutes, stirring occasionally. Stir in nuts. Pour into buttered loaf pan, 9x5x3 inches. Let set until firm. *Makes 1 pound (32 squares).*

Fudge Clusters (Pictured below, left): Follow recipe (above) except—substitute 2 cups pecans or almonds for the chopped nuts. Drop by teaspoonfuls onto waxed paper. Let stand until firm. *Makes 4 dozen.*

Chocolate-Mint Balls: Follow recipe (left) except—add 1 teaspoon peppermint extract with the nuts. Cool; form into balls. Dip in a variety of chopped nuts, colored sugars, chocolate shot or other colorful candies. (If candies and nuts do not stick to fudge, dip in unbeaten egg white first.) *Makes 3 dozen.*

Ribbon Fudge (Pictured below, center): Pour Chocolate Fudge (left) into buttered square pan, 8x8x2 inches. Pour Opera Fudge (page 49) on top, making two layers. Let set until firm. Cut into 1-inch squares. *Makes 64 squares.*

Marshmallow-Nut Fudge (Pictured below, right): Follow recipe (left) except—stir in 1 cup miniature marshmallows with the nuts. *Makes 32 squares.*

OPERA FUDGE

Pictured above.

3 tablespoons butter or margarine
3 tablespoons milk
1 package Betty Crocker Creamy White Frosting Mix
Walnut halves

Melt butter with milk in top of double boiler. Blend in frosting mix (dry mix) until smooth. Heat over rapidly boiling water 5 minutes, stirring occasionally. Pour into buttered loaf pan, 9x5x3 inches. Press walnut halves on top. Let set until firm. *Makes 1 pound (32 squares).*

Cherry Opera Fudge: Follow recipe (above) except—stir in ½ cup candied cherry halves before pouring into pan.

Peppermint Wafers (*Pictured below, right*): Follow recipe (above) except—add ½ teaspoon peppermint extract and food coloring as desired; omit nuts. Drop by teaspoonfuls onto waxed paper, making rounded flat shapes.* *Makes about 4 dozen.*

Crunchy Mocha Drops: Follow recipe (above) except—blend 1 to 2 tablespoons instant coffee into the butter and milk. Stir in 1½ cups toasted flaked coconut after removing from heat. Drop by teaspoonfuls onto waxed paper. *Makes 4 to 5 dozen.*

Lemon Opera Fudge: Follow recipe (above) except—use our Lemon Velvet Frosting Mix.

Lemon Wafers: Follow recipe (above) except—use our Lemon Velvet Frosting Mix; omit nuts. Drop by teaspoonfuls onto waxed paper, making rounded flat shapes.* *Makes about 4 dozen.*

Keep frosting over hot water while making wafers.

CARAMEL FUDGE

2 tablespoons butter or margarine
2 tablespoons plus 1 teaspoon water
1 package Betty Crocker Golden Caramel Frosting Mix
½ cup chopped nuts

Melt butter with water in top of double boiler. Blend in frosting mix (dry mix) until smooth. Heat over rapidly boiling water 5 minutes, stirring occasionally. Stir in nuts. Pour into buttered loaf pan, 9x5x3 inches. Let set until firm. *Makes 1 pound (32 squares).*

Caramel Pralines: Follow recipe (above) except—substitute 1 cup pecan halves for the chopped nuts. Drop by teaspoonfuls onto waxed paper. *Makes 3 dozen.*

Caramel-Hazelnut Fudge: Follow recipe (above) except—use hazelnuts for nuts.

CREAMY VANILLA FONDANT

Mix with fork Betty Crocker Creamy White Frosting Mix (dry mix), ½ cup soft butter or margarine and 1 teaspoon vanilla. Work into a ball with hands. Knead 20 to 30 times on board lightly dusted with confectioners' sugar. Fondant may be divided and tinted different colors as desired with food coloring. Knead again to distribute color in each portion. Shape into balls or slices.

To make balls: shape into 1-inch balls. Press tops into or roll completely in finely crushed peppermint stick candy, chopped nuts, multicolored candies or flaked coconut. *Makes about 4 dozen.*

To make slices: roll into pencil-like strips about ¾ inch in diameter. Roll strips in finely crushed peppermint stick candy, chopped nuts, multicolored candies or finely chopped coconut. Carefully cut ½-inch slices, using a sharp knife. *Makes about 6 dozen.*

Toasted Almond Bonbons: Follow recipe (above) except—omit vanilla and add ½ cup finely chopped toasted almonds. Shape into 1-inch balls. Roll balls in more finely chopped toasted almonds, if desired. *Makes about 4 dozen.*

Peppermint Creams: Follow recipe (above) except—omit vanilla and add ½ teaspoon peppermint extract.

Fondant-filled Dates: Make Creamy Vanilla Fondant (above). Use to fill pitted dates. Chill.

CREAMY CHOCOLATE FONDANT

Mix with fork Betty Crocker Chocolate Fudge Frosting Mix (dry mix), ½ cup soft butter or margarine and 1 teaspoon vanilla. Work into a ball with hands. Knead 20 to 30 times on board lightly dusted with confectioners' sugar. Press fondant into rectangle, 8x7 inches. Press flaked coconut, chopped nuts, chocolate shot or multicolored candies on top of fondant. Cut into 1-inch squares or 2x½-inch fingers. *Makes about 4½ dozen.*

Chocolate Bonbons: Follow recipe (above) except—mold fondant around whole pieces of candied fruit, cherries, ginger, pineapple, walnut or pecan halves. Garnish candies with flaked coconut pressed on top or roll in finely chopped nuts, chocolate shot, etc. *Makes about 5 dozen.*

Chocolate-Nut Creams: Follow recipe (above) except—add ½ cup finely chopped nuts. Shape fondant into 1-inch balls. Roll in mixture of cinnamon and sugar. *Makes about 5 dozen.*

COFFEE AND RUM BALLS

1 package Betty Crocker Golden Caramel Frosting Mix
½ cup soft butter or margarine
2 teaspoons instant coffee
½ teaspoon rum flavoring
⅔ cup finely chopped pecans

Mix all ingredients except pecans with fork. Work into a ball with hands. Knead 20 to 30 times on board lightly dusted with confectioners' sugar. Shape into 1-inch balls; roll in chopped pecans. *Makes about 5 dozen.*

CREAMY PEANUT BUTTER FONDANT

Mix with fork Betty Crocker Creamy White Frosting Mix (dry mix), ½ cup soft butter or margarine and ½ cup peanut butter. Work into a ball with hands. Knead 20 to 30 times on board lightly dusted with confectioners' sugar. Shape into balls or squares.

To make balls: shape into 1-inch balls. Roll in toasted flaked coconut. *Makes about 4 dozen.*

To make squares: press fondant into rectangle, 8x7 inches. Press toasted flaked coconut or chopped peanuts on top. Cut into 1-inch squares. *Makes about 4½ dozen.*

Children's Surprises

CHEERIOS-FUDGE CONFECTIONS

1 package Betty Crocker Chocolate Fudge Frosting Mix
½ cup soft butter or margarine
2 teaspoons hot water
½ teaspoon vanilla
2 cups Cheerios

In large bowl, combine frosting mix (dry mix), butter, water and vanilla with fork or fingers until thoroughly blended. Add Cheerios; mix well. With hands, shape into 1-inch balls. Balls may be rolled in ½ cup crushed Cheerios. *Makes about 4 dozen.*

CHEERIOS-PEANUT BUTTER FUDGE BALLS

1 package Betty Crocker Chocolate Fudge Frosting Mix
½ cup creamy peanut butter
¼ cup soft butter or margarine
2 tablespoons hot water
½ teaspoon vanilla
2 cups Cheerios

In large bowl, combine frosting mix (dry mix), peanut butter, butter, water and vanilla with fork or fingers until thoroughly blended. Add Cheerios; mix well. With hands, shape into 1-inch balls. If desired, roll balls in ½ cup crushed Cheerios. *Makes about 4 dozen.*

FROZEN CHEERIOS SQUARES

1 package Betty Crocker Chocolate Malt Frosting Mix
¼ cup butter or margarine
3 tablespoons hot water
½ teaspoon vanilla
3 cups Cheerios
½ cup peanuts

In large bowl, combine frosting mix (dry mix), butter, water and vanilla until thoroughly blended. Stir in Cheerios and peanuts. Spread in a lightly buttered square pan, 9x9x2 inches. Freeze for 2 to 3 hours. Cut into 1½-inch squares; serve frozen. *Makes 3 dozen.*

Betty Crocker Note: If storing for more than a day, keep covered in freezer.

JELLY-COCONUT DIPS

Heat oven to 350°. Prepare any flavor Betty Crocker Layer Cake Mix as directed on package. Pour batter into greased and floured jelly roll pan, 15½x10½x1 inch. Bake *25 to 30 minutes.* Cool in pan.

Cut into 1½-inch squares. Dip sides and tops into jelly softened by heating over hot water. Roll in plain or toasted coconut. Or roll in finely chopped nuts. *Makes about 70 dips..*

Variation: Frost cake in pan. Cut into squares. Sprinkle with plain or toasted coconut or finely chopped nuts. Serve from pan.

Betty Crocker Note: Cakes are easier to cut *before* sprinkling with coconut.

BANANA POPS

2 tablespoons butter or margarine
3 tablespoons water
1 package Betty Crocker Chocolate Fudge Frosting Mix
4 bananas

Melt butter with water in top of double boiler. Add frosting mix (dry mix) and stir until smooth. Heat over rapidly boiling water 5 minutes, stirring occasionally. Peel bananas, cut crosswise into three or four pieces and place each on a wooden skewer. Dip in fudge mixture or spread mixture on with spatula. Roll in chopped nuts, candies or flaked coconut (toasted, if desired). Chill until fudge coating is firm.

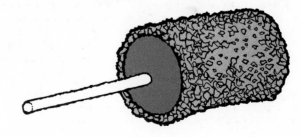

FUDGY CARAMEL APPLES

Pictured above.

7 or 8 medium apples
2 tablespoons butter or margarine
3 tablespoons water
1 package Betty Crocker Golden Caramel Frosting Mix

Wash and dry apples; insert wooden skewers in them. Melt butter with water in top of double boiler. Add frosting mix (dry mix); stir until smooth. Heat over boiling water 5 minutes, stirring occasionally. Remove from heat, keeping caramel mixture over hot water. Dip apples one at a time in caramel mixture, coating apples evenly. If desired, immediately dip each caramel apple in chopped nuts. Add a few drops hot water if caramel mixture becomes too thick. Frost last two or three apples with spatula. *Makes 7 or 8.*

Betty Crocker Note: Apples may be coated with frosting prepared as directed on package. Spread with spatula.

ANGEL S'MORES

Bake Betty Crocker Angel Food Cake Mix in two loaf pans, 9x5x3 inches, as directed on inner packet. Cool. Remove from pans.

When completely cool, cut into 1-inch slices. Top each slice with milk chocolate candy bar squares (use 1-ounce candy bars). Place marshmallow halves on chocolate squares. Place s'mores on baking sheet about 4 inches from broiler 1 to 2 minutes, or just until marshmallows brown. Serve immediately. *Each loaf makes 9 s'mores.*

TOASTED CAKE WEDGES

Cut leftover cake into wedges or squares. Split and spread cut surface with soft butter. Sprinkle with a sugar-cinnamon mixture. Toast in broiler 1 to 2 minutes about 3 inches from heat. Serve immediately.

SELF-FROSTED COCONUT BARS

Heat oven to 350°. Prepare any flavor Betty Crocker Layer Cake Mix as directed on package. Pour batter into greased and floured jelly roll pan, 15½x10½x1 inch. Sprinkle 2 cups flaked coconut over top of batter. Bake *25 to 30 minutes.* Cool.

Sprinkle confectioners' sugar over top of cake while still slightly warm, if desired. Cut into bars to serve. *Makes 18 to 24 bars.*

HONEY COCONUT BARS

Heat oven to 350°. Slice leftover cake (chiffon or layer cake) into strips, 3x1½ inches. Coat each strip with soft butter and honey. Roll in flaked coconut. Place strips on baking sheet. Bake *10 to 12 minutes.* Serve warm.

MARGUERITES

Heat oven to 350°. Prepare Betty Crocker Fluffy White Frosting Mix as directed on package. Fold in 1 cup chopped nuts. Drop by tablespoonfuls onto 40 soda crackers.

Bake *4 to 6 minutes,* or until light brown. *Makes 40.*

Betty Crocker Note: Any leftover fluffy frosting may be used in this way.

LITTLE TREATS

Bake your favorite flavor Betty Crocker Layer Cake Mix in paper baking cups as directed on package. Finish in one of the following ways.

Chocolate-Mint Cupcakes: Immediately after removing cupcakes from oven, top each with a chocolate-covered mint patty. When the patty melts, spread lightly for marbled mint frosting.

Little Clown Cupcakes: Make faces on frosted cupcakes with bits of candied fruit.

Porcupine Cupcakes: Stick peanut halves or slivered almonds into frosted cupcakes.

Flower Cupcakes: Arrange miniature marshmallows, pillow mints, tiny gumdrops or sliced candied cherries in flower design on frosted cupcakes. Cut green gumdrops or green candied cherries for leaves and stems.

Butterfly Cupcakes: Slice off top of cupcake crosswise. Frost cut side with our Fluffy White Frosting Mix or whipped cream. Cut top slice in half crosswise; insert each piece in frosting or whipped cream at 45-degree angle to resemble butterfly wings.

Top Hats: Cut cones from tops of cupcakes. Fill with prepared packaged pudding, replace tops and dust with confectioners' sugar.

Good Fortune Cupcakes: Write fortunes on narrow strips of paper; fold into small squares and wrap in plastic wrap. Cut a slit along top *edge* of each cupcake; insert fortune so that a small portion shows.

Frost cupcakes. If desired, decorate with "butterflies": Drain mandarin orange segments well; place two on frosted top of each cupcake to resemble butterfly wings. Use thin strips of green gumdrops for the antennae.

"YOUR OWN CHOICE" CUPCAKES

Frost cupcakes with your favorite flavor Betty Crocker Satin ready-to-spread Frosting and garnish with:

Crushed peppermint candy

Pieces of mint patty or pastel mints

Animal crackers

Chopped nuts

Walnut halves

Slivered almonds

Toasted coconut

Tinted coconut

Colored sugars

Colored nonpareils

Chocolate sprinkles

Grated orange peel or lemon peel

Peppermint candy canes

Maraschino cherries

Pillow mints

Semisweet chocolate pieces

Gumdrops and other candies

Candied fruit

S'MORE CUPCAKES

Bake Betty Crocker Dark Chocolate Fudge Cake Mix in paper baking cups as directed on package. Just as cupcakes come from oven, place a half marshmallow on top of each. Put back in oven 3 to 5 minutes, or until marshmallows soften and start to melt. Remove from oven and press a chocolate kiss in the center of each marshmallow. Serve warm or cold.

SUGAR 'N SPICE CUPCAKES

Prepare Betty Crocker Honey Spice Cake Mix as directed on package. Pour batter into paper baking cups. Sprinkle batter lightly with confectioners' sugar, a little cinnamon (so some white sugar is still visible) and chopped nuts (about 1 teaspoon for each cupcake). Bake as directed for cupcakes. Serve warm or cold.

COCONUT-JELLY CUPCAKES

Bake Betty Crocker Yellow Cake Mix in paper baking cups as directed on package. Cool. Spread tops with tart red jelly and sprinkle with coconut.

For another children's treat, try Ice Cream Cone Cakes (page 60).

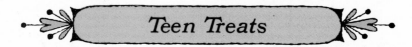

Teen Treats

BANANA DAISY SUNDAE

1 package Betty Crocker Dark Chocolate Fudge Cake Mix
Bananas
Ice cream
Dark Chocolate Fudge Sauce (below)

Bake cake in oblong pan, 13x9x2 inches, as directed on package. Cool. Cut into squares. Place a banana slice on each of the four corners of each piece. In the center, place a small scoop of your favorite flavor ice cream. Pour Dark Chocolate Fudge Sauce over the ice cream.

Dark Chocolate Fudge Sauce:

1 package Betty Crocker Dark Chocolate Fudge Frosting Mix
2 tablespoons light corn syrup
3 tablespoons soft butter or margarine
⅔ cup milk

Combine frosting mix (dry mix), corn syrup and butter in top of double boiler. Add milk gradually. Heat over rapidly boiling water 5 minutes, stirring occasionally. Store sauce covered in refrigerator. *Makes 1 pint.*

Ice Cream Sandwiches: Bake cake and cut into squares. Cut each square to make three equal layers. Cut a pint brick of ice cream into squares that will fit between the three cake slices and place the cake and ice cream alternately on individual oval banana split dishes. Arrange banana pieces at the ends of the plates. Pour Dark Chocolate Fudge Sauce over the top of cake and ice cream.

DIPSY DOODLES

They're the teen-age rage! Bite-size cake mix snacks and crackers served with little bowls of gaily colored frosting dips—some made with cream cheese, some with sour cream or fruity flavorings. Mix and match to taste.

Prepare Butter Mix Cookies (page 108) except—divide dough in half. Add 1 square (1 ounce) unsweetened chocolate, melted and cooled, to one half; knead in until dough is uniformly colored. Shape both yellow and chocolate dough into several 1-inch rolls. Cut into slices ⅛ inch thick. Place on ungreased baking sheet. Bake *6 to 8 minutes.* Cool.

Serve with an assortment of sweet dips (below). Keep covered with plastic wrap until serving time to prevent drying.

Suggested dips:
Creamy Cheese Frosting (page 20)
Brown Satin Frosting (page 138)
Caramel Fluff Topping (page 94)
Raspberry or Strawberry Frosting (page 20)
Lemon, Orange or Lime Frosting (page 20)
Fluffy Sour Cream Topping, using Cherry Fluff Frosting Mix (page 94)

Chocolate Fudge Soda

CHOCOLATE SAUCE

1 package Betty Crocker Chocolate Fudge Frosting Mix
2 tablespoons light corn syrup
3 tablespoons soft butter or margarine
⅔ cup milk

Combine frosting mix (dry mix), corn syrup and butter in top of double boiler. Add milk gradually. Heat over rapidly boiling water 5 minutes, stirring occasionally. Store sauce covered in refrigerator. *Makes 1 pint.*

Continental Cocoa: Mix 2 cups milk, ¼ teaspoon cinnamon and ⅓ cup Chocolate Sauce (above). Heat, but do not boil. Place a marshmallow in each cup and pour cocoa over it. *3 or 4 servings.*

Chocolate Fudge Milk Shake: Combine ½ cup cold milk and 3 tablespoons Chocolate Sauce (above). Add 2 to 4 large scoops vanilla ice cream; mix just enough to blend. Serve immediately. *Makes 1 shake.*

Chocolate-Mint Shake:

1 cup cold milk
¼ cup Chocolate Sauce (left)
½ teaspoon vanilla
2 or 3 drops peppermint extract
2 or 3 scoops vanilla ice cream

Combine milk, Chocolate Sauce and flavorings. Add ice cream; shake until smooth and blended. *Makes 1 shake.*

Chocolate Fudge Soda: Combine 2 tablespoons Chocolate Sauce (left) and ¼ cup carbonated water in large glass. Add 1 or 2 large scoops vanilla or chocolate ice cream. Pour ¼ cup carbonated water over ice cream; blend slightly. Serve immediately. *Makes 1 soda.*

Chocolate-Nog:

1 egg, well beaten
¼ cup Chocolate Sauce (left)
1 cup milk
½ teaspoon vanilla
Nutmeg

Combine egg and Chocolate Sauce; beat. Beat in milk and vanilla. Serve cold in tall glasses; sprinkle each with a dash of nutmeg. *2 servings.*

Chocolate Fudge Milk Shake

GOLDEN CARAMEL SAUCE

1 package Betty Crocker Golden Caramel Frosting Mix
2 tablespoons light corn syrup
3 tablespoons soft butter or margarine
⅔ cup milk

Combine frosting mix (dry mix), corn syrup and butter in top of double boiler. Stir in milk gradually. Heat over rapidly boiling water 5 minutes, stirring occasionally. Store sauce covered in refrigerator. *Makes 1 pint.*

Caramel-Pecan Sauce: Follow recipe (above) except—after removing from heat, stir in 1 cup pecans.

Caramel-Cream Parfaits: Fill parfait glasses, making alternate layers of Golden Caramel Sauce (above), butter pecan ice cream and whipped cream. Freeze until serving time. Top with whipped cream and garnish with pecan halves.

Caramel-Cream Parfait

Golden Caramel Sauce over vanilla ice cream

CHOCOLATE MALT BANANA SPLIT

Bake Betty Crocker Chocolate Malt Cake Mix in oblong pan, 13x9x2 inches, as directed on package. Cool. Slice lengthwise into ½-inch strips. Cut strips in half. Cut bananas in half lengthwise.

Place 1 banana slice and 1 cake strip on each side of 3 tiny scoops of ice cream (use a variety of flavors) on long narrow dish or regular dessert plate. Top with a variety of sauces (such as chocolate, crushed pineapple, butterscotch, marshmallow), berry preserves and nuts. Top with whipped cream and a cherry.

ICE CREAM AND CAKE PARFAITS

A wonderful way to serve leftover cake.

Fill parfait glasses, making alternate layers of small cubes of cake, ice cream and drained fruit or berries* (layer them in that order). When parfait glass is full, top with a spoonful of ice cream and a piece of fruit or berry. (This may be frozen.)

**Fresh, frozen (thawed) or canned raspberries or strawberries may be used.*

Betty Crocker Note: For a quick snack, serve in colorful paper cups, flat-bottomed ice cream cones, gay coffee mugs or other dessert dishes.

"CHOO CHOO" BIRTHDAY TRAIN

Pictured below.

Heat oven to 350°. Grease and flour six small loaf pans, 4½x2¾x1¼ inches, and one square pan, 8x8x2 inches, or one round layer pan, 9x1½ inches. Prepare Betty Crocker Devils Food Cake Mix as directed on package. Fill each loaf pan half full of batter and pour remaining batter into square or layer pan. Bake loaves *20 to 25 minutes* and square or layer as directed on package. Cool.

Prepare Betty Crocker Chocolate Fudge Frosting Mix as directed on package. Place each small loaf upside down on individual aluminum foil "plates" or large serving tray. Frost sides and tops of loaves. Decorate with hard candy circle mints for wheels and candleholders, red 1-inch gumdrop for smokestack. Use candles on engine and first car. "Fill" each additional car with one of these: red cinnamon candies, nonpareils, peanuts and colored decorators' sugar.

Place in line down center of table. Serve on aluminum foil "plates," one for each child, or cut in half to serve two.

Betty Crocker Note: If no loaf pans are available, bake in square pans, 8x8x2 inches or 9x9x2 inches, or oblong pan, 13x9x2 inches; cut into 4x2½-inch pieces; frost and decorate as above.

A DAY-AT-THE-ZOO CAKE

Bake any flavor Betty Crocker Layer Cake Mix in oblong pan, 13x9x2 inches, as directed on package. Remove from pan and cool.

Prepare Betty Crocker Chocolate Fudge Frosting Mix as directed on package. Frost sides and top of cake (frosting on top should be about ¼ inch thick).

Decorate by spacing animal crackers about 1 inch apart around top edge of cake, pressing animals gently into frosting to hold upright. Between each animal place a gumdrop, using assorted colors.

Form a rectangle in center of cake by setting candles in frosting (candleholders may be used). Use the number of candles appropriate to the child's birthday.

Decorate sides of cake by pressing additional animal crackers flat against frosting around bottom edge. Alternate crackers with gumdrops in assorted colors.

"CUT-UP" CLOWN CAKE

Prepare any flavor Betty Crocker Layer Cake Mix as directed on package. Divide batter evenly between greased and floured round layer pan, 9x1½ inches, and square pan, 8x8x2 inches. Bake as directed on package for 9-inch round layers. Cool.

Cut cakes as shown below.

Arrange on large tray or aluminum foil-covered board. (Clown is approximately 16 inches long.)

Frost and finish cake as shown.

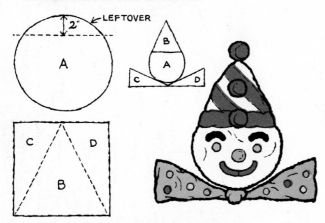

Prepare Betty Crocker Fluffy White Frosting Mix as directed on package. Tint 1 cup blue and ¼ cup red. Frost entire face and hat with remaining frosting. Use blue frosting for bow tie. Shape a knot at center of tie. Use red frosting for brim and diagonal stripes on hat. (You may prefer to frost bow tie before arranging pieces next to face.)

Gumdrop trim:

Eyebrows: Roll 2 long black gumdrops long and flat; form arches.

Eyes: Use 2 large green gumdrops.

Nose: Use large red or orange gumdrop.

Mouth: Roll 2 large red gumdrops flat. Press and join together; cut out to shape smile.

Pompons: Place 3 large red gumdrops in a vertical line at top, center and bottom of hat.

Bow Tie: Use small gumdrops of varied colors to form polka dot effect.

> *Betty Crocker Note:* For ease in rolling gumdrops, use sugar (this will prevent sticking).

BOZO CLOWN CAKE

Prepare any flavor Betty Crocker Layer Cake Mix as directed on package except—reserve ¼ cup batter. Pour remaining batter into two greased and floured round layer pans, 8 or 9x1½ inches. Bake as directed. Pour reserved batter into greased and floured 3-inch custard cup; bake with cake *15 to 20 minutes.* Cool.

Prepare Betty Crocker Fluffy White Frosting Mix as directed on package. Reserve 1½ cups; tint remaining frosting light green. Fill and frost cake with green frosting, heaping it in mounds on top for ruffle.

Frost cupcake white; set in center of cake. Frost cone for hat.

Make Decorator Icing (page 24) with remaining white frosting. Tint ¼ cup pink. Make hat brim and ruff, using star tip. Add white trim with flower tip. Decorate with gumdrop slices.

Cupcake Clowns: Follow recipe (above) except—bake cake in paper baking cups as directed on package. Cool. Remove papers. Holding each cupcake with fork, frost entirely with green-tinted frosting. Top with frosted cone for hat. Decorate individual "clowns" as directed above, or use pieces of miniature gumdrops for faces. Serve each on a doily.

ICE CREAM CONE CAKES

Pictured opposite.

Prepare any flavor Betty Crocker Layer Cake Mix as directed on package. Pour scant ¼ cup of batter into each of 30 flat-bottomed waffle ice cream cones, filling *scant ½ full.* (If cones are filled more than this, batter will run over top.) Set in oblong or square baking pan. Bake as directed for cupcakes. Cool.

Frost with any flavor Betty Crocker Frosting Mix prepared as directed on package. Decorate with candies, nonpareils, etc., or top with a scoop of ice cream. *Makes about 30 medium cones.*

> *Betty Crocker Note:* These waffle ice cream cones may be purchased at many supermarkets.

Pictured from top to bottom: Honey Bear Cake, Ice Cream Cone Cakes, Big Top Circus Cake

HONEY BEAR CAKE

Pictured on page 61.

Heat oven to 350°. Prepare any flavor Betty Crocker Layer Cake Mix as directed on package. Pour into greased and floured jelly roll pan, 15½x10½x1 inch. Bake *25 to 30 minutes.* Cool.

Cut cake as shown in diagram. On large aluminum foil-covered cardboard or two baking sheets taped together and covered with aluminum foil, arrange cake pieces to resemble bear with balloon in hand (see picture).

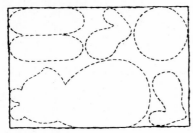

Prepare Betty Crocker Golden Caramel Frosting Mix as directed on package. Frost bear and balloon, joining all parts. Sprinkle balloon with decorators' sugar. Join balloon to bear's paw with shoestring licorice. Use large black gumdrop for nose. Cut a marshmallow into thirds; use one third for the eye, and a chocolate chip for the pupil.

CALICO PONY CAKE

Bake Betty Crocker Devils Food Cake Mix in oblong pan, 13x9x2 inches, as directed on package. Remove from pan and cool.

Cut cake as shown in diagram. Cover top of very large breadboard with bright paper and hold it in place with plastic wrap. Arrange cake pieces as shown in sketch.

Prepare Betty Crocker Chocolate Fudge Frosting Mix as directed on package. Frost entire cake, joining all parts. Arrange pastel-colored flat mint wafers for pony's spots and use shoestring licorice for bridle, harness and tail.

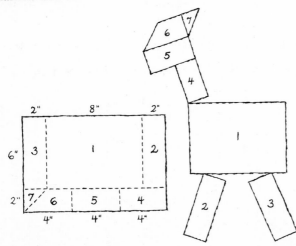

PUPPY DOG CAKE

Prepare any flavor Betty Crocker Layer Cake Mix as directed on package. Pour into one greased and floured square pan, 8x8x2 inches, and one round layer pan, 8x1½ inches. Batter should be the same depth in both pans (check level with a wooden pick). Bake as directed on package. Cool.

Cut body, paw and collar from square cake and head, tail and ear from round cake as shown. Arrange cake pieces on a tray as shown in sketch, turning ear and tail pieces over so they are in proper position.

Prepare Betty Crocker Fluffy White Frosting Mix as directed on package. Frost entire dog, joining all parts. Melt 2 squares (2 ounces) semisweet chocolate. Using small spatula, spread chocolate over frosting on ears and collar. Draw eyes and mouth with melted chocolate. Outline paws and legs (see sketch) with pieces of black licorice sticks. For his nose, anchor a large gumdrop with a wooden pick.

BIG TOP CIRCUS CAKE

Pictured on page 61.

Bake Betty Crocker Devils Food Cake Mix in two round layer pans, 8 or 9x1½ inches, as directed on package. Cool.

Prepare 1 package Betty Crocker Chocolate Fudge and 1 package Betty Crocker Creamy White Frosting Mix as directed on packages. Fill and frost cake with chocolate frosting.

Divide white frosting into 4 parts; tint one part red, one yellow, one green and one blue. Use animal crackers for the animals, straws for uprights of canopy and a peppermint candy stick, if desired, in center of cake. Animals may be arranged inside on "stands" made from dabs of yellow frosting pressed through decorating cone with star tip (see page 25). Make a ring around top of cake with same tip and frosting.

Make canopy by scalloping edge of an 11-inch circle of peppermint striped paper. Cut between 2 scallops to center and overlap to make cupped canopy. Fasten with transparent tape or paper clip. Rest canopy on top of straw "poles."

Decorate side of cake with other animal crackers. Make different colored cages, using writing tip and star tip and the remaining tinted frosting (see page 25).

Children's Cakes—Especially for Girls

DOLL CAKE

Pictured on page 65.

2 packages Betty Crocker White Cake Mix
2 packages Betty Crocker Fluffy White Frosting Mix
5½ cups sifted confectioners' sugar
Red food coloring
6-inch doll

Bake cake mixes in three round layer pans, 8x1½ inches, and 12 to 18 paper baking cups as directed on package, preparing one package at a time. Cool.

Place layers on aluminum foil-covered cardboard circle or cake plate. Trim layers just enough to give a rounded effect for skirt. Wrap doll below waist with aluminum foil or plastic wrap. Cut hole in center of layers large enough and deep enough for doll to stand waist deep.

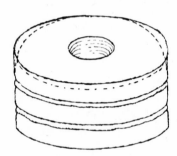

Prepare 1 package of frosting mix as directed on package. Tint very light pink. Transfer to large bowl and blend in 2 cups sifted confectioners' sugar, 1 cup at a time. Fill and frost layers. Set doll in hole.

Repeat with second package of frosting mix except— blend in 1 to 1½ cups more sifted confectioners' sugar. Use leaf tip (see page 25) to make 5 rows of scallop designs for ruffled skirt. Tint icing slightly deeper pink; use half with same tip to continue scallop design. Tint remaining icing deeper pink and complete skirt. Use star tip for flower trim on skirt, if desired.

The Cradle Cake (page 119) could be served for a little girl's birthday party.

HANSEL AND GRETEL'S CAKE

Pictured on page 65.

Bake any flavor Betty Crocker Layer Cake Mix in oblong pan, 13x9x2 inches, as directed on package. Remove from pan and cool. Measure 5 inches along length of cake; cut crosswise. Cut diagonally across remaining piece as shown in diagram A.

Prepare Betty Crocker Fluffy White Frosting Mix as directed on package. Tint yellow, pink or green. Use 9x5-inch piece for base of house, 9-inch side for front. Place triangles upright on base as shown in diagram B. Trim corners and base so pieces fit smoothly. (The pointed roof of the house will be slightly off center.) Use frosting to hold house together; frost entire house. Decorate as follows:

Use ½ cup toasted coconut for roof.

Use row of chocolate chips (point side in) where roof joins base.

Use milk chocolate candy bar for doors, windows and panes.

Place dragées around windows and panes.

Surround house with green coconut grass and lollipop trees, if desired.

To serve cake, cut slices from roof section first.

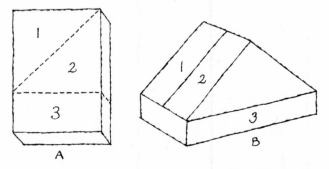

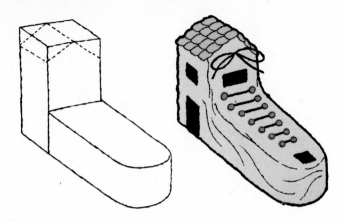

SHOE CAKE

Heat oven to 350°. Prepare Betty Crocker Yellow Cake Mix as directed on package except—use 2 tablespoons less water. Pour batter into two greased and floured loaf pans, 9x5x3 inches. Bake *35 to 40 minutes*. Cool.

Place one loaf on serving plate or tray; stand second loaf upright against horizontal loaf as shown. If desired, round corners of horizontal loaf to resemble toe of shoe. Cut corners of upright loaf to form peak of roof.

Prepare Betty Crocker Fluffy White Frosting Mix as directed on package. Tint desired color. Frost shoe.

To decorate, use pillow mints or wafers for roof; red cinnamon candies or pillow mints for eyelets of shoe; red or black shoestring licorice for shoelace; milk chocolate squares or pillow mints for the door and windows.

BOW-DOTTED CAKE

Bake any flavor Betty Crocker Layer Cake Mix in two round layer pans, 8 or 9x1½ inches, as directed on package. Cool.

Prepare Betty Crocker Fluffy White Frosting Mix as directed on package. Reserve ½ cup. Fill and frost cake with remaining frosting.

To the ½ cup frosting add ½ to ¾ cup sifted confectioners' sugar and a few drops red food coloring. Use this frosting to outline shape of bows with decorating or envelope cone (see page 24) on top and sides or around top edge of cake. Fill in bows with more frosting, if desired. A candle may be placed in the center of each bow.

MARIGOLD CAKE

Bake any flavor Betty Crocker Layer Cake Mix in oblong pan, 13x9x2 inches, as directed on package. Remove from pan; cool.

Prepare Betty Crocker Fluffy White Frosting Mix as directed on package. Cut cake lengthwise in half; stack pieces to make an oblong loaf, using frosting as filling. To make cake as level as possible, place bottoms together with cut edges opposite each other. Frost sides and top of cake.

To make marigold on top of cake, use circles of gumdrops, fruit slices, jelly beans or almonds. Use a green candy stick for the stem, upon which green spearmint leaves may be placed.

For a birthday, the appropriate number of candles may be inserted into the flower or stem.

SLICK CHICK CAKE

Bake any flavor Betty Crocker Layer Cake Mix in two round layer pans, 9x1½ inches, as directed on package. Cool.

Prepare Betty Crocker Fluffy White Frosting Mix as directed on package. Fill layers with frosting. Cut cake in half; on tray or large serving plate, arrange halves of cake in form of chicken as shown in sketch. Frost cake with remaining frosting.

Decorate tail section of cake with lemon and orange candy slices placed alternately in semicircular rows. Use a yellow candy stick broken in half for legs. Cut circle of lemon slice for the eye. One lemon slice will make a wing, comb or beak.

Pictured at top, left: Hansel and Gretel's House; top, right: Sailboat Cake; bottom, left: Camelot Knight's Cake; bottom, right: Doll Cake

DREAM VILLAGE

Bake any flavor Betty Crocker Layer Cake Mix in oblong pan, 13x9x2 inches, as directed on package. Remove from pan; cool.

Prepare Betty Crocker Fluffy White Frosting Mix as directed on package. Tint, if desired. Cut cake lengthwise in half. On large tray or aluminum foil-covered cardboard arrange pieces, placing bottoms together with cut edges down (see diagram). Use frosting as filling. Frost entire loaf.

Decorate 4 sides of loaf to resemble a village scene. Use various kinds of candy to make buildings, trees, flowers, grass, etc. For example, use:

Tiny round candies for pebbles and stones

Lollipops for trees and bushes

Candy flowers for flowers, pieces of gumdrop for stems

Flat round candies broken in half for tile roofs

Gumdrops flattened out and cut into various shapes for buildings.

To celebrate a birthday or special occasion, place candles around top of cake or use long tapers attached to side of cake.

FAIRY CROWN CAKE

Pictured at left.

Bake Betty Crocker Lemon Chiffon Cake Mix as directed on package. Cool. Remove from pan. Trim top to make level and place top side up on serving plate.

Prepare Betty Crocker Fluffy White Frosting Mix as directed on package; reserve ½ cup. Frost cake with remaining frosting, using up-and-down strokes of spatula on sides of cake and radiating strokes from center on top. Drop spoonfuls of the reserved frosting around the top edge of cake, swirling each into a peak to resemble the point of a crown. To decorate cake, place silver dragées on each point of crown. Press more dragées and sliced jewel-colored gumdrops on cake as desired.

HOPSCOTCH CAKE

Bake any flavor Betty Crocker Layer Cake Mix in oblong pan, 13x9x2 inches, as directed on package. Cool.

Cut cake into 8 pieces (4 squares and 4 rectangles) as shown in diagram. On large platter or aluminum foil-covered cardboard, place cake pieces in favorite hopscotch pattern or follow pattern in sketch.

Prepare Betty Crocker Fluffy White Frosting Mix as directed on package. Divide into 3 parts. Tint 2 parts your favorite colors; leave 1 part white. Frost pieces of cake.

If desired, decorate cake with candles on each piece representing numbers or outline numbers on each piece with small candies.

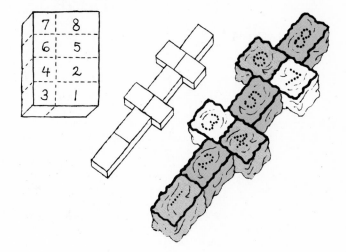

Children's Cakes—Best for Boys

BASEBALL MITT CAKE

1 package Betty Crocker Yellow Cake Mix
1 package Betty Crocker Golden Caramel Frosting Mix
1 package Betty Crocker Fluffy White Frosting Mix
Licorice rope candy

Prepare cake mix as directed on package. Pour half the batter into greased and floured round layer pan, 8 or 9x1½ inches, and remaining batter into 15 to 18 paper baking cups. Bake as directed on package. Cool. Remove papers from cupcakes.

Place your right hand on right side of layer and carefully trace around it with a wooden pick or trace pattern from baseball mitt. Enlarge size of fingers and extend them to make baseball mitt (see diagram). Cut away cake to make fingers of glove. Hollow palm of mitt slightly.

Prepare frosting mixes as directed on packages. Frost top and sides of mitt with caramel frosting. Cut licorice into short strips and lay between fingers for laces. Frost baseball cupcakes on tops and sides with white frosting. Draw stitching lines on baseballs using a decorating cone and Chocolate Decorator Icing (page 69). Place one ball in the palm of the mitt. Put candles in the other balls and arrange around the mitt.

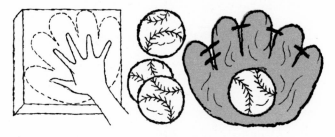

PIRATE CHEST BIRTHDAY CAKE

Pictured at right.

Heat oven to 350°. Prepare any flavor Betty Crocker Layer Cake Mix as directed on package. Pour batter into greased and floured jelly roll pan, 15½x10½x1 inch. Bake *25 to 30 minutes.* Cool.

Cut into three 5-inch strips. Prepare Betty Crocker Chocolate Fudge Frosting Mix as directed on package except—add 3 more tablespoons butter. Fill and frost cake, stacking to make a three-layered oblong cake. Outline chest top with gold or silver dragées. Place gold foil-covered chocolate coins around edge as if falling out of chest (stick in frosting). Use some coins around edge of plate as candleholders (melt wax and stick candle to coin).

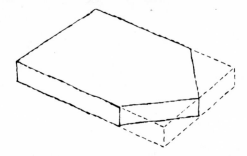

CAMELOT KNIGHT'S CAKE

Pictured on page 65.

Bake any flavor Betty Crocker Layer Cake Mix in oblong pan, 13x9x2 inches, as directed on package. Remove from pan and cool. Trim off corners as shown above to make a shield shape.

Prepare Betty Crocker Creamy White Frosting Mix as directed on package. Leave ⅓ white; tint small amount red; color remaining frosting a medium green. Frost in stripes (see picture). Accent stripes with silver dragées, red cinnamon candies or chocolate pieces. Frost sides of cake with remaining frosting.

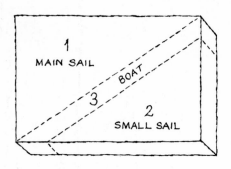

SATELLITE CAKE

1 package Betty Crocker Yellow Cake Mix
¾ cup peanut butter
½ cup hot water
1 package Betty Crocker Creamy White Frosting Mix
Red and green cherries

Bake cake in two round layer pans, 9x1½ inches, as directed on package. Cool.

Add peanut butter and hot water to frosting mix (dry mix). Beat until smooth. If necessary, add a few drops more water for spreading consistency. Frost cake.

Make "satellites" to orbit around cake by sticking wooden picks into red and green cherries. Place on top of cake and use as candleholders.

Peanut Butter 'n Jelly Cake: Follow recipe (above) except—split cake to make 4 layers (see page 20). Spread ⅓ cup tart jelly between each layer to within ¼ inch of edge.

DRUM CAKE

Bake any flavor Betty Crocker Layer Cake Mix in two round layer pans, 8 or 9x1½ inches, as directed on package. Cool.

Prepare Betty Crocker Fluffy White Frosting Mix as directed on package. Fill and frost cake.

Press striped peppermint candy sticks at angles into frosting all around sides of cake. Set a maraschino cherry at ends of each stick. If you like, cross two candy sticks on top of cake for drumsticks.

SAILBOAT CAKE

Pictured on page 65.

Bake any flavor Betty Crocker Layer Cake Mix in oblong pan, 13x9x2 inches, as directed on package. Remove from pan and cool.

Cut cake diagonally in half, forming two triangles, 1 and 2, as illustrated in diagram. From triangle 2, cut a 2-inch strip (3) parallel to first cut. Arrange pieces as shown in picture.

Prepare Betty Crocker Fluffy White Frosting Mix as directed on package. Frost sides and top of cake. Use peppermint sticks for the mast and sprinkle boat (3) with colored decorators' sugar.

Betty Crocker Note: A tray covered with blue paper and transparent plastic wrap forms plate and background for sailboat.

CORRAL CAKE

Pictured on cover.

Bake Betty Crocker Yellow Cake Mix in two round layer pans, 8 or 9x1½ inches, as directed on package. Cool.

Prepare Betty Crocker Golden Caramel Frosting Mix as directed on package except—substitute crunchy peanut butter for the butter. If frosting is too thick, add a few drops hot water. Fill layers and frost sides and top of cake.

Encircle sides of cake with penny-size chocolate rolls placed 2 inches apart for the posts and black shoestring licorice 1½ inches apart for the wires. Weave "wires" under and over alternate "posts." On top of cake write name and age of child with small pieces of string licorice. Make a circle around age with additional licorice. Small birthday candles placed at angles in a group make a "bonfire."

To serve, use scissors to cut licorice "wire." Allow one chocolate roll per serving.

Other cakes appropriate for a boy's birthday party are Football Cake (page 104), Twin Pennant Cakes (page 104) or Gone Fishing Cake (page 101).

Teen-agers' Cakes

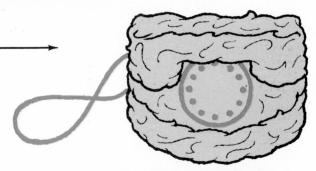

PARTY LINE CAKES

Bake Betty Crocker Yellow Cake Mix in oblong pan, 13x9x2 inches, as directed on package. Remove from pan; cool.

Cut 1-inch slice from each end of cake and reserve for hand grip of telephone. Shape ovals for base and cut 2 circles for ear and mouth pieces (see diagram). Cut circles in half horizontally to make 4 circles.

Prepare Betty Crocker Fluffy White Frosting Mix as directed on package. Tint pink. (To make sure that hand grip of telephone doesn't weaken or collapse, insert a long thin wooden pick or skewer full length through the handle.) Frost bases first; assemble cake as 2 telephones with receivers on hook, frosting cake pieces as they are assembled. Use red cinnamon candies for the dial and red licorice laces for the phone cord and circle of dial.

LEMON CHANTILLY FLAMBEAU

Bake Betty Crocker Lemon Velvet Cake Mix in two round layer pans, 8 or 9x1½ inches, as directed on package. Cool.

Fill and frost with Lemon Chantilly (below). Decorate top with Lemon Cup (below) and chopped pistachio nuts. Chill.

Just before serving, arrange Frosted Grapes (page 23) around base of cake.

Lemon Chantilly: Add 1 package Betty Crocker Lemon Velvet Frosting Mix (dry mix) to 2 cups whipping cream in small mixer bowl. Chill at least 1 hour. Blend; beat until stiff. To 1 cup whipped mixture fold in ½ cup chopped green grapes, well drained, and ½ cup chopped pistachio nuts. Fill cake. Frost cake with remaining whipped mixture.

Lemon Cup: Cut top off lemon; scoop out inside. Snip top edge in zigzag fashion to look like tulip. Place on frosted cake. Just before serving, place 4 to 6 sugar cubes, which have been soaked in lemon extract, in lemon cup. Ignite.

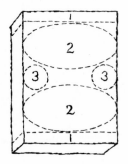
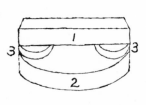

TELEGRAM CAKE

Pictured on page 70.

Bake any flavor Betty Crocker Layer Cake Mix in oblong pan, 13x9x2 inches, as directed on package. Remove from pan and cool.

Prepare Betty Crocker Creamy White Frosting Mix as directed on package. Tint pale yellow. Frost cake.

Using a decorating or envelope cone (see page 24) and Chocolate Decorator Icing (below) write a "telegram" message.

Chocolate Decorator Icing:

1 square (1 ounce) unsweetened chocolate
1 teaspoon butter or margarine
1 cup sifted confectioners' sugar
1 to 2 tablespoons boiling water

Melt chocolate and butter over hot water. Remove from heat. Blend in sugar and 1 tablespoon water. Beat until smooth. Add more boiling water, a teaspoonful at a time, until of desired consistency.

ZODIAC CAKE

Pictured on page 70.

Bake Betty Crocker Dark Chocolate Fudge Cake Mix in two round layer pans, 9x1½ inches, as directed on package. Cool.

Prepare Betty Crocker Fluffy White Frosting Mix as directed on package except—fold in ¼ teaspoon peppermint extract, if desired. Reserve ¼ cup frosting. Fill layers and frost sides and top of cake with remaining frosting.

Add 6 to 7 tablespoons sifted confectioners' sugar to reserved ¼ cup frosting. Use decorating cone and writing tip (see page 25). Decorate chocolate mint patties with signs of the zodiac. Place patties in circle around top edge of cake in the correct order. Point an arrow, made with tiny red cinnamon candies, in direction of the appropriate zodiac sign. Use quarter of a mint for head of arrow.

RECORD CAKE

Bake any flavor Betty Crocker Layer Cake Mix in two round layer pans, 8 or 9x1½ inches, as directed on package. Cool.

Prepare Betty Crocker Chocolate Fudge Frosting Mix and Betty Crocker Creamy White Frosting Mix as directed on package. Spread white frosting between layers; reserve 1 cup.

Frost top and sides of cake with chocolate frosting, reserving ⅓ cup for decorating.

Frost center of cake with a small amount of white frosting to resemble label on a record; leave at least 2 inches on outer edge with chocolate frosting. To give effect of grooves on record, draw tines of fork through chocolate frosting on top of cake.

Decorate cake, using writing tip (see page 25). Use the reserved chocolate frosting to write "Happy Birthday" and make two or three notes and a dot for record hole on "label." White frosting may be used to decorate sides of cake with musical symbols. Use pipe cleaners to make two small dancers on cake.

Betty Crocker Note: The remaining white frosting may be used to frost cupcakes or graham crackers. Decorate with remaining chocolate frosting.

BLACK MAGIC TOP HAT

Prepare 2 packages any flavor Betty Crocker Layer Cake Mix, 1 package at a time, as directed. Bake in four round layer pans, 8 or 9x1½ inches, as directed on package. Cool.

In 2 of the layers, cut a hole 4 inches in diameter through the center. On an 18-inch length of ribbon or colored string tie small party favors; wrap in plastic wrap, leaving a 6-inch length of ribbon extending out.

Prepare 2 packages Betty Crocker Dark Chocolate Fudge Frosting Mix, 1 package at a time, as directed. Frost edge of a 12-inch cake plate. Fill layers with frosting (the two layers with holes should be on top).

Frost sides of cake. Place the ribbon with favors into the hole of cake, leaving a 2-inch length extending over the top of cake. Replace one of the cut cake circles so that the top of cake is even. Frost top of cake.

Place miniature marshmallows (about 80) around the first layer of cake to form a hatband. Decorate with marshmallow rabbit, if desired.

SWEET SIXTEEN CAKE

Pictured opposite.

Prepare Betty Crocker Yellow Cake Mix as directed on package. Pour batter into greased and floured jelly roll pan, 15½x10½x1 inch. Bake *25 to 30 minutes*. Remove from pan; cool.

Cut cake as shown in diagram. Use cookie cutter to cut out heart or make your own heart-shaped design.

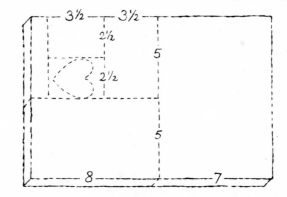

Prepare Betty Crocker Cherry Fluff Frosting Mix as directed on package. Spread a thin layer of frosting on top of each piece of cake, stacking pieces in decreasing size. Frost sides of bottom layer with frosting; cover frosting with shredded coconut. Repeat, frosting sides of each layer and covering with coconut until all 4 layers are finished. Reserve enough frosting for heart-shaped piece of cake.

Attach heart to top of cake with long thin wooden picks. Frost heart with remaining frosting. Using red food coloring, paint a large "16" on heart. If desired, surround base of cake with Frosted Flowers, using sweetheart roses (page 118). Place thin pink and white candles of varying sizes on two of the layers.

Other cakes for teen-age parties are Twin Pennant Cakes (page 104), Braque Guitar Cake (page 138) or Football Cake (page 104).

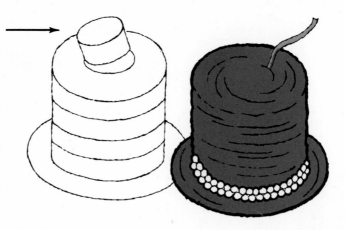

Pictured from top to bottom: Sweet Sixteen Cake, Zodiac Cake, Telegram Cake

After-20 Cakes

MY FAIR LADY CAKES

Bake Betty Crocker White Cake Mix in two round layer pans, 8 or 9x1½ inches, as directed on package. Cool. Prepare Betty Crocker Cherry Fluff Frosting Mix as directed on package. Place each layer on an individual serving plate and frost, using petal design (see page 81).

Using roses, violets or shattered carnations, make Frosted Flowers (page 118). Arrange in two nosegays on two 4-inch white doilies. Tie with ribbon streamers. Place off-center on top of each cake, allowing streamers to fall onto serving plates.

GRANDMOTHER'S PATCHWORK QUILT CAKE

Prepare Betty Crocker Marble Cake Mix as directed on package. Blend marbling mixture into 1½ cups batter. Divide remaining batter into thirds. To ⅓ add a few drops red food coloring and ¼ teaspoon peppermint extract. To another third add a few drops green food coloring. Leave remaining third plain.

Spoon batter into greased and floured oblong pan, 13x9x2 inches. Marble and bake as directed on package. Remove from pan and cool. Frost sides and top with Creamy Cheese Frosting (page 20).

Score top of cake with knife to make 15 squares. Decorate alternate squares with decorators' sugars or multicolored nonpareils. Decorate other squares with flowers made of gumdrops, marshmallows, nuts or mints. Chill several hours.

FEATHER IN YOUR HAT CAKE

Place this on a level white cake plate—it will look like a hat brim.

Bake Betty Crocker Yellow Cake Mix in two round layer pans, 9x1½ inches, as directed on package. Cool.

Fill and frost cake with Betty Crocker Vanilla Satin ready-to-spread Frosting.

Form a hatband by using corn candy. Place one with point up and one with point down, alternating around base of cake. For the side decoration of the hat, roll out one large gumdrop in sugar. Trim to shape of feather. Cut slashes on sides. Pull alternate strips out and back to resemble ruffled feather. Repeat with a large green gumdrop. Place on band of hat. Small ribbons or decorated canapé picks may be added, if desired.

> *Betty Crocker Note:* Use slim up and down strokes, made close together, to frost the cake. This will produce the straw hat effect.

MOTHER'S HATBOX CAKE

Bake 2 packages any flavor Betty Crocker Layer Cake Mix, one at a time, in two round layer pans, 9x1½ inches, as directed on package. Cool.

Prepare 2 packages Betty Crocker Fluffy White Frosting Mix, one at a time, as directed on package. Tint half of frosting from 1 package pink. Trim rounded tops of layers to make them level. Fill and frost 3 layers with the white frosting, spreading it very smooth. Frost top layer with pink frosting, smoothing it to resemble hatbox cover.

Across top, place red shoestring licorice tied in a bow; tuck ends of licorice into side of frosted cake just under the top layer. Cut 4-inch strips of red shoestring licorice; press 1 inch apart into frosting on sides of 3 bottom layers, making vertical stripes. If desired, write name across top of cake.

Slice and serve the two top layers first and then the two bottom layers.

For other birthday ideas for Mom and Dad, see Calendar Cakes (pages 96 to 110).

Pictured from top to bottom: Mother's Hatbox Cake, Feather in Your Hat Cake, Grandmother's Patchwork Quilt Cake

ROSES ARE RED CAKE

Pictured on cover.

Prepare Betty Crocker Angel Food Cake Mix as directed on package except—add ¼ teaspoon soluble fluid rose and 4 drops red food coloring to the water before adding to mix. Pour batter into ungreased tube pan, 10x4 inches. Bake as directed on package. Cool. Remove from pan.

Prepare Betty Crocker Fluffy White Frosting Mix as directed on package. Fold in ½ cup dairy sour cream, ⅛ teaspoon soluble fluid rose and 4 drops red food coloring. Frost sides and top of cake. Decorate with silver dragées or Frosted Flowers, using roses (page 118). *Or* pour and spread with Rose Glaze (below).

Rose Glaze: Blend 4¾ cups sifted confectioners' sugar with 2 tablespoons light corn syrup, ⅛ teaspoon soluble fluid rose, 3 to 4 drops red food coloring and ¼ cup hot water. Beat until smooth. Add hot water, one teaspoon at a time, until of glaze consistency.

Betty Crocker Note: Soluble fluid rose is available in the pharmacy department of most drugstores.

VIOLETS ARE BLUE CAKE

Bake Betty Crocker White Cake Mix in two round layer pans, 8 or 9x1½ inches, as directed on package. Cool.

Fill with Grape Filling (below).

Prepare Betty Crocker Fluffy White Frosting Mix as directed on package. Frost sides and top of cake.

With candied violets and green spearmint leaves, form a design to resemble a nosegay of violets on top of cake. Scatter individual violet buds and leaves around side of cake. Stems may be cut from leaves and leaves cut in half for smaller sizes as desired.

Grape Filling:

1 cup grape juice
3 tablespoons honey
2 tablespoons cornstarch
2 teaspoons lemon juice

Mix grape juice, honey and cornstarch in saucepan. Cook over low heat until thick and clear, stirring constantly. Remove from heat. Stir in lemon juice. Chill thoroughly before filling cake.

LADY BALTIMORE CAKE

Prepare Betty Crocker White Cake Mix as directed on package except—add 1 teaspoon almond extract to batter. Pour batter into two greased and floured round layer pans, 8 or 9x1½ inches. Bake as directed. Cool.

Prepare Betty Crocker Fluffy White Frosting Mix as directed on package. Into ⅓ of the frosting blend ⅓ cup finely cut raisins, ⅓ cup figs or dates, cut into thin strips, and ⅓ cup chopped walnuts. Spread between layers and over top of cake. Frost sides and top of cake with remaining frosting.

Garnish with walnut halves or put two walnut halves together with frosting. Place birthday candle between halves. Stand walnuts with candle in icing around top edge of cake. Repeat for desired number of candles.

LORD BALTIMORE CAKE

Prepare Betty Crocker Yellow Cake Mix as directed on package except—add 1 tablespoon grated orange peel to batter. Pour batter into two greased and floured round layer pans, 8 or 9x1½ inches. Bake as directed. Cool.

Prepare Betty Crocker Cherry Fluff Frosting Mix as directed on package. Into ⅓ of the frosting, mix ¼ cup *each* toasted chopped pecans and almonds, and ¼ cup chopped maraschino cherries. Spread between layers. Frost sides and top with remaining frosting. Garnish with almonds and cherries.

CHOCOLATE BUTTER-MALLOW CAKE

Bake Betty Crocker Dark Chocolate Fudge Cake Mix in two round layer pans, 8 or 9x1½ inches, as directed on package. Cool.

Fill and frost top of cake with Butterscotch Filling (below).

Prepare Betty Crocker Fluffy White Frosting Mix as directed on package. Frost sides and top of cake, reserving a small amount of frosting. Around top edge of cake arrange flat chocolate peppermint patties. Write a message for Dad such as "Hi Pop," "Happy Dad's Day" or "Happy Birthday," making one letter on each patty. Use a wooden pick and reserved white frosting for "writing."

Butterscotch Filling:

1 cup brown sugar (packed)
3 tablespoons flour
1 cup milk
2 egg yolks, slightly beaten
2 tablespoons butter or margarine
1 teaspoon vanilla
½ cup chopped nuts

Combine brown sugar and flour in saucepan. Gradually stir in milk. Cook over medium heat, stirring constantly, until mixture thickens and boils. Boil 1 minute, stirring constantly. Remove from heat. Slowly stir at least half of hot mixture into egg yolks. Blend into remaining hot mixture in saucepan. Boil 1 minute more, stirring constantly. Remove from heat and blend in butter and vanilla. Cool. Spread filling on cake. Sprinkle with nuts.

DAD'S PLAID CAKE

Bake Dad's favorite flavor Betty Crocker Layer Cake Mix in two round layer pans, 8 or 9x1½ inches, as directed on package. Cool.

Prepare Betty Crocker Fluffy White Frosting Mix as directed on package. Fill and frost cake.

Dip a piece of white sewing thread in food coloring; stretching it taut, press into frosting. Repeat. Use new thread for each color. Make up your own plaid design.

GIFT-WRAPPED CAKE

Pictured above.

Bake Betty Crocker Yellow Cake Mix in oblong pan, 13x9x2 inches, as directed on package. Remove from pan and cool.

Cut cake in half crosswise; split each half into two layers to make four layers in all. Spread each layer with strawberry or raspberry jam; stack.

Prepare Betty Crocker Fluffy White Frosting Mix as directed on package. Reserve 1½ cups for Decorator Icing (page 24). Frost sides and top of cake with remaining frosting. Tint ½ cup Decorator Icing pink, ¼ cup green and ¼ cup yellow. Leave remaining icing white.

With petal tip (see page 25) and pink icing make ribbon and bow.

With writing tip and green icing make stems; with leaf tip, make leaves.

With petal tip and white icing make blossoms; with writing tip, make lily of the valley.

With star tip and yellow icing make rosettes.

Betty Crocker Note: If decorating cone is not available, reserve only ½ cup frosting; tint light pink. Draw outline of "ribbon" on cake with wooden pick. Fill in with pink frosting, using small spatula. Decorate center of bow with Gumdrop Roses (page 24).

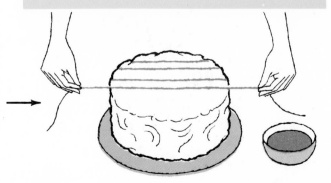

WHEN COMPANY COMES

In these days of relaxed, informal entertaining, the only thing that's more fun than a party is lots of parties. Think of a party occasion—big, small, casual or highbrow—don't you think of a cake?

Always welcome for dessert, cake lends an especially festive air to entertaining. Whatever kind you like, you'll find in this chapter. Not-too-elaborate cakes for coffee and brunch. The pretty and dainty ones for ladies only. The all-around favorites for dinner parties. And gala cakes that can solo for late-evening dessert parties.

Then, because variety is the spice of party planning, some interesting recipes for pies and refrigerator desserts are also included.

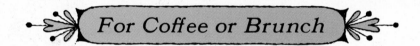

For Coffee or Brunch

STREUSEL COFFEE CAKE

Pictured on cover.

1 package Betty Crocker Yellow Cake Mix
¼ cup firm butter
1 cup brown sugar (packed)
¾ cup chopped walnuts
3 eggs
1½ cups dairy sour cream (12 ounces)

Heat oven to 350°. Measure ⅔ cup of cake mix (dry mix) into small bowl. Cut in the butter. Mix in brown sugar and walnuts. Set aside.

Beat eggs lightly with a fork; stir in sour cream. Blend in remaining cake mix (dry mix), scraping bowl often. (Batter will be thick and slightly lumpy.) Pour half the batter into greased and floured oblong pan, 13x9x2 inches; sprinkle half the topping over batter. Spoon and gently spread remaining batter into pan; top with remaining topping mixture. Bake *40 to 45 minutes.*

Flavor variations

Orange: Mix 2 tablespoons grated orange peel into cake batter.

Lemon: Mix 2 tablespoons grated lemon peel into cake batter.

Cranberry: Fold 1 cup chopped fresh cranberries into cake batter.

Mocha: Blend 1 to 2 tablespoons instant coffee into cake batter.

Spice: Blend 1 teaspoon cinnamon and ¼ teaspoon nutmeg into cake batter.

Raisin: Stir 1 cup raisins into cake batter.

Pan variations

Use two round layer pans, 9x1½ inches. Bake *40 to 45 minutes.*

Use two loaf pans, 9x5x3 inches. Bake *40 to 45 minutes.*

Use one tube pan, 10x4 inches. Bake *60 to 65 minutes.*

Betty Crocker Note: Coffee cake may be drizzled with Thin Confectioners' Sugar Icing: Combine 1 cup sifted confectioners' sugar, 1 to 2 tablespoons warm water and ½ teaspoon vanilla.

Pictured at left: Golden Rich Coffee Cake; at right: French Breakfast Puffs, Upside-down Pecan Loaf

CARAMEL-NUT CAKE RING

Pictured on page 4.

3 tablespoons butter or margarine, melted
1 tablespoon warm water
⅓ cup brown sugar (packed)
⅔ cup broken walnuts
1 package Betty Crocker Yellow Cake Mix

Heat oven to 350°. Grease and flour a 6-cup ring mold. Combine butter, water and brown sugar; spread in bottom of mold. Sprinkle with walnuts. Prepare cake mix as directed on package except—use 2 tablespoons less water. Pour half the batter over nuts in mold.

Bake *30 to 35 minutes.* Immediately loosen cake from edges of pan. Invert onto cake plate; let stand 2 minutes. Remove pan; cool. To serve, fill bowl with whipped butter or softened cream cheese and place in center of cake. *8 servings.*

Bake remaining batter in 8-inch layer pan as directed on package.

Betty Crocker Note: For a delicious dessert, try this made with any of our chocolate layer cake mixes; serve with whipped cream or Hard Sauce (page 105).

UPSIDE-DOWN PECAN LOAF

Pictured on page 77.

Heat oven to 350°. Grease and flour sides only of two shiny loaf pans, 9x5x3 inches. Combine 6 tablespoons butter or margarine, melted, ½ cup brown sugar (packed), 1 cup broken pecans and 2 tablespoons light corn syrup. Spread evenly in pans.

Prepare Betty Crocker Yellow Cake Mix as directed on package except—use 2 tablespoons less water. Pour into prepared pans. Bake *35 to 40 minutes.* Invert cakes immediately onto plate or tray; let stand 2 minutes. Remove pans. Slice and serve warm. *8 servings from each loaf.*

Individual Pecan Cakes: Place 2 teaspoons butter, melted, 2 teaspoons brown sugar and 3 pecan halves in each muffin cup. Prepare Betty Crocker Yellow Cake Mix as directed on package except—pour batter into prepared muffin cups. Bake *25 to 30 minutes.* Invert cakes onto rack. Let pan stand over cakes 1 minute; remove pan. Serve warm. *Makes 30 to 36 cakes.*

GOLDEN RICH COFFEE CAKE

Pictured on page 77.

Heat oven to 350°. Prepare Betty Crocker Yellow Cake Mix as directed on package except—use 2 tablespoons less water. Pour half the batter into greased and floured tube pan, 10x4 inches; sprinkle with half the Filling (below). Repeat, sprinkling top with remaining Filling. Bake *50 to 60 minutes,* or until wooden pick inserted in center comes out clean. Cool 30 minutes; remove from pan. Serve warm. *16 to 20 servings.*

Filling: Mix together ½ cup brown sugar (packed), ½ cup chopped nuts and 1 teaspoon cinnamon.

Poppy Seed Coffee Cake: Follow recipe (above) except—blend 3 tablespoons poppy seed into batter. Pour half the batter into prepared pan; sprinkle Vienna Revel (below) over batter. Spread remaining batter over Revel. Bake as directed. Sprinkle top with confectioners' sugar.

Vienna Revel: Stir together ⅓ cup brown sugar (packed), 2 teaspoons cinnamon and ½ teaspoon instant coffee.

OLD-FASHIONED APPLE SPICE CAKE

1 package Betty Crocker Honey Spice Cake Mix
3 cups thinly sliced tart apples, pared or unpared
¼ cup sugar
2 teaspoons cinnamon

Heat oven to 350°. Prepare cake mix as directed on package. Pour batter into greased and floured oblong pan, 13x9x2 inches. Arrange sliced apples over batter. Mix sugar and cinnamon; sprinkle over apples.

Bake *40 to 45 minutes.* Serve warm, plain or with whipped butter.

Betty Crocker Note: For a family dessert, serve warm with whipped cream or ice cream.

MOLASSES SPICE CAKE

Bake Betty Crocker Honey Spice Cake Mix in oblong pan, 13x9x2 inches, as directed on package. Cool 5 minutes; cut cake into squares or diamonds and prick holes in entire surface with fork. Mix ⅓ cup sugar and 1 teaspoon cinnamon; sprinkle over cake.

Combine ½ cup light molasses, 2 tablespoons butter or margarine and ½ cup water; heat slowly in heavy saucepan until of glaze consistency. Pour warm glaze over cake. If desired, sprinkle confectioners' sugar over cake.

SINGED ANGEL WINGS

Bake Betty Crocker Angel Food Cake Mix as directed on package. Cool. Remove from pan.

Brush cut sides of cake wedges with melted butter. Lightly brown both sides under broiler (1 minute per side). Serve with Orange Sauce (page 106).

KAFFEEKLATSCH PANCAKES

½ package Betty Crocker Yellow Cake Mix
  (about 2½ cups)
1 cup water
1 egg
¼ cup Gold Medal Flour (regular or Wondra)

Combine cake mix (dry mix) with remaining ingredients in small mixer bowl. Blend at low speed on mixer; beat 2 minutes medium speed. Drop batter onto lightly greased griddle, using ¼ cup for each pancake. Bake until edges turn golden brown; turn and finish baking. *Makes 12 pancakes.*

For brunch, serve pancakes with marmalades, jellies, honey, fruit-flavored syrups or fresh fruit with sour cream topping.

For dessert, serve with ice cream and sundae sauce, ice cream and thawed frozen fruit or whipped cream.

Waffles: Follow recipe (above) except—pour batter into lightly greased waffle iron. Bake according to manufacturer's directions. *Makes about three 12-inch waffles.*

Betty Crocker Note: To make pancakes ahead of time, place baked pancakes between folds of towels on baking sheet. Cover top with aluminum foil and set aside. Twenty minutes before serving, place on baking sheet in single layer and heat *for about 20 minutes at 300°.*

FRENCH BREAKFAST PUFFS

Pictured on page 77.

Heat oven to 350°. Prepare Betty Crocker Yellow Cake Mix as directed on package. Pour batter into greased small-size muffin pans or make small cupcakes by filling greased muffin pans ⅓ to ½ full. Bake *15 to 20 minutes.*

Melt 1 cup butter or margarine in small saucepan. Stir together 3 teaspoons cinnamon and 1½ cups sugar in another bowl. Remove cupcakes from pan while still warm. Dip 18 to 20 cupcakes into the melted butter, then into sugar-cinnamon mixture. Serve warm. *Makes 18 to 20 puffs.*

Freeze the remaining cupcakes for later use.

COUNTRY LOAF SLICES

Heat oven to 350°. Prepare Betty Crocker Yellow Cake Mix as directed on package except—use 2 tablespoons less water. Pour batter into two greased and floured shiny loaf pans, 9x5x3 inches. Bake *35 to 40 minutes.* Cool.

Cut each loaf into ½- to ¾-inch slices. Spread each with butter, then with a cinnamon-sugar mixture, honey, jelly or jam. Place on baking sheet. Heat *about 5 minutes at 350°.*

French Toasted Country Loaf: Follow recipe (above) except—after loaves have cooled, cut each loaf into 1-inch slices; place on tray and allow to "dry" 1 hour; turn once. Beat 2 eggs; stir in ½ cup milk and ¼ teaspoon salt. Dip slices in egg mixture; place on greased griddle. Fry until golden brown on each side. Serve hot for breakfast or brunch with butter and syrup, jam or confectioners' sugar.

For Luncheon or Dessert

CHERRIES À LA CRÈME

1 package Betty Crocker White Cake Mix
1½ cups whipping cream
⅓ cup confectioners' sugar
1 teaspoon almond extract
1 can (1 pound 5 ounces) cherry pie filling

Bake cake in two round layer pans, 8 or 9x1½ inches, as directed on package. Cool. Split cake to make 4 layers (see page 20).

Whip cream with confectioners' sugar. Fold in almond extract. Spread the whipped cream mixture between each of the two split layers; frost tops of each. Place the filled and frosted layers on two serving plates. Spoon half of pie filling on top of each. Spread to within 1 inch of edge. Refrigerate. *Each layer makes 8 servings.*

Equally easy and delicious fruit and cake combinations:

Betty Crocker Yellow Cake Mix with blueberry pie filling

Betty Crocker Honey Spice Cake Mix with peach pie filling

Betty Crocker Lemon Velvet Cake Mix with pineapple pie filling

Betty Crocker Devils Food Cake Mix with apricot pie filling

CHOCOLATE REFRIGERATOR DESSERT

1 package Betty Crocker White Cake Mix
1 package (about 4 ounces) chocolate pudding and pie filling
1 cup whipping cream
⅓ cup confectioners' sugar
½ cup chopped nuts, if desired

Bake cake in layers as directed on package. Cool. Line bottom of square baking dish, 8x8x2 inches, with strips of cake. (Use one layer.)

Cook pudding as directed on package. Cool. Whip cream with confectioners' sugar; fold into cooled pudding. Pour over cake strips in baking dish. Sprinkle nuts over top. Chill several hours. *9 servings.*

Freeze second layer for later use.

Betty Crocker Note: If desired, pour plain pudding over cake and spread whipped cream over pudding.

PINK CHECKERBOARD CAKE

Pictured below, left.

Grease and flour two round layer pans, 9x1½ inches. Make circle dividers for center of pans by folding two pieces of foil, 13x6 inches, lengthwise twice, forming two strips, each 13x1½ inches. Shape strips into 4-inch circles; fasten each with a paper clip. Place a foil circle divider in center of each prepared pan.

Prepare Betty Crocker White Cake Mix as directed on package. Divide batter in half. Tint half light pink and blend in ½ teaspoon almond extract. Fill center of foil divider in one pan with pink batter and the outer circle with white batter. Fill center in other pan with white batter and outer circle with pink. (Batter in both inner and outer circles should be level.) Remove foil dividers and bake as directed on package. Cool.

Prepare Betty Crocker Cherry Fluff Frosting Mix as directed on package. Use layer with white center as bottom layer; fill and frost cake.

Betty Crocker Note: If 8-inch round layer pans are used, shape foil dividers into 3½-inch circles.

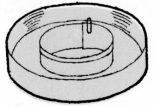 

LEMON-ORANGE CHIFFON CAKE

Bake Betty Crocker Lemon Chiffon Cake Mix in ungreased tube pan, 10x4 inches, as directed on package. Cool. Remove from pan.

Split cake to make three layers (see page 20) and fill with Orange Filling (page 88). Use 1 cup of filling between each layer and the remaining filling on top. Whip 1 cup whipping cream with ¼ cup confectioners' sugar. Frost sides of cake. Sprinkle sides with toasted almonds, if desired. Chill until serving time. *12 to 16 servings.*

VANILLA FRUIT BAVARIAN

Prepare Butter Crunch (below). Press 2 cups *hot* Butter Crunch in bottom of square pan, 8x8x2 inches. Cool.

Layer 1 cup sliced strawberries or bananas in bottom of shell; pour half of Vanilla Fluff (below) over fruit. Layer 1 cup more sliced strawberries or bananas on top; cover with remaining Vanilla Fluff. Sprinkle remaining Butter Crunch over top. Chill 2 hours. *9 servings.*

Butter Crunch:

½ cup butter or margarine
¼ cup brown sugar (packed)
1 cup Gold Medal Flour (regular or Wondra)
½ cup chopped pecans, walnuts or flaked coconut

Heat oven to 400°. Mix all ingredients with hands. Spread in oblong pan, 13x9x2 inches. Bake *15 minutes.* Remove from oven; stir with spoon. *Makes 2½ cups.*

Vanilla Fluff:

2 teaspoons unflavored gelatin
½ cup water
1 package Betty Crocker Fluffy White Frosting Mix
1½ cups whipping cream
½ teaspoon nutmeg

Soften gelatin in water. Dissolve over hot water. Cool to room temperature. Blend frosting mix (dry mix), whipping cream and nutmeg; chill thoroughly. Beat medium high speed on mixer just until mixture starts to thicken. Gradually add gelatin mixture. Beat just until stiff; *do not overbeat. Makes about 3 cups.*

Lemon-Orange Bavarian: Follow recipe (above) except —use Betty Crocker Lemon Fluff Frosting Mix and 2 cans (11 ounces each) mandarin orange segments, drained; omit strawberries or bananas.

Cherry-Fruit Bavarian: Follow recipe (above) except— use Betty Crocker Cherry Fluff Frosting Mix and 2 cans (1 pound each) pitted Bing cherries, drained; omit strawberries or bananas.

PETAL CAKE

Pictured above.

Bake any flavor Betty Crocker Layer Cake Mix in two round layer pans, 8 or 9x1½ inches, as directed on package. Cool.

Add 1 package Betty Crocker Fluffy White Frosting Mix (dry mix) to 1½ cups whipping cream in small mixer bowl. Chill 1 hour. Blend; beat until stiff.

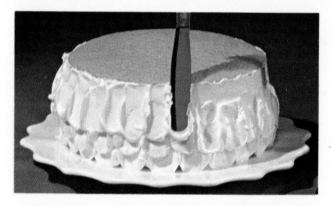

Place about 1 teaspoon frosting on tip of small flexible spatula. Beginning at base of cake, form small petal by pressing spatula with frosting against side of cake. Repeat to form petals in rows around cake; overlap each petal slightly. Use slightly larger amounts of frosting for petals on top of cake. Refrigerate.

LEMON CHIFFON WALDORF

Bake Betty Crocker Lemon Chiffon Cake Mix in ungreased tube pan, 10x4 inches, as directed on package. Cool. Remove from pan.

Prepare for filling (page 82). Cook 1 package (3½ ounces) lemon pudding and pie filling and fold into beaten egg whites as directed. Cool. Fill cake.

Whip 1½ cups whipping cream with ⅓ cup confectioners' sugar until stiff; frost sides and top of cake.

How to Fill an Angel Food Cake

It is important to have cake *completely cool*, or filling will weigh it down; make cake the day before you plan to fill it, if possible.

1. Place a 10-inch angel food cake upside down on plate or waxed paper. About 1 inch from top, slice entire top from cake. Lift off and put aside.

4. Completely fill cavity with chilled filling. Push filling well into cake hollow to avoid "holes" in cut slices.

2. Cut down into the cake 1 inch from outer edge, and 1 inch from center hole, leaving a substantial "wall" of cake about 1 inch thick.

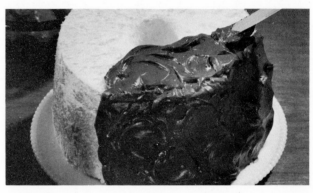

5. Replace top of cake and press gently. Cover top and sides as directed in individual recipe.

3. Remove center with a curved knife or spoon, being careful to leave a base of cake at bottom 1 inch thick. Place cake on serving plate.

6. Decorate as desired and chill until well set (4 hours or more). Cut into 12 to 16 servings.

ANGEL FOOD WALDORF

Bake Betty Crocker Angel Food Cake Mix in ungreased tube pan, 10x4 inches, as directed on package. Cool. Remove from pan. Prepare for filling (page 82). Fill and frost with Cocoa Fluff Filling and Topping (below).

Cocoa Fluff Filling and Topping:

3 cups chilled whipping cream
1½ cups confectioners' sugar
¾ cup cocoa
¼ teaspoon salt
⅔ cup toasted slivered almonds

Blend cream, sugar, cocoa and salt in chilled bowl; beat until stiff. Fold half of almonds into half the Cocoa Fluff; use this to fill cake. Frost cake with remaining Cocoa Fluff; sprinkle sides and top of cake with remaining almonds.

ALMOND-PEACH ANGEL FOOD WALDORF

Bake Betty Crocker Angel Food Cake Mix in ungreased tube pan, 10x4 inches, as directed on package. Cool. Remove from pan.

Prepare for filling (page 82). Fill with Almond-Peach Filling (below). Whip 1½ cups whipping cream with ⅓ cup confectioners' sugar just until stiff. Frost sides and top of cake; garnish with almonds and reserved peach slices.

Almond-Peach Filling:

1 package (12 ounces) frozen sliced peaches, thawed and drained (reserve syrup)
1 teaspoon lemon juice
2 packages (3 ounces each) peach-flavored gelatin
½ cup toasted slivered almonds, chopped
½ teaspoon almond extract
6 drops red food coloring
6 drops yellow food coloring
1 cup whipping cream, whipped

Reserve 6 peach slices for garnish; sprinkle with lemon juice and refrigerate until ready to use. Crush remaining peaches with a potato masher; set aside. To reserved peach syrup, add enough boiling water to make 2 cups. Pour over gelatin in large bowl; stir until gelatin dissolves. Stir in crushed peaches, almonds, almond extract and food colorings. Chill, stirring occasionally, until mixture mounds when dropped from spoon, about 1 hour. Beat high speed on mixer until foamy and light. Fold in whipped cream.

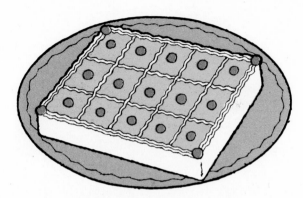

ORANGE LATTICE CAKE

Bake Betty Crocker White Cake Mix in an oblong pan, 13x9x2 inches, as directed on package. Remove from pan and cool.

Gently spread Orange Filling (page 88) on top of cake. Whip 1 cup whipping cream with ¼ cup confectioners' sugar until stiff. With decorating cone, flute whipped cream around edge of cake and form lattice work on top to indicate number of servings. Place maraschino cherry on each serving. Chill until serving time. *12 to 15 servings.*

Betty Crocker Note: Leftover dessert should be stored in the refrigerator.

LEMON-LIME CHIFFON CAKE

Bake Betty Crocker Lemon Chiffon Cake Mix in ungreased tube pan, 10x4 inches, as directed on package. Cool. Remove from pan. Split cake to make two layers. Fill and frost with Lime Filling (below). Make a wreath on top with fresh mint leaves or green leaf gumdrops. Chill until serving time. *12 to 16 servings.*

Lime Filling:

2 egg yolks
¼ cup sugar
⅛ teaspoon salt
3 tablespoons lime juice
1 teaspoon grated lime peel
Green food coloring
1½ cups whipping cream

Mix egg yolks, sugar, salt and lime juice in top of double boiler. Cook over hot water 6 to 8 minutes, stirring constantly, until thickened. Remove from heat and cool. Add lime peel and enough green food coloring to give desired shade of green. Whip cream; fold in the cooled lime mixture.

ALMOND ANGEL REFRIGERATOR DESSERT

1 package (about 3½ ounces) vanilla pudding and pie
  filling
1 teaspoon almond extract
1 cup whipping cream, whipped
1 can (13½ ounces) pineapple tidbits, drained
Betty Crocker Angel Food Cake (about half)*
Toasted slivered almonds
Chopped drained maraschino cherries

Cook pudding as directed on package. Add extract.
Cool. Fold in whipped cream and pineapple. Tear cake
into small pieces; place in baking dish, 11½x7½x1½
inches. Pour whipped cream mixture over pieces.
Garnish with almonds and cherries. Chill several hours
or overnight. *8 to 10 servings.*

*Our Lemon Chiffon Cake may be substituted—it makes an
equally delicious dessert!*

FRUIT DESSERT FREEZE

1 package Betty Crocker Creamy White Frosting Mix
2 cups whipping cream
1 can (8¾ ounces) crushed pineapple, drained
1 large banana, peeled and sliced
1 can (11 ounces) mandarin orange segments, drained
⅓ cup halved maraschino cherries
⅓ cup chopped dates
⅓ cup chopped pecans
2 tablespoons lemon juice

Add frosting mix (dry mix) to whipping cream; chill.
Beat until soft peaks form. Fold in remaining ingredients. Pour into two refrigerator trays or a square pan,
9x9x2 inches. Freeze until firm. Cut into squares. *12
servings.*

Frozen Fruit Salad: Follow recipe (above) except—add
⅓ cup mayonnaise to frosting mix and whipping cream
before beating.

LEMON CHEESECAKE

Pictured at left.

Graham cracker crust
1 can Betty Crocker Lemon Satin ready-to-spread
  Frosting
1 cup creamed cottage cheese (small curd)
1 cup dairy sour cream

Prepare your favorite graham cracker crust except—
reserve 3 tablespoons of mixture for topping. Press
larger portion firmly over bottom of square pan, 9x9x2
inches. In mixer bowl combine remaining ingredients.
Beat high speed on mixer until well blended, about 1
minute. Pour into pan; sprinkle with reserved crumbs.
Freeze overnight. If desired, garnish with strawberries,
peaches, small bunches of green seedless grapes or other
fruit. *9 to 12 servings.*

Chocolate Cheesecake: Follow recipe (above) except—
use Betty Crocker Chocolate Satin ready-to-spread
Frosting.

Orange Cheesecake: Follow recipe (above) except—use
Betty Crocker Vanilla Satin ready-to-spread Frosting
and add 1 can (6 ounces) frozen orange juice concentrate, slightly softened. In large mixer bowl, beat at high
speed about 2 minutes.

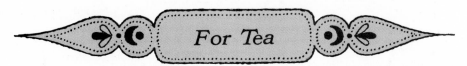

For Tea

SETTING THE FORMAL TEA TABLE

Arrange the table with simple elegance, placing the tea service at one end, coffee service at the other. Accompaniments for each should be nearby. The food is placed so that it can be passed easily to guests. Guests may stand or be seated; they may be invited to help themselves.

Tea Menu

White Nut Pound Cake (below)
Gâteaux Bonbons (right)
Fancy Cookies and Bars
Salted Nuts   Peppermint Wafers (page 49)
Tea   Coffee

WHITE NUT POUND CAKE

Pictured on page 87.

Heat oven to 350°. Grease and flour a tube pan, 10x4 inches, bundt pan or 2-quart anodized aluminum mold. Prepare Betty Crocker White Cake Mix as directed on package except—use 2 tablespoons less water. Add 1 teaspoon almond extract, if desired. Fold in ½ cup finely chopped nuts. Pour batter into prepared pan. Bake *45 to 55 minutes*, or until wooden pick inserted into center comes out clean. Cool 10 minutes; remove from pan. When cool, slice thinly and spread with butter or softened cream cheese, if desired.

Betty Crocker Note: To retain moistness, store cake in plastic wrap or freeze and use as needed.

GÂTEAUX BONBONS

Pictured on cover.

Prepare Betty Crocker White Cake Mix as directed on package except—tint half the batter pink. Using the tinted batter for half the cupcakes, bake small cupcakes (fill paper baking cups ⅓ to ½ full or use small size muffin pans, if available). Bake *15 to 20 minutes at 350°*. Cool; remove papers.

Heat to boiling 2 jars (12 ounces each) apricot preserves with ¼ cup water; strain. Place glaze in top of double boiler. Keep over hot water. One at a time, place cupcakes upside down on cooling rack over large bowl. With small measuring cup, pour warm apricot glaze over each cupcake, so that tops and sides are completely covered. (Glaze which drips off cupcakes into bowl can be heated and used again until all cupcakes are thinly glazed.)

When apricot glaze is set, pour Chocolate Glaze (below) over half of cupcakes and Pastel Glaze (below) over remaining cupcakes. Follow directions for glazing (above). When glaze is set, use decorating cone and writing tip (see page 25) to make designs. Use Chocolate and White Decorator Icings (below) on pastel-glazed cupcakes and White and Pastel Decorator Icings (below) on chocolate-glazed cupcakes.

Chocolate Glaze: In top of double boiler, combine all but 1 cup Betty Crocker Chocolate Fudge Frosting Mix (dry mix), ⅓ cup milk and 1 tablespoon light corn syrup. Heat over hot (not boiling) water until thin and syrupy. (If glaze is too thick, add more milk, 1 teaspoon at a time, until of desired consistency.)

Pastel Glaze: Follow recipe for Chocolate Glaze (above) except—use Betty Crocker Creamy White Frosting Mix. Tint as desired.

Chocolate Decorator Icing: Combine the 1 cup reserved Chocolate Fudge Frosting Mix and 1 tablespoon hot water. Beat until smooth. Add a few more drops of hot water if necessary.

White and Pastel Decorator Icings: Follow recipe for Chocolate Decorator Icing (above) except—use reserved Creamy White Frosting Mix. Tint half.

Betty Crocker Note: If a decorating cone is not available, snip off a tiny corner from an envelope. Fill with frosting and use to decorate cupcakes.

For Petits Fours, see page 116.

TOASTED TRIO CAKE

Ideal for a tea or shower. Pictured above, left.

Heat oven to 350°. Prepare Betty Crocker White Cake Mix as directed on package. Spread batter in greased and floured jelly roll pan, 15½x10½x1 inch. Bake *25 to 30 minutes.* Cool. Frost with Toasted Trio Topping (below). To serve, cut cake into 1½-inch squares. *Makes 70 squares.*

Toasted Trio Topping: Heat oven to 500°. Prepare Betty Crocker Fluffy White Frosting Mix as directed on package. Fold in 1 teaspoon grated lemon peel. Spread frosting on cake, forming two slight ridges with knife to mark cake into three parts. Sprinkle one part with ¼ cup chopped nuts, one part with a mixture of 1 tablespoon sugar and ¼ teaspoon cinnamon and one part with ⅓ cup flaked coconut. Place in oven for 3 to 5 minutes, or until topping is lightly browned. (Be careful not to burn.)

Betty Crocker Note: Cake may be made ahead and frosted just before it is toasted.

CHOCOLATE MELTAWAYS

Pictured opposite.

1 package Betty Crocker Devils Food Cake Mix
¼ cup water
2 eggs
¼ cup soft butter or margarine
¼ cup brown sugar (packed)
½ cup chopped nuts
1 package Betty Crocker Creamy White Frosting Mix
3 squares (3 ounces) unsweetened chocolate

Heat oven to 375°. Combine half the cake mix (dry mix), the water, eggs, butter and brown sugar in mixing bowl; mix thoroughly. Blend in remaining cake mix. Stir in nuts. Spread in greased and floured jelly roll pan, 15½x10½x1 inch. Bake *20 to 25 minutes.* Cool.

Prepare frosting mix as directed on package; spread on cake. Melt chocolate and spread evenly over frosting. Chill. Cut into 1½-inch squares before chocolate is completely firm. *Makes 70.*

DATE MERINGUE BARS

Pictured at left.

1 package (8 ounces) pitted dates, cut up (about 1⅓ cups)
2 tablespoons sugar
¾ cup water
¼ cup chopped nuts
½ cup soft butter
1 package Betty Crocker Devils Food Cake Mix
1 package Betty Crocker Fluffy White Frosting Mix

Mix dates, sugar and water in saucepan. Cook over low heat, stirring constantly, until thickened, about 7 minutes. Remove from heat and add nuts. Cool.

Heat oven to 350°. Cut butter into cake mix (dry mix). Reserve ⅓ cup cake mixture; press and flatten remaining mixture on bottom of ungreased jelly roll pan, 15½x10½x1 inch. Bake *10 to 12 minutes,* or until lightly browned.

Spread date filling over baked mixture. Cover with frosting mix prepared as directed on package. Sprinkle top with remaining ⅓ cup cake mixture. Bake *about 25 minutes,* or until topping is golden brown. Cool. Cut into 1½-inch squares. Store in refrigerator. *Makes 70.*

Date-Lemon Meringue Bars: Follow recipe (above) except—use Betty Crocker Yellow Cake Mix and Betty Crocker Lemon Fluff Frosting Mix.

Date-Cherry Meringue Bars: Follow recipe (above) except—use Betty Crocker White Cake Mix and Betty Crocker Cherry Fluff Frosting Mix.

Betty Crocker Note: When cutting bars, dip knife in hot water to prevent frosting from sticking.

FILLED TEA SQUARES

Heat oven to 350°. Prepare Betty Crocker Devils Food Cake Mix as directed on package. Spread batter evenly in two greased and floured jelly roll pans, 15½x10½x1 inch. Bake *12 to 15 minutes.* Cool.

Spread one sheet cake with jam, using ½ cup cherry jam on half of cake and ½ cup apricot jam on other half. Place other sheet cake on top.

Prepare Betty Crocker Creamy White Frosting Mix as directed on package. Tint half of frosting pink with food coloring. Frost cherry-filled section with pink frosting; frost apricot-filled section with white. Sprinkle half of each frosting with chopped nuts or chocolate shot; leave other half plain.

Cut one half into 1½-inch squares, the other half into nine 3-inch squares; cut each 3-inch square into four small triangles. *Makes about 24 squares and 36 triangles.*

For individual frozen desserts, elegant to serve at a tea, try Coconut-Cherry Mousse (page 91).

Pictured from top to bottom: White Nut Pound Cake, Gâteaux Bonbons and Petits Fours, Chocolate Meltaways

JOSEPHINES

Prepare dough for Cream Cheese Cookies (page 43), using Betty Crocker Yellow Cake Mix. Chill dough 1 hour. With stockinet-covered rolling pin, roll out on cloth-covered board to ⅛-inch thickness. With fluted pastry wheel, cut oblongs, 2x1½ inches. Bake as directed *6 to 8 minutes*. Or, use a round fluted cookie cutter to cut rounds 1½ inches in diameter. Bake *about 5 minutes*.

Prepare Betty Crocker Creamy White Frosting Mix as directed on package. Divide in half. To one half, add ¼ cup cocoa and blend thoroughly. Tint white frosting, if desired. Fill and frost cookies (stacking one on top of another), alternating colors.

Decorate tops with nuts, decorators' sugars and chocolate shot. *Makes about 9 dozen cookies.*

Other cookies and bars appropriate for a tea may be found on pages 43 to 48 and page 108.

For Dinner

FRUIT PARFAIT ANGEL CAKE

Bake Betty Crocker Angel Food Cake Mix in ungreased tube pan, 10x4 inches, as directed on package. Cool. Remove from pan. Split cake to make three layers (see page 20). Reassemble layers with one of the fillings below or right. Whip 1½ cups whipping cream with ⅓ cup confectioners' sugar. If desired, tint cream to match filling. Frost sides and top of cake. Garnish with fruit. Chill until serving time. *12 to 16 servings.*

Orange Filling:

1 cup sugar
½ teaspoon salt
¼ cup cornstarch
1 cup orange juice
2 tablespoons butter or margarine
2 tablespoons grated orange peel, if desired
2 tablespoons lemon juice

Mix sugar, salt and cornstarch in saucepan. Stir in orange juice slowly. Bring to boil, stirring constantly. Boil 1 minute. Remove from heat; stir in butter and orange peel. Gradually add lemon juice. Cool.

Pineapple Filling:

Few drops green food coloring
1 can (8¾ ounces) crushed pineapple, drained
2 teaspoons unflavored gelatin
2 tablespoons cold water
½ cup whipping cream, whipped

Add green food coloring to pineapple; mix well. Soften gelatin in cold water. Place over hot water until gelatin is dissolved and mixture is clear. Combine with pineapple. Chill. When partially set, fold in whipped cream.

Fruit Cocktail Filling:

1 can (1 pound) fruit cocktail, drained
¼ teaspoon almond extract
½ cup whipping cream, whipped

Fold fruit cocktail and almond extract into whipped cream.

Raspberry Filling:

1 teaspoon unflavored gelatin
1 tablespoon cold water
1 cup thick raspberry jam
½ cup whipping cream, whipped

Soften gelatin in cold water. Place over hot water until gelatin is dissolved and mixture is clear. Stir into the jam. Chill. When partially set, fold in whipped cream.

Betty Crocker's Best Filled Layer Cakes

Over the years we've found the following recipes to be our most popular for filled layer cakes. Mixes are used for the cakes and frostings, "start-from-scratch" recipes for the fillings—to bring you the best of both.

BUTTER-NUT FILLED WHITE CAKE

Bake Betty Crocker White Cake Mix in two round layer pans, 8 or 9x1½ inches, as directed on package. Cool. Fill layers with Butter-Nut Filling (below).

Prepare Betty Crocker Fluffy White Frosting Mix as directed on package. Frost sides and top of cake. Garnish with whole or chopped nuts.

Butter-Nut Filling:

½ cup sugar
1 tablespoon flour
3 tablespoons orange juice
½ cup butter or margarine
¼ cup chopped dates or raisins
2 egg yolks, beaten
½ cup chopped nuts

Mix sugar, flour, orange juice, butter and dates in saucepan. Cook over low heat, stirring, until mixture boils. Boil 1 minute. Remove from heat. Pour at least half of hot filling into egg yolks, stirring constantly. Then stir into hot mixture in saucepan. Bring to boil. Remove from heat and add nuts. Cool.

LEMON-FILLED COCONUT CAKE

Pictured on cover.

Bake Betty Crocker White Cake Mix in two round layer pans, 8 or 9x1½ inches, as directed on package. Cool.

Spread Lemon Filling (below) between layers. Prepare Betty Crocker Fluffy White Frosting Mix as directed on package. Frost sides and top of cake. Sprinkle frosted cake with about 1 cup coconut, tinted pale yellow (see page 19).

Lemon Filling:

¾ cup sugar
3 tablespoons cornstarch
¼ teaspoon salt
¾ cup water
1 tablespoon grated lemon peel
1 tablespoon butter or margarine
⅓ cup lemon juice

Mix sugar, cornstarch and salt in saucepan. Gradually add water. Bring to boil and boil 1 minute, stirring constantly. Remove from heat and stir in lemon peel and butter. Gradually add lemon juice. Chill until spreading consistency, about 1 hour.

CHOCOLATE-FILLED CHOCOLATE CURL CAKE

Pictured below.

Prepare Betty Crocker White Cake Mix as directed on package except—fold 2 squares (2 ounces) unsweetened chocolate, coarsely shaved, into batter. Pour batter into two greased and floured round layer pans, 8 or 9x1½ inches. Bake as directed on package. Cool.

Fill layers with Dark Chocolate Filling (below). Prepare Betty Crocker Fluffy White Frosting Mix as directed on package. Frost sides and top of cake. Sprinkle top with more shaved chocolate.

Dark Chocolate Filling:

1 cup sugar
⅓ cup light cream
2 tablespoons butter or margarine
2 squares (2 ounces) unsweetened chocolate, cut up
2 egg yolks, beaten

In saucepan, mix sugar, cream, butter and chocolate. Cook over medium heat, stirring constantly, until chocolate and butter are melted. Stir at least half of hot mixture into egg yolks. Blend into remaining mixture in saucepan. Boil 1 minute, stirring constantly. Remove from heat and cool.

Betty Crocker Note: To shave chocolate, pare thin shavings from chocolate bar or square with potato parer or sharp knife.

DARK CHOCOLATE CREAM CAKE

Bake any chocolate flavor Betty Crocker Cake Mix in two round layer pans, 8 or 9x1½ inches, as directed on package. Cool.

Split to make 4 layers (page 20). Fill and frost with Chocolate Fluff Topping (page 94). Chill 2 to 3 hours; garnish with toasted slivered almonds before serving, if desired.

Equally delicious variations include:

Betty Crocker Lemon Velvet Cake Mix with Lemon Velvet Fluff Topping (page 94).
Betty Crocker Honey Spice Cake Mix with Caramel Fluff Topping (page 94).
Betty Crocker White or Yellow Cake Mix with Vanilla Fluff Topping (page 94).

ORANGE-FILLED LEMON CAKE

Bake Betty Crocker Lemon Velvet Cake Mix in two round layer pans, 8 or 9x1½ inches, as directed on package. Cool.

Spread bottom layer with Orange Filling (page 88). Top with second layer.

Prepare Betty Crocker Fluffy White Frosting Mix as directed on package. Frost sides and top of cake. Tint 1 cup coconut pale yellow with food coloring (see page 19); lightly coat sides of cake. Decorate top with candy orange or lemon slices.

CHOCOLATE RIBBON CAKE

Pictured below.

Prepare Betty Crocker Marble Cake Mix as directed on package except—pour half of yellow batter into greased and floured round layer pan, 8 or 9x1½ inches. To the other half of batter, blend in marbling mixture. Pour into another greased and floured round layer pan, 8 or 9x1½ inches. Bake as directed on package. Cool.

Split to make 4 layers (page 20). Whip 1½ cups whipping cream with ⅓ cup confectioners' sugar. Fill and frost cake, alternating yellow and chocolate layers. Decorate with Chocolate Curls (page 23). Chill.

SOUR CREAM CHEESECAKE

Graham cracker crust
1 package (8 ounces) cream cheese, softened
1½ cups dairy sour cream
1 package Betty Crocker Lemon Fluff Frosting Mix
1 package (10 ounces) frozen strawberries

Heat oven to 350°. Prepare your favorite graham cracker crust except—reserve ⅓ cup of mixture for topping. Press larger portion evenly over bottom of square pan, 8x8x2 inches. In large mixer bowl, beat cream cheese and sour cream until blended.

Prepare frosting mix as directed on package. Gradually beat into cream cheese-sour cream mixture. Pour into crust. Sprinkle top with reserved crumb mixture. Bake 35 *minutes*. Cool; then chill. Top with thawed strawberries. *9 to 12 servings.*

EGYPTIAN-FILLED WHITE CAKE

Pictured below.

Bake Betty Crocker White Cake Mix in two round layer pans, 8 or 9x1½ inches, as directed on package. Cool.

Spread Egyptian Filling (below) between layers and on top of cake. Whip ½ cup whipping cream with 2 tablespoons confectioners' sugar. Spread on sides of cake. Chill.

Egyptian Filling:
⅔ cup light cream
⅔ cup sugar
2 egg yolks
½ cup chopped dates
½ teaspoon vanilla
½ cup chopped toasted almonds

In saucepan, mix cream, sugar, egg yolks and dates. Cook over low heat until slightly thickened, 6 to 7 minutes, stirring constantly. Remove from heat; add vanilla and nuts. Cool until thick enough to spread.

Betty Crocker Note: Let filling set before spreading whipped cream on sides of cake.

Pictured from left to right: Chocolate Ribbon Cake, Egyptian-filled White Cake, Whipped Cream-filled Chocolate Cake, Coconut-Cherry Mousse, Sour Cream-filled Mocha Cake

DOUBLE CHERRY BAKED ALASKA PIE

Bake your favorite 9-inch pie shell in metal pie pan. Cool. Fill with 1 quart cherry-nut ice cream, slightly softened. Place in freezer.

Prepare Betty Crocker Cherry Fluff Frosting Mix as directed on package. With frosting, cover ice cream completely, to edge of crust. Freeze until serving time, at least 3 hours.

Heat oven to 500°. Place pie in oven for 3 to 5 minutes, or until lightly browned. Serve at once. *6 to 8 servings.*

Betty Crocker Note: Ice cream must be very firm before placing in oven. Cover ice cream completely to edge of crust to insure insulation during baking.

Other flavor combinations:

Chocolate, strawberry or peppermint ice cream with our Fluffy White Frosting Mix;
French vanilla or pistachio ice cream with our Lemon Fluff Frosting Mix.

WHIPPED CREAM-FILLED CHOCOLATE CAKE

Pictured below.

Bake Betty Crocker Dark Chocolate Fudge Cake Mix in two round layer pans, 8 or 9x1½ inches, as directed on package. Cool.

Split cake to make 4 layers (see page 20). Fill with Whipped Cream Filling (below).

Prepare Betty Crocker Dark Chocolate Fudge Frosting Mix as directed on package. Frost sides and top of cake. Sprinkle chopped nuts on top, if desired. Chill.

Whipped Cream Filling: Whip 1 cup whipping cream with ¼ cup confectioners' sugar and 1 teaspoon vanilla. Fold in ⅓ cup chopped nuts, if desired.

Betty Crocker Note: Spread filling ½ inch from edges of cake layers. Refrigerate leftover cake.

COCONUT-CHERRY MOUSSE

Pictured below.

Prepare Betty Crocker Cherry Fluff Frosting Mix as directed on package except—use ½ cup *cold* water. Beat until fluffy, about 3 minutes. On high speed, gradually beat in 1½ cups whipping cream. Continue beating until soft peaks form. Fold in 1 cup shredded coconut and the packet of cherries. Pour into paper baking cups set in muffin pans. Sprinkle with more coconut and garnish with maraschino cherry halves. Freeze. *Makes 12.*

Betty Crocker Note: Mixture may be frozen in an ice cube tray or square pan, 8x8x2 inches. *Makes about 1 quart.*

Lemon-Pineapple Mousse: Follow recipe (above) except—use Betty Crocker Lemon Fluff Frosting Mix and add 1 can (8¾ ounces) crushed pineapple, drained; omit coconut.

Mocha-Almond Mousse: Follow recipe (above) except—use Betty Crocker Fluffy White Frosting Mix and add 1 tablespoon instant coffee to frosting mix before beating. Fold in ½ cup roasted almonds; omit coconut. Garnish with almonds.

SOUR CREAM-FILLED MOCHA CAKE

Pictured below.

Heat oven to 375°. Prepare Betty Crocker Spice 'n Apple Cake Mix as directed on package except—add 1 tablespoon instant coffee to dry mix. Pour into greased and floured jelly roll pan, 15½x10½x1 inch. Bake *15 to 20 minutes.* Cool.

Cut cake into three 5-inch strips. Fill with Rich Sour Cream Filling (below). Prepare Betty Crocker Creamy White Frosting Mix as directed on package except—add 1 teaspoon instant coffee to dry mix. Frost sides and top of cake. Chill.

Rich Sour Cream Filling: Blend 3 egg yolks, ½ cup dairy sour cream and ½ cup sugar in saucepan. Cook over low heat, stirring constantly, until mixture begins to simmer. Simmer several minutes, stirring constantly, until mixture is very thick. Remove from heat; chill.

VELVET CREAM CAKE

Bake any flavor Betty Crocker Layer Cake Mix in two round layer pans, 9x1½ inches, as directed on package. Cool. Split cake to make 4 layers (see page 20).

Add 2 cups any flavor Betty Crocker Creamy-type Frosting Mix (dry mix) to 1½ cups whipping cream and 1 teaspoon vanilla in small mixer bowl. Chill 1 hour. Blend; beat until stiff. Spread between layers. Frost top with Thin Icing (below), letting some drizzle down sides. Sprinkle top with chopped nuts, if desired. Chill. *12 to 14 servings.*

Thin Icing: Blend remaining frosting mix (dry mix), 2 to 3 tablespoons hot water and 1 tablespoon light corn syrup. Beat until smooth. Add 1 to 2 teaspoons more water, if necessary.

Betty Crocker Note: See page 17 for an easy way to insure a neat cake plate.

For Dessert and Coffee

ALOHA PINEAPPLE RING CAKE

½ cup butter or margarine
1 cup brown sugar (packed)
1 can (1 pound 4½ ounces) pineapple slices, well drained
Maraschino cherries and pecan halves, if desired
1 package Betty Crocker Yellow Cake Mix
2 cups whipping cream
½ cup confectioners' sugar

Heat oven to 350°. Melt half of butter in a round layer pan, 9x1½ inches, and half in a 6-cup ring mold. Sprinkle half of brown sugar into each pan. In each pan arrange pineapple slices; place cherry in center of each.

Prepare cake mix as directed on package. Pour half the batter over fruit in each pan. Bake *35 to 45 minutes.* Invert layer at once on serving plate and ring mold on cooling rack. Leave pans over cakes a minute.

When cool, place ring on top of layer. Whip cream with confectioners' sugar until stiff. Spread on sides of cake and fill center. Chill until serving time. *12 servings.*

Double Pineapple Upside-down Cake (Pictured on cover): Follow recipe (above) except—bake cake in two round layer pans, 9x1½ inches, as directed on package. Put layers together and frost sides with sweetened whipped cream.

GREAT GRAPE CAKE

1 package Betty Crocker Yellow Cake Mix
1 package Betty Crocker Lemon Fluff Frosting Mix
1 cup whipping cream
1 cup fresh or canned seedless grapes, halved
½ cup chopped walnuts
1 can (11 ounces) mandarin orange segments, drained or 1 large banana, peeled and sliced

Bake cake in two round layer pans, 9x1½ inches, as directed on package. Cool. Split to make 4 layers (page 20).

Prepare frosting mix as directed on package. Set aside to cool. Whip cream until it holds stiff peaks; fold into frosting. Reserve 1 cup of mixture. To remaining frosting mixture, fold in grapes, walnuts and other fruit. Fill layers; spread top of cake with reserved frosting. Garnish cake with fruit and walnut halves. Chill.

COCONUT-PECAN GOURMET CAKE

Bake Betty Crocker German Chocolate Cake Mix in two round layer pans, 8 or 9x1½ inches, as directed on package. Cool.

In small mixer bowl, add contents of Betty Crocker Coconut-Pecan Frosting Mix packet (dry mix) to 1 cup dairy sour cream; chill.

Beat frosting mixture low speed on mixer until blended. Fold in coconut-pecan mixture. Fill layers and frost top of cake. Chill.

Coconut-Pecan Supreme: Follow recipe (above) except —substitute 1 cup whipping cream for the sour cream. Chill. Beat medium speed until soft peaks form.

PINEAPPLE CREAM CAKE

1 package Betty Crocker White Cake Mix
1 can (1 pound 4½ ounces) crushed pineapple, drained (reserve syrup)
2 tablespoons cornstarch
1 cup whipping cream
¼ cup confectioners' sugar

Heat oven to 350°. Prepare cake mix as directed on package. Pour batter into greased and floured jelly roll pan, 15½x10½x1 inch. Bake *25 to 30 minutes.* Cool.

Mix pineapple syrup with cornstarch, a little at a time. Bring to boil; boil 1 minute. Remove from heat and cool. Stir in crushed pineapple and spread evenly over cake. Whip cream with confectioners' sugar until stiff. Spread over pineapple topping. Chill. *About 18 servings.*

CHOCOLATE SUNDAE PIE

Pictured below.

One 9-inch baked pie shell
1 package Betty Crocker Chocolate Fudge Frosting Mix
1½ cups whipping cream
Syrup (below)
⅓ cup finely chopped nuts

Allow pie shell to cool. Measure 1 cup frosting mix (dry mix) and set aside. Add remaining frosting mix (dry mix) to whipping cream. Chill.

Prepare Syrup; pour into pie shell, reserving 2 tablespoons. Brush over bottom and sides. Sprinkle with nuts. Beat chilled frosting mix and cream until stiff. Pour over nuts. Drizzle the reserved Syrup over top. Marble top by drawing a spatula back and forth across top of pie. Freeze. Remove from freezer 20 minutes before serving. *10 to 12 servings.*

Syrup: Add 2 tablespoons hot water and 1 teaspoon light corn syrup to the 1 cup frosting mix. Beat until smooth.

Betty Crocker Note: Our Dark Chocolate Fudge or Chocolate Malt Frosting Mixes may also be used in this recipe.

Lemon Sundae Pie: Follow recipe (above) except—use Betty Crocker Lemon Velvet Frosting Mix. Line pie shell and decorate with pistachio nuts.

Mocha Sundae Pie: Follow recipe (above) except—use Betty Crocker Golden Caramel Frosting Mix and add 2 teaspoons instant coffee to the whipping cream. Line pie shell with ½ square (½ ounce) unsweetened chocolate, grated; omit nuts.

Angel Food Cake Toppings

CHOCOLATE FLUFF TOPPING

Combine any Betty Crocker Chocolate Creamy-type Frosting Mix (dry mix) with 2 cups whipping cream and 1 teaspoon vanilla. Chill thoroughly. Whip until soft peaks form. Refrigerate until serving time. Use ¼ to ⅓ cup for each serving. Sprinkle with toasted almonds, if desired. *12 to 16 servings.*

Caramel Fluff Topping: Prepare Chocolate Fluff Topping (above) except—use Betty Crocker Golden Caramel Frosting Mix. Sprinkle with toasted almonds, chopped pecans or shaved chocolate, if desired.

Lemon Velvet Fluff Topping: Prepare Chocolate Fluff Topping (above) except—use Betty Crocker Lemon Velvet Frosting Mix.

Lemon-Cherry-Nut Fluff: Fold into Lemon Velvet Fluff Topping (above) 1 cup chopped well-drained maraschino cherries and 1 cup chopped walnuts.

Lemon-Orange Fluff: Fold into Lemon Velvet Fluff Topping (above) 1 can (11 ounces) mandarin orange segments, drained, and 1 cup chopped walnuts.

Vanilla Fluff Topping: Prepare Chocolate Fluff Topping (above) except—use Betty Crocker Creamy White Frosting Mix. Serve with any fresh fruit.

Minted Fluff Topping: Flavor Vanilla Fluff Topping (above) with ½ teaspoon peppermint extract; tint a delicate green.

Hawaiian Fluff Topping: Fold into Vanilla Fluff Topping (above) ½ cup flaked coconut, ⅓ cup chopped nuts and 1 can (8¾ ounces) crushed pineapple, well drained.

Strawberry Chantilly Fluff Topping: Prepare Chocolate Fluff Topping (above) except—use Creamy White Frosting Mix. Fold in 1 tablespoon lemon juice and 1 cup crushed fresh strawberries (about 1 quart), well drained.

Coconut-Pecan Fluff Topping: Prepare Chocolate Fluff Topping (above) except—use frosting mix from Betty Crocker Coconut-Pecan Frosting Mix. Fold in coconut-pecan mixture. If desired, drizzle chocolate syrup over top.

WHIPPED CREAM TOPPING

Combine 1 cup whipping cream, ¼ cup confectioners' sugar and ½ teaspoon vanilla. Chill. Whip until stiff. Refrigerate until serving time. (Use ¼ to ⅓ cup for each serving.)

COCOA WHIPPED CREAM TOPPING

Combine 1 cup whipping cream, ½ cup confectioners' sugar and ¼ cup cocoa. Chill. Whip until stiff. Refrigerate until serving time.

CARAMEL WHIPPED CREAM TOPPING

Combine 2 cups whipping cream, ¾ cup brown sugar (packed) and 1 teaspoon vanilla. Chill; whip until stiff. Refrigerate until serving time. Sprinkle each serving with shaved chocolate, if desired.

ORANGE CUSTARD WHIPPED CREAM TOPPING

2 eggs, beaten
½ cup sugar
⅓ to ½ cup orange juice
1 tablespoon grated orange peel
1 cup whipping cream
½ cup toasted chopped almonds

Cook eggs, sugar and orange juice over hot water until thick (about 15 minutes). Remove from heat. Stir in orange peel. Cool. Whip cream; fold cream and almonds into orange mixture. Refrigerate until serving time.

TROPICAL FRUIT WHIPPED CREAM TOPPING

1 package (about 3½ ounces) vanilla instant pudding
1 cup whipping cream
1 can (13½ ounces) mixed tropical fruits, drained (reserve about ½ cup syrup)

Blend pudding (dry mix), whipping cream and reserved syrup in small mixer bowl. Beat about 1 minute medium speed on mixer, until fluffy. *Do not overbeat.* Fold in fruit. Refrigerate until serving time.

FLUFFY SOUR CREAM TOPPING

1 package Betty Crocker Fluffy White Frosting Mix
½ cup dairy sour cream
½ cup drained chopped fruit
⅓ cup chopped nuts

Prepare frosting mix as directed on package. Fold in remaining ingredients. Refrigerate until serving time.

> **Flavor variations:**
>
> Betty Crocker Fluffy White Frosting Mix with fresh grapes and nuts
> Betty Crocker Lemon Fluff Frosting Mix with sliced bananas and walnuts
> Betty Crocker Cherry Fluff Frosting Mix with cherries and almonds

LEMON GRAHAM CRUNCH TORTE

1 cup graham cracker crumbs
½ cup finely chopped nuts
⅓ cup brown sugar (packed)
⅓ cup butter or margarine, melted
1 teaspoon cinnamon
1 package Betty Crocker Lemon Velvet Cake Mix
1½ cups whipping cream
⅓ cup confectioners' sugar
1½ teaspoons vanilla
⅛ to ¼ teaspoon yellow food coloring

Heat oven to 350°. Grease and flour *sides only* of two round layer pans, 9x1½ inches, or square pans, 8x8x2 inches. Mix crumbs, nuts, brown sugar, butter and cinnamon. Press mixture evenly into prepared pans.

Prepare cake mix as directed on package. Pour batter over mixture in pans. Bake *30 to 35 minutes*. Cool in pans 5 minutes, then turn upside down on racks; remove pans. Cool. Split cake to make 4 layers (see page 20).

Whip cream, confectioners' sugar, vanilla and food coloring until stiff. Use ½ cup whipped cream between each layer, placing one crumb-topped layer in the middle and one on top. Frost sides with remaining whipped cream. Chill. *12 servings.*

CARD PARTY CAKES

Heat oven to 350°. Prepare any flavor Betty Crocker Layer Cake Mix as directed on package. Pour batter into greased and floured jelly roll pan, 15½x10½x1 inch. Bake *25 to 30 minutes*. Cool in pan.

Prepare Betty Crocker Creamy White Frosting Mix as directed on package. Tint as desired with food coloring. Frost cake. With sandwich or cookie cutters, cut into heart, diamond, club and spade shapes. If desired, sprinkle with finely chopped nuts or toasted coconut.

Or cut cake into squares. Place a cutter on top; use as an outline and sprinkle candies or nuts into a design on top of each square. (Frosting should be soft, so that candies will adhere to it.) Or dip cutter into food coloring; then press into frosting.

Betty Crocker Note: If card design cutters are shallow, use as patterns only and cut around them with a sharp knife. Cake will crumble and break if too much pressure is put on it.

SWEET AND SIMPLE SOUR CREAM CAKE

Pictured below.

Bake Betty Crocker Devils Food Cake Mix in two round layer pans, 8 or 9x1½ inches, as directed on package or in two square pans, 8x8x2 inches or 9x9x2 inches, as directed for 9-inch layers. Cool.

In small mixer bowl, combine ⅔ cup dairy sour cream with Betty Crocker Creamy White Frosting Mix (dry mix); chill.

Blend ¼ cup soft butter into chilled frosting mix. Beat 1 minute low speed on mixer. *Do not overbeat* or frosting will be too thin. Spread between cake layers and on top, leaving sides unfrosted. Decorate with Chocolate Leaves or Chocolate Curls (page 23). Chill.

Other cake and frosting combinations:

Betty Crocker White or Yellow Cake Mix with Chocolate Fudge or Dark Chocolate Fudge Frosting Mix
Betty Crocker Honey Spice Cake Mix with Golden Caramel Frosting Mix
Betty Crocker Lemon Velvet Cake Mix with Lemon Velvet Frosting Mix
Betty Crocker Chocolate Malt Cake Mix with Chocolate Malt Frosting Mix

CALENDAR CAKES

Check the calendar—if there's a holiday coming up, plan to celebrate! And what better way to celebrate than with cake, especially decorated for the occasion?

We've included many longtime favorites among our calendar cakes; these recipes are like old friends, always nice to see again with each new year. There are the Sweetheart Cupcakes for Valentine's Day and the Easter Bunny Cake for Easter. The traditional Christmas choices, like fruitcakes and steamed puddings. The patriotic favorites for February and the Fourth. Plus many other ideas for making merry with cake every single month.

Happily we go round the calendar now, season by season, ending up with the fifth and favorite "holly" season.

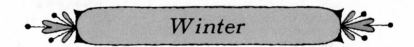

Winter

CLOCK STRIKES TWELVE CAKE

Bake any flavor Betty Crocker Layer Cake Mix in two round layer pans, 9x1½ inches, as directed on package. Cool.

Prepare Betty Crocker Fluffy White Frosting Mix as directed on package; tint with food coloring, if desired. Fill and frost cake. Place gumdrops, licorice circles or other favorite candies on frosted cake to resemble face of clock. Use shoestring licorice for hands of clock.

CONFETTI CUPCAKES

Bake any flavor Betty Crocker Layer Cake Mix in paper baking cups as directed on package. Cool. Remove papers from 16 cupcakes. Tint ½ cup shredded coconut green, ½ cup pink and ½ cup yellow (see page 19). Sprinkle a large serving plate with untinted shredded coconut.

Prepare Betty Crocker Fluffy White Frosting Mix as directed on package. Place each cupcake on tines of fork and frost entire surface. Sprinkle each with about 1 tablespoon tinted coconut.

Place cupcakes in a circle around edge of plate. Just before serving, place desired number of ice cream balls in center. Sprinkle balls with remaining coconut.

> *Betty Crocker Note:* There is enough frosting to frost 16 cupcakes completely and the tops of the remaining cupcakes.

PEPPERMINT BELL CAKE

1 package Betty Crocker Angel Food Cake Mix
¼ teaspoon peppermint extract
Red food coloring
1 package Betty Crocker Fluffy White Frosting Mix
½ to ¾ cup crushed peppermint stick candy
Red cinnamon candies, if desired

Prepare cake mix as directed on package except—during last ½ minute of mixing, add peppermint extract and a few drops red food coloring. Pour batter into ungreased tube pan, 10x4 inches. Bake as directed on package. Cool. Remove from pan.

Prepare frosting mix as directed on package; frost cake. Coat sides of cake with crushed candy, reserving 3 tablespoons. Dip bell cookie cutter into red food coloring; press into frosting, making an imprint on top of cake. Repeat, dipping cookie cutter each time into red food coloring, until there is a circle of bells (5 or 6) on top of cake.

Fill in bells with reserved crushed peppermint candy. Cinnamon candies may be used for clappers. Place artificial holly between bells to tie them together.

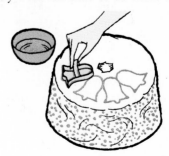

ESKIMO IGLOO CAKE

Bake any flavor Betty Crocker Layer Cake Mix in two round layer pans, 8x1½ inches, as directed on package. Cool. Cut each layer in half.

Prepare Betty Crocker Fluffy White Frosting Mix as directed on package. Spread frosting on one side of three halves. Set halves side by side on their cut edges with frosting between to form a long rounded cake. Frost the rounded top and ends with the remaining frosting.

In top of double boiler, heat 1 square (1 ounce) unsweetened chocolate and ¼ teaspoon shortening until melted.

To make ice blocks on igloo, mark icing into squares by dripping chocolate mixture from end of teaspoon.

To serve cake, cut crosswise in half, then cut from either flat end of cake to center This gives flat slices of cake, each with frosting on top and sides.

VALENTINE CAKE

Bake any flavor Betty Crocker Layer Cake Mix in two round layer pans, 8 or 9x1½ inches, as directed on package. Cool.

Prepare Betty Crocker Cherry Fluff Frosting Mix as directed on package. Spread half of frosting between layers and on top of cake. Tint remaining frosting deep pink with red food coloring. Outline a heart on top of cake and fill it in with ⅓ cup of the tinted frosting. Frost sides of cake with remaining tinted frosting.

Coconut Valentine Cake: Fill and frost cake with Betty Crocker Fluffy White Frosting Mix. Fill heart outlined on top of cake with pink-tinted coconut (see page 19), red decorators' sugar or chopped maraschino cherries.

HAVE A HEART CAKE

Bake any flavor Betty Crocker Layer Cake Mix in one square pan, 8x8x2 inches, and one round layer pan, 8x1½ inches, as directed on package. Cool. Place square cake on a large serving tray or plate. Cut the round layer in half. Place each half against the top corners of the square cake to form a heart.

Frost cake with Betty Crocker Cherry Fluff Frosting Mix prepared as directed on package. Cover top of cake well, especially over cut sections. If desired, decorate cake with red cinnamon candies, writing a message such as "Be Mine."

Betty Crocker Note: The cake may be baked in two heart-shaped layer pans; follow package directions for 8-inch round layer pans.

SWEETHEART CUPCAKES

Bake any flavor Betty Crocker Layer Cake Mix in paper baking cups as directed on package. Cool.

Prepare Betty Crocker Fluffy White Frosting Mix as directed on package. Divide in thirds. Leave ⅓ white; tint ⅓ pink and ⅓ red. Frost cupcakes. Decorate with candy hearts of various sizes (available in candy stores).

CHERRY MOUSSE ANGEL FOOD

1 package Betty Crocker Angel Food Cake Mix
1 pint whipping cream (2 cups)
½ cup confectioners' sugar
16 maraschino cherries, well drained and cut up
   (3-ounce bottle)
½ cup chopped walnuts
2 tablespoons cherry syrup

Bake cake in ungreased tube pan, 10x4 inches, as directed on package. Cool. Remove from pan. Whip cream with confectioners' sugar until stiff. Fold in cherries, walnuts and cherry syrup. Spread on top and sides of cake. Refrigerate until served.

Betty Crocker Note: Cake may be frosted, then frozen until ready to use.

LINCOLN LOG CAKE

Follow directions for Bûche de Noël (page 109). Decorate with maraschino cherries or red hatchets.

MINIATURE LINCOLN LOGS

Bake Betty Crocker White Cake Mix in paper baking cups as directed on package. Cool. Remove papers. Prepare Betty Crocker Chocolate Fudge Frosting Mix as directed on package. To form log, put two cupcakes together end-to-end with frosting. Frost sides, leaving ends of logs (tops of cupcakes) unfrosted. With small spatula make strokes in frosting to resemble bark. Decorate each log with a hatchet cut from red construction paper. Garnish plate with stemmed red cherries, if desired. *Makes 12 to 15 logs.*

LIME RIBBON DELIGHT

Pictured at left.

1 package Betty Crocker White Cake Mix
1 package (3 ounces) lime-flavored gelatin
1 cup hot water
½ cup fruit juice or water
½ cup drained crushed pineapple
¼ cup chopped nuts
Few drops lemon juice
1 cup whipping cream
¼ cup confectioners' sugar

Bake cake in two round layer pans, 9x1½ inches, as directed on package. Cool.

Dissolve gelatin in hot water. Add fruit juice and chill until almost firm. Add pineapple, nuts and lemon juice.

Place two strips of aluminum foil across the bottom of each layer pan, letting strips extend over edge. Replace cake layers, placing one layer back in pan upside down and the other right side up. (This will make a better looking cake when gelatin layers are put together.) Spoon the fruit gelatin over the two layers. Chill until firm.

Whip cream with confectioners' sugar. Lift cake layers out of pans, using extended edges of foil. Stack layers gelatin side up. Frost sides with whipped cream.

Refrigerate until serving time. Decorate with miniature white clay pipes for St. Patrick's Day.

SHAMROCK DESIGNER CAKE

Prepare Betty Crocker Angel Food Cake Mix as directed on package except—tint batter light green and fold in ¼ teaspoon peppermint extract after mixing. Pour batter into an ungreased tube pan, 10x4 inches. Bake as directed. Cool. Remove from pan.

Prepare Betty Crocker Fluffy White Frosting Mix as directed on package. Frost sides and top of cake.

Dip shamrock cookie cutter into green food coloring; then press into frosting, making an imprint on top of cake. Repeat, dipping cookie cutter each time into green food coloring, until there is a circle of shamrocks (4 or 5) on top of cake.

MARDI GRAS CAKE

Bake Betty Crocker Confetti Angel Food Cake Mix in ungreased tube pan, 10x4 inches, as directed on package. Cool. Remove from pan.

Prepare Betty Crocker Fluffy White Frosting Mix as directed on package. Frost sides and top of cake.

Select 3 or 4 cookie cutters of different designs. Place food coloring in small shallow dishes. Dip cookie cutter into food coloring; press into cake. Repeat over top and sides of cake. Using a second cookie cutter and another food coloring, repeat process, overlapping existing design. Repeat again with third and fourth cookie cutter and food coloring.

Spring

SPRING BONNET CAKE

Prepare any flavor Betty Crocker Layer Cake Mix as directed on package. Bake in one round layer pan, 8x1½ inches, and one round layer pan, 9x1½ inches, as directed on package. Cool.

Frost 9-inch layer with Betty Crocker Fluffy White Frosting Mix prepared as directed on package. Trim the other layer down to 6-inch diameter. Place on top of 9-inch layer. Reserve ½ cup frosting. Frost 6-inch layer with remaining frosting.

Tint reserved frosting with food coloring and use to make a contrasting ribbon around the base of the 6-inch layer. Decorate hat, using gumdrops, dragées, chocolate pieces, red cinnamon candies, pillow mints or nuts.

MINIATURE EASTER BONNETS

Bake any flavor Betty Crocker Layer Cake Mix in paper baking cups as directed on package. Cool. Remove papers.

Prepare Betty Crocker Fluffy White Frosting Mix as directed on package. Divide into 4 equal parts. Leave one part white; tint the remaining portions pink, yellow and green.

Place each cupcake upside down in center of flattened cupcake paper or doily. Frost sides and bottoms of each cupcake to resemble the crown of a hat (the doily or paper is the hat brim) in matching or contrasting color. *Makes 5 or 6 of each color.*

Decorate each hat with one of the following:

A row of chocolate pieces, dragées, red cinnamon candies or pillow mints around base of crown to resemble a band.

Coconut or colored decorators' sugar sprinkled over frosted cupcake.

Gumdrops or nuts cut or shaped to resemble petals of flowers.

Decorated cocktail picks to resemble feathers.

EASTER BUNNY CAKE

Pictured below.

Bake any flavor Betty Crocker Layer Cake Mix in two round layer pans, 8 or 9x1½ inches, as directed on package. Cool. Prepare Betty Crocker Fluffy White Frosting Mix as directed on package. Cut one layer in half; put halves together with frosting. Stand cake upright on cut edge.

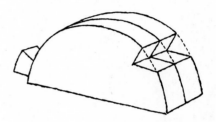

With a sharp knife, cut a notch about a third of the way around the semicircle, forming the rabbit's head. Save cutout piece for the tail. Secure in place with a wooden pick. Frost rabbit with remaining frosting. Sprinkle generously with shredded coconut.

Make ears of white paper; color inside pink with crayon. Use pink jelly beans or gumdrops for eyes and nose. Coconut tinted green (see page 19) or paper grass and a few Easter eggs (jelly beans) form an attractive nest around the bunny.

Freeze other layer for later use.

April shower cake ideas may be found on pages 117 and 118.

EASTER BASKET CAKE

Pictured at left.

Bake Betty Crocker Lemon Chiffon Cake Mix in ungreased tube pan, 10x4 inches, as directed on package. Cool. Remove from pan. Decorate cake as a basket (see below). Fill basket with green-tinted coconut "grass" (see page 19) and candy Easter eggs.

To make basket: Use a sharp knife to cut a shallow sloping slice from outer edge to center of cake. (Make center cut no deeper than ½ inch.) Fill hole made by tube pan with cut cake.

To frost basket: Prepare Betty Crocker Fluffy White Frosting Mix as directed on package. Tint pale yellow. Frost sides of cake and lightly frost top. Make a basket weave pattern in frosting on sides of cake by drawing inch-long horizontal and vertical lines with tines of fork.*

For basket handle: Fashion handle of pipe cleaners or coat hangers. Wrap with several strips of aluminum foil. Then wrap handle with pastel yellow ribbon; secure ribbon with transparent tape. Tie mauve ribbon on top. Press handle into top of cake basket.

*If frosting sticks to fork while decorating basket, dip fork in hot water.

MAYPOLE CENTERPIECE CAKE

Bake Betty Crocker Lemon Chiffon Cake Mix* in ungreased tube pan, 10x4 inches, as directed on package. Cool. Remove from pan.

Frost with Betty Crocker Lemon Fluff Frosting Mix prepared as directed on package.

With melted wax or florists' clay, secure a 12- to 15-inch taper candle in center hole of cake. Attach pastel-colored ribbons to top of candle. Arrange a circle of paper dolls around base of cake plate. Drape a ribbon over the hand of each doll.

*Try our White or Confetti Angel Food Cake Mix in this recipe, if you prefer, and frost with our Fluffy White or Cherry Fluff Frosting Mix.

EASTER EGGS

Pictured above.

1 package Betty Crocker Creamy White Frosting Mix
5 tablespoons soft butter or margarine
3 tablespoons flour
2 tablespoons hot water
Food coloring, if desired
Chocolate Fudge Coating (below), if desired

Combine frosting mix (dry mix), butter and flour. Add hot water; blend thoroughly. Divide mixture into several parts and tint desired colors. Knead each colored mixture 20 to 30 times on board lightly dusted with confectioners' sugar. Divide and shape into different sized eggs (use ½ to 1½ tablespoons of mixture for each egg). Chill; decorate with Icing: Blend ½ cup sifted confectioners' sugar and 1 to 2 teaspoons water—use in decorating cone (see page 24). *Or* cover with Chocolate Fudge Coating.

Chocolate Fudge Coating: Melt 2 tablespoons soft butter or margarine with 6 tablespoons water in top of double boiler. Add 1 package Betty Crocker Chocolate Fudge Frosting Mix (dry mix); stir until smooth. Heat over rapidly boiling water about 5 minutes, stirring occasionally. Remove from heat, keeping over hot water so that it will not thicken. Place fondant eggs on fork over chocolate mixture and pour chocolate over entire egg. Place on rack to set.

MAY BASKET CUPCAKES

Bake any flavor Betty Crocker Layer Cake Mix in paper baking cups as directed on package. Cool.

Frost cupcakes with Betty Crocker Lemon Fluff Frosting Mix prepared as directed on package. For each daisy, place a small yellow gumdrop in center of cupcake. For petals, use six miniature marshmallows.

For handle of each basket, shape pastel-colored pipe cleaner in "U" shape. Insert in edges of cupcake. Tie a tiny ribbon atop each handle, if desired.

CHERRY BLOSSOM CAKE

Prepare Betty Crocker White Cake Mix as directed on package. Divide batter in half; tint one half a delicate pink with red food coloring and flavor with ½ teaspoon almond extract. Bake one white layer and one pink layer in round layer pans, 8 or 9x1½ inches, as directed on package. Cool. Split cake to make 4 layers (page 20).

Prepare Betty Crocker Cherry Fluff Frosting Mix as directed on package. Reserve ½ cup frosting. Fill and frost cake, alternating pink and white layers.

To make cherry blossoms: Tint reserved frosting a deep pink with red food coloring. For each petal, half fill a teaspoon with frosting and with second teaspoon ease each petal onto cake. Make 5 petals per flower. (There is enough frosting for 8 or 9 blossoms.) Sprinkle centers with yellow decorators' sugar or silver dragées.

FLAG DAY CUPCAKES

Bake any flavor Betty Crocker Layer Cake Mix in paper baking cups as directed on package. Cool.

Frost cupcakes with Betty Crocker Fluffy White Frosting Mix prepared as directed on package. Leave a third of the cupcakes white, sprinkle another third with red decorators' sugar and the remaining third with blue decorators' sugar. In center of each, place a miniature American flag.

STRAWBERRY SHORTCAKE

Pictured at right.

Bake Betty Crocker Yellow Cake Mix in round layer pans, 8 or 9x1½ inches, as directed on package. Cool. Place one layer on serving plate upside down; cover with sweetened strawberries. Top with other layer right side up; cover with more strawberries. Top with sweetened whipped cream.

> **Betty Crocker Note:** Wash, drain and hull fresh strawberries; add sugar and let stand at room temperature about one hour. Use 1 quart (4 cups) of strawberries in all.

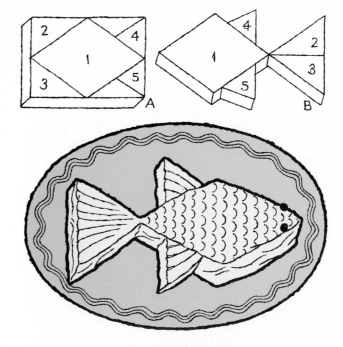

GONE FISHING CAKE

Bake any flavor Betty Crocker Layer Cake Mix in oblong pan, 13x9x2 inches, as directed on package. Remove from pan and cool.

Cut cake into diamond shape (see diagram A); remove cutout piece to serving platter or aluminum foil-covered cardboard. Make tail with 2 of the corners; make fins from remaining corners (see diagram B).

Prepare Betty Crocker Lemon Velvet Frosting Mix as directed on package; frost cake. To make scales, invert a teaspoon and press tip into frosted cake. Repeat in rows. A gumdrop or jelly bean may be used for the eye.

For a Father's Day cake, see pages **72** and **75** in the Birthday section.

Summer

RED, WHITE AND BLUE CAKE

Bake Betty Crocker Angel Food Cake Mix in ungreased tube pan, 10x4 inches, as directed on package. Cool. Remove from pan and dust top of cake with confectioners' sugar.

Serve wedges of angel food with fresh raspberries (or strawberries) and blueberries; top with sweetened whipped cream.

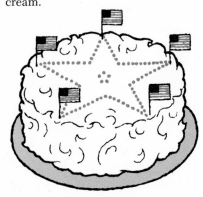

U.S.A. BIRTHDAY CAKE

Bake any flavor Betty Crocker Layer Cake Mix in two round layer pans, 9x1½ inches, as directed on package. Cool.

Prepare Betty Crocker Fluffy White Frosting Mix as directed on package. Fill and frost layers.

Make a five-pointed star on top of cake. First, place five wooden picks 5 inches apart on outside edge of cake to mark the star points; then place another five wooden picks halfway between outer picks and 2½ inches from edge of cake. Form star by drawing lines in frosting between picks; remove picks.

Outline star with red cinnamon candies. Place five red cinnamon candies in center for a tiny star.

Decorate cake with miniature state flags or United States flags.

FIRECRACKERS

Bake Betty Crocker White Cake Mix in paper baking cups as directed on package. Cool. Remove papers.

Prepare Betty Crocker Creamy White Frosting Mix as directed on package.

To form each firecracker, put two cupcakes together end-to-end with frosting. Frost sides, leaving ends of firecrackers (tops of cupcakes) unfrosted. Sprinkle generously with red decorators' sugar before frosting sets. Decorate each with a red candle stuck into one end. *Makes 12 to 15 firecrackers.*

LAZY DAISY CAKE

Bake any flavor Betty Crocker Layer Cake Mix in two round layer pans, 8 or 9x1½ inches, as directed on package. Cool.

Prepare Betty Crocker Lemon Fluff Frosting Mix as directed on package. Fill and frost cake.

Snip top of each of 3 marshmallows into 6 sections, cutting about ¾ of way through each. Spread sections, pinching gently, so that they resemble petals. Arrange at one side on top of frosted cake. In center of each flower, place small yellow gumdrop; at sides, make leaves with green gumdrops.

Betty Crocker Note: To cut marshmallows easily, dip scissors in hot water between cuttings.

Brown-eyed Susan Cake: Follow recipe (above) except —for each flower, use 6 sliced almonds for petals and a chocolate chip for center.

For summer sports cakes, see Baseball Mitt Cake (page 67), Sailboat Cake (page 68) and Gone Fishing Cake (page 101).

LUAU PALM TREE CAKE

Bake Betty Crocker Yellow Cake Mix in two round layer pans, 8x1½ inches, as directed on package. Cool.

Prepare Betty Crocker Fluffy White Frosting Mix as directed on package. Fill and frost cake.

Sprinkle sides of cake thickly with shredded fresh coconut° (1½ to 2 cups). On top of cake arrange a coconut palm tree, using cinnamon stick or chocolate candy roll as trunk, slices of green peppermint gumdrops as leaves and chocolate pieces as coconuts.

To Prepare Fresh Coconut:

Pierce three holes at one end. Drain out milk. Heat coconut for *30 minutes at 350°.* Cool. Break shell with hammer or chisel; remove. Break meat in pieces. Pare off brown skin; shred white meat.

°*1½ to 2 cups canned or packaged coconut may be used in place of fresh coconut.*

For cakes to take on a picnic, see pages 34 to 36.

PEACHES AND VELVET CREAM CAKE

Pictured below, right.

1 package Betty Crocker Yellow Cake Mix
1 package Betty Crocker Creamy White Frosting Mix
1½ cups whipping cream
1 cup finely chopped fresh peaches, well drained°
Thin Icing (below)

Bake cake in two round layer pans, 9x1½ inches, as directed on package. Cool. Split cake to make 4 layers (page 20).

Add 2 cups frosting mix (dry mix) to whipping cream. Chill 1 hour; whip until stiff. Fold in peaches. Spread between layers. Spread top with Thin Icing; let some drizzle down sides. Chill. Just before serving, garnish top edge of cake with slices of fresh peaches. *12 to 14 servings.*

Thin Icing: Blend remaining frosting mix, 2 to 3 tablespoons hot water and 1 tablespoon light corn syrup. Beat until smooth.

°*Two packages (10 ounces each) frozen sliced peaches, thawed and well drained, or 1 can (1 pound) sliced peaches, well drained, may be used in place of fresh peaches. These, too, should be finely chopped.*

Strawberries and Velvet Cream Cake: Follow recipe (above) except—use Betty Crocker White Cake Mix. Substitute 1 cup crushed fresh strawberries°° (about 1 quart), well drained, for the peaches. Garnish top of cake with several whole strawberries.

°°*Two packages (10 ounces each) frozen sliced strawberries, thawed and well drained, may be used in place of fresh strawberries. To serve, spoon extra strawberries over each slice.*

Summer Mint Velvet Cream Cake: Follow recipe (above) except—use Betty Crocker White Cake Mix; omit peaches. Fold 2 squares (2 ounces) unsweetened chocolate, grated, a few drops green food coloring and ¼ teaspoon peppermint extract into whipped cream filling. Tint Thin Icing light green. Garnish top of cake with a wreath of Chocolate Curls (page 23).

Betty Crocker Note: For a neat cake plate, see page 17.

BERRY BASKET CAKE

Bake Betty Crocker Yellow Cake Mix in two round layer pans, 9x1½ inches, as directed on package. Cool.

Heat oven to 400°. Place one layer on a baking sheet. Make Meringue (below). Pile mounds of meringue around the top edge of cake for a basket effect. Bake *8 to 10 minutes*, or until delicately browned. Serve warm or cold with fresh sweetened berries heaped in the center. *6 to 8 servings.*

Freeze the other layer for another dessert.

Meringue:
3 egg whites
¼ teaspoon cream of tartar
6 tablespoons sugar
½ teaspoon vanilla

Beat egg whites with cream of tartar until frothy. Gradually beat in sugar, a little at a time. Continue beating until stiff and glossy. *Do not underbeat. Beat until all sugar is dissolved.* Fold in vanilla.

BACK TO SCHOOL CAKE

Bake Betty Crocker Chocolate Malt Cake Mix in oblong pan, 13x9x2 inches, as directed on package. Remove from pan and cool.

Prepare Betty Crocker Chocolate Fudge Frosting Mix as directed on package. Frost sides and top of cake.

Arrange peppermint candy sticks along edge of cake to form border of slate. Write figures or words (2+2=4, one, cat, etc.) on top of cake with Icing: Combine ½ cup sifted confectioners' sugar with 1 to 2 teaspoons warm water—just enough to make icing easy to force through decorating cone yet hold its shape.

Autumn

HOMECOMING CAKE

Bake any flavor Betty Crocker Layer Cake Mix in oblong pan, 13x9x2 inches, as directed on package. Remove from pan and cool. Place on large tray or breadboard which has been covered with aluminum foil.

Prepare Betty Crocker Fluffy White Frosting Mix as directed on package. Frost sides and top of cake. Sprinkle entire top of cake with green decorators' sugar.

With wooden pick, draw lines across top of cake to make yard and goal lines. Pennants and goal posts can be made with wooden skewers, lollipop sticks or paper straws. Cut tiny flags from colored construction paper, using school colors. Crossbars on the goal posts can be fastened with transparent tape, candle wax or glue.

FOOTBALL CAKE

Heat oven to 350°. Prepare Betty Crocker Devils Food Cake Mix as directed on package except—use 2 tablespoons less water. Pour batter into two greased and floured loaf pans, 9x5x3 inches. Bake *35 to 40 minutes.* Let cool in pans 10 minutes; remove from pans and cool thoroughly.

To achieve the effect of a football field, use a rectangular plate. (A cardboard rectangle covered with green paper and cellophane could also be used.)

Prepare Betty Crocker Chocolate Fudge Frosting Mix as directed on package. Cut rounded tops off cakes (see diagram A). Assemble as shown in diagram B, using a thin layer of frosting between pieces. Trim corners of cake to form the football.

Place football cake in middle of plate; frost on all sides. Use strips of cut marshmallows for the lacing on football. Use white drinking straws across plate for yard lines. Small pennants may also be attached to half a straw and inserted in football.

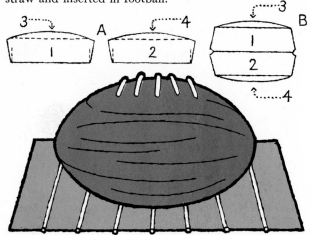

TWIN PENNANT CAKES

Heat oven to 350°. Prepare your favorite flavor Betty Crocker Layer Cake Mix as directed on package. Pour batter into greased and floured jelly roll pan, 15½x10½x1 inch. Bake *25 to 30 minutes.* Remove from pan and cool.

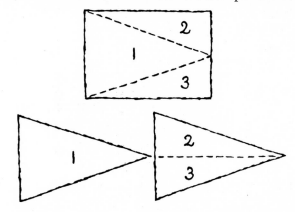

Cut cake as shown in diagram. The sides of the large cake become the center line of the second pennant. Place each cake on a large platter or aluminum foil-covered cardboard as shown in sketch. Frost each pennant cake with half of Betty Crocker Fluffy White Frosting Mix prepared as directed on package and tinted with food colorings to match favorite school colors. With wooden pick, lightly draw in frosting the school names of your choice; outline names with decorators' sugar, food coloring, chocolate pieces or shoestring licorice.

If desired, press long wooden sticks or peppermint sticks into sides of pennant cakes and attach small felt streamers or bows at corners of each pennant.

BLACK CAT CUPCAKES

Bake any flavor Betty Crocker Layer Cake Mix in paper baking cups as directed on package. Cool.

Prepare Betty Crocker Fluffy White Frosting Mix as directed on package. Tint orange, using 1 to 2 drops *each* red and yellow food coloring. Frost cupcakes.

For each cat, slice a 1-inch black gumdrop into 3 pieces. Use small rounded end slice for head and largest slice for body; cut tail and ears from third slice.

Spicy Apple Butter Cake (page 39) and Johnny Appleseed Cake (page 36) are especially appropriate at this time of year.

PUMPKIN CAKE WITH HARD SAUCE

Bake Pilgrim Pumpkin Cake (page 36). Top warm squares with Hard Sauce (below).

Hard Sauce:
½ cup soft butter or margarine
1 egg white
½ package (about 1¾ cups) Betty Crocker Creamy
   White Frosting Mix
½ teaspoon rum flavoring, if desired

Blend butter, egg white and frosting mix (dry mix) in small mixer bowl. Beat 1 minute high speed on electric mixer or by hand until light and fluffy. Blend in flavoring. Chill until hard. *Makes 1½ cups.*

To Make Hard Sauce Hobgoblins:
Shape chilled Hard Sauce into 1-inch balls. Use gumdrops, hard candies, raisins, whole cloves, chocolate pieces and candied fruits to make eyes, noses, mouths and hats. Refrigerate.

HARVEST PUMPKIN

Bake any flavor Betty Crocker Layer Cake Mix in two round layer pans, 8x1½ inches, as directed on package. Cool.

Prepare 2 packages Betty Crocker Fluffy White Frosting Mix, 1 package at a time, as directed.

Reserve ½ cup frosting and tint green. Tint remaining frosting orange with ¼ teaspoon *each* red and yellow food coloring. Fill and frost cake; frost sides and top with more frosting to make pumpkin shape. Make grooves with spatula. Use half a banana, frosted with green frosting, for stem. Anchor in center of cake with wooden picks.

FESTIVE CRANBERRY CAKE

Bake Betty Crocker White Cake Mix in two round layer pans, 9x1½ inches, as directed on package. Cool.

Split cake to make 4 layers (see page 20). Whip 1½ cups whipping cream with ⅓ cup confectioners' sugar until stiff. Spread each layer with ¼ of sweetened whipped cream. Then spoon ¼ of 1 jar (14 ounces) cranberry-orange relish over each layer; swirl relish into the whipped cream; stack. Chill 1 to 2 hours before serving. *12 to 16 servings.*

Cranberry-Pineapple Cake: Follow recipe (above) except—do not split layers. Combine 1 can (8¾ ounces) crushed pineapple and 1 jar (14 ounces) cranberry-orange relish. Drain any excess liquid. Spread ⅓ cup whipped cream between layers; cover with half the cranberry mixture. Frost top and sides of cake with remaining whipped cream, using a thin layer only over top. Cover top with remaining cranberry mixture. Chill. *12 to 16 servings.*

CRANBERRY ANGEL CAKE

Bake Betty Crocker Angel Food Cake Mix in ungreased tube pan, 10x4 inches, as directed on package. Cool. Remove from pan. Split cake to make 3 layers (see page 20).

Spread half of 1 jar (14 ounces) cranberry-orange relish between each layer, working quickly. Whip 1½ cups whipping cream with ⅓ cup confectioners' sugar; tint with red food coloring, if desired. Frost sides and top of cake. Chill several hours before serving. *12 to 15 servings.*

For a delicious family treat at Thanksgiving or Christmas, serve Mincemeat Upside-down Cake (page 32).

AUTUMN CHRYSANTHEMUM CAKE

Pictured at right.

Prepare Betty Crocker Yellow Cake Mix as directed on package except—fold 2 tablespoons grated orange peel into batter. Pour into two greased and floured square pans, 8x8x2 inches, or two round layer pans, 9x1½ inches. Bake as directed on package. Cool.

Fill layers with Mincemeat Filling (below). Prepare Betty Crocker Fluffy White Frosting Mix as directed on package. Frost cake. Top with Orange Chrysanthemum (below).

Mincemeat Filling:

2 tablespoons brown sugar
2 tablespoons cornstarch
¼ cup orange juice
¾ cup water
1 cup prepared mincemeat
1 tablespoon grated orange peel

In saucepan mix brown sugar and cornstarch. Gradually stir in orange juice and water. Stir in mincemeat. Cook over medium heat until thickened. Remove from heat. Add orange peel. Cool.

Orange Chrysanthemum: You will need about ¾ pound large candy orange slices. With knife or scissors cut each of 8 candy slices lengthwise into 2 thin slices (see diagram A); dip in sugar. With curved rim as guide, cut each thin slice into 4 slender curved petals, leaving them attached at one end (see diagram B); dip into sugar after each cut. To form flower, place each group of four petals on frosted cake with tips toward edge of circle, curving upward (see picture). Cut separate petals to fill in; bend some into loops for center.

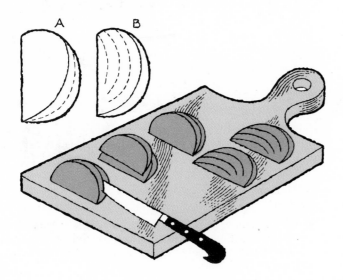

STEAMED ORANGE PUDDING

Prepare Betty Crocker Yellow Cake Mix as directed on package except—add 1 tablespoon grated orange peel. Pour batter into 12 well-greased custard cups (6-ounce size). Cups should be only ⅔ full. Tie waxed paper or aluminum foil loosely over tops. Steam 30 minutes (see page 107).

Serve warm, inverted in dessert dishes; pour hot Orange Sauce (below) over each.

Orange Sauce:

1 cup sugar
2 tablespoons cornstarch
¼ teaspoon salt
1 cup orange juice
¼ cup lemon juice
¾ cup boiling water
1 tablespoon butter or margarine
1 teaspoon <u>each</u> grated orange and lemon peel

Mix sugar, cornstarch and salt in saucepan. Stir in juices and water. Boil 1 minute, stirring constantly. Remove from heat. Stir in butter and grated peel. Keep hot until serving time. *Makes 2 cups.*

FRUITED STEAMED PUDDING

1 package Betty Crocker Honey Spice Cake Mix
⅓ cup shortening
4 eggs
1 tablespoon rum flavoring
½ cup mixed candied fruit
½ cup cut-up dates
½ cup diced prunes
½ cup cut-up figs
½ cup chopped walnuts

Grease two 1½-quart oven-glass bowls. Blend cake mix (dry mix), shortening, eggs and rum flavoring. Beat 2 minutes medium speed on mixer. Add fruits and nuts. Blend 1 minute low speed.

Pour into bowls. Tie waxed paper or aluminum foil loosely over tops. Steam 2½ to 3 hours (below). Serve hot with Celestial Sauce (at right) or Hard Sauce (page 105). Store unused pudding in refrigerator not longer than ten days. To reheat, place covered bowl in pan with boiling water; simmer for 1 hour. *6 servings from each pudding.*

HOW TO STEAM

In steamer, in deep well or tightly covered pan on surface of range.
Arrange a rack about 2 inches above bottom of pan. Add about 1 inch of water. Cover and bring water to boil. Place molds on rack. Replace cover. When water is again boiling, reduce heat enough so that water is just boiling.

In covered roasting pan.
Arrange a rack about 2 inches above bottom of pan. Add about 1 inch boiling water; cover. Place pan in 500° oven. When water is again boiling, place molds on rack. Replace cover. After 10 minutes, reduce temperature to 350°.

CHOCOLATE STEAMED PUDDING

Prepare Betty Crocker Devils Food Cake Mix as directed on package. Pour batter into three well-greased cans (2½-cup size). Tie waxed paper or aluminum foil loosely over tops. Steam 1½ hours (see below). Remove from cans.

Slice pudding and serve warm with Hard Sauce (page 105) or Celestial Sauce (below). *9 to 12 servings.*

Celestial Sauce:
1 package Betty Crocker Creamy White Frosting Mix
1 cup soft butter or margarine
1 cup whipping cream, whipped
2 tablespoons rum or brandy flavoring

Beat frosting mix (dry mix) and butter until creamy. Fold in whipped cream. Heat, stirring constantly; boil until foamy. Remove from heat. Stir in flavoring. Serve immediately. *Makes 2½ to 3 cups.*

Betty Crocker Note: Leftover sauce may be stored covered in refrigerator and reheated in top of double boiler or served cold, if desired.

Notes on Steaming

1. Steam must surround mold.
2. Do not have so much water in steamer that it touches mold.
3. If it is necessary to add more water during steaming, lift lid quickly and add boiling water.
4. Do not remove cover during steaming (unless more water must be added); the pudding may fall if you do.

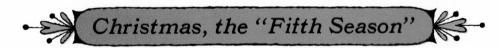

Christmas, the "Fifth Season"

HOLIDAY CUPCAKES

Bake Betty Crocker White Cake Mix in paper baking cups as directed on package. Cool.

Prepare Betty Crocker Fluffy White Frosting Mix as directed on package. Decorate, using one of the suggestions at right.

Candle Cupcakes: Frost cupcakes. Set a small red candle in center of each and decorate with "holly" (use red cinnamon candies or cut berries from candied cherries; cut leaves from green candied cherries, citron or angelica).

Merry Christmas Cupcakes: Frost cupcakes. Decorate top of each with one letter made from red cinnamon candies. Arrange cupcakes on large serving tray to spell out "Merry Christmas."

SANTA LUCIA CROWN

Pictured on page 111.

Bake Betty Crocker Angel Food Cake Mix in ungreased tube pan, 10x4 inches, as directed on package. Cool; remove from pan.

Split cake to make 3 layers (see page 20). Fill with Lingonberry Filling (below). Frost with Fluffy Cream Frosting (below). Refrigerate. Surround cake with a dozen 12-inch slim candles.

Lingonberry Filling:
1½ cups lingonberries
¾ cup sugar
1 tablespoon cornstarch
¼ cup water

Wash and drain lingonberries. Combine sugar and cornstarch in saucepan. Add water and lingonberries. Bring to a boil and simmer for 10 minutes. Cool.

Fluffy Cream Frosting: Add 1 package Betty Crocker Fluffy White Frosting Mix (dry mix) to 1½ cups whipping cream in small mixer bowl. Chill 1 hour. Blend; beat until soft peaks form.

Also for Christmas

Another cake appropriate at Christmastime is the Peppermint Bell Cake (page 96). For variations, use Christmas cookie cutters such as tree, reindeer, Santa, star or angel in place of bell cutter.

DELLA ROBBIA CAKE

Pictured on page 5.

Bake Betty Crocker Lemon Velvet Cake Mix in two round layer pans, 9x1½ inches, as directed on package. Cool. Split cake to make 4 layers (see page 20).

Add 1 package Betty Crocker Fluffy White Frosting Mix (dry mix) to 1½ cups whipping cream in small mixer bowl. Chill at least 1 hour. Blend; beat until stiff. Fold 1 cup frosting mixture into 1 jar (10 ounces) Nesselrode. Spread between layers.

Frost sides and top of cake with remaining frosting mixture. Decorate top of cake with a wreath of fruit-shaped Modern Marzipan (page 131).

BUTTER MIX COOKIES

Pictured on page 111.

⅓ cup soft butter*
½ cup shortening*
2 egg yolks
½ teaspoon vanilla
1 package any flavor Betty Crocker Layer Cake Mix**

Heat oven to 375°. Mix butter, shortening, egg yolks and vanilla. Thoroughly blend in cake mix (dry mix), ⅓ at a time. (If dough is dry, add 1 to 1½ teaspoons water and blend well.) Finish dough in one of the following ways and bake on ungreased baking sheet. Cool cookies slightly before removing from baking sheet. *Makes 6 to 8 dozen.*

*Do not use all butter or all shortening.

Pressed: Place dough in cookie press and force through press onto baking sheet. Decorate with colored sugar or dragées. Bake *8 to 10 minutes.*

Rolled: Gather ¼ of dough together with fingers. Press firmly into a ball. Flatten with hand and roll out ⅛ inch thick on lightly floured cloth-covered board. (Use a stockinet-covered rolling pin.) Cut with cookie cutters. Repeat, using remaining dough. Bake *6 to 8 minutes.* Frost or decorate as desired.

Refrigerated: Press and mold dough into a long smooth roll about 2 inches in diameter. Roll in finely chopped nuts, decorators' sugar, coconut or grated chocolate. Wrap in waxed paper and chill until stiff (several hours or overnight). With a sharp thin knife, cut in slices ⅛ inch thick. Bake *6 to 8 minutes.*

Molded: Add ½ cup chopped nuts, candied cherries or fruit, dates, raisins, chocolate or butterscotch chips to dough. Form *scant* teaspoonfuls of dough into balls. (These small cookies will have attractive cracked tops after baking.) Bake *8 to 12 minutes.*

Surprise: Wrap 1 level teaspoonful of dough around filling (candied cherry, date, gumdrop). Bake *8 to 10 minutes.* Frost tops with any flavor Betty Crocker Creamy-type Frosting Mix prepared as directed on package. Decorate with chopped nuts, flaked coconut or decorators' sugar.

Betty Crocker Note: If dough is too soft, chill slightly. Baking sheets should be cool before re-using. Store cookies in airtight container.

**For Marble, follow directions (above) using only yellow mix. Divide dough in half; into one half, knead marbling mixture and 1 teaspoon soft butter. Leave remaining dough plain. Shape as desired.

Other cookies appropriate for holiday serving can be found in the Snacking with Sweets chapter.

CHRISTMAS HOLLY WREATHS

Pictured on page 111.

Heat oven to 350°. Prepare any flavor Betty Crocker Layer Cake Mix as directed on package. Spread batter in greased and floured jelly roll pan, 15½x10½x1 inch. Bake *25 to 30 minutes,* or until wooden pick inserted in center comes out clean. Cool in pan.

With a large biscuit or doughnut cutter, cut wreaths out of cake. (If cutters are shallow, use them as patterns instead; cut around them with a sharp knife.)

Prepare Betty Crocker Fluffy White Frosting Mix as directed on package. Tint green. Frost wreaths and decorate with red cinnamon candies. Frost the holes from centers; dip in chopped nuts, plain or toasted coconut.

SANTA'S SLEDS

Pictured on page 111.

Heat oven to 350°. Prepare Betty Crocker Lemon Chiffon Cake Mix as directed on package. Pour batter into two ungreased loaf pans, 9x5x3 inches. Bake *45 to 55 minutes.* Cool; remove from pans and cut into 1½-inch slices. Trim rounded tops to make rectangles.

Prepare Betty Crocker Fluffy White Frosting Mix as directed on package. Frost top and sides of cake slices. Sprinkle with shredded coconut. Place each slice on top of two J-shaped candy canes, so that the canes make "runners" for each "sled." If desired, decorate tops with candied cherries or holiday candies. *Makes 12 "sleds."*

> **Betty Crocker Note:** Frosting or coconut or both may be divided and tinted several colors, if desired.

FLAMING POINSETTIA CAKE

Pictured on page 111.

Bake Betty Crocker White Cake Mix in two round layer pans, 8x1½ inches, as directed on package. Cool.

Prepare Betty Crocker Fluffy White Frosting Mix as directed on package. Reserve ⅔ cup frosting. Fill and frost cake with remaining frosting.

Using paste food coloring, tint reserved frosting a deep red. Drop 5 mounds of red frosting around center of cake; with a spoon, pull up to form petals of poinsettia. Drop 5 smaller mounds between and slightly overlapping first mounds; pull up to form slightly smaller petals. Sprinkle flower with red decorators' sugar.

Cut a small cup from one end of a lemon; remove pulp. Insert cup in center of poinsettia. Just before serving, soak 2 sugar cubes in lemon extract and yellow food coloring. Place in lemon cup; ignite.

BÛCHE DE NOËL

Pictured on page 111.

Heat oven to 350°. Prepare Betty Crocker Yellow Cake Mix as directed on package except—use 2 tablespoons less water. Pour batter into two greased and floured loaf pans, 9x5x3 inches. Bake *35 to 40 minutes.* Cool. Remove from pans.

Trim off edges and top of one cake to make a rounded log shape. Cut cake lengthwise into 3 layers. Reassemble log, filling layers with French Silk Frosting (page 129); spread on sides and top of log. Frost ends with Mocha Frosting (below). With wooden pick or fork, make markings to resemble bark; outline circles on ends of log. If desired, decorate with spearmint leaves and red cinnamon candies for vine effect. Chill.

Serve other loaf as desired.

Mocha Frosting: Dissolve 1 teaspoon instant coffee in 1 tablespoon hot water. Stir into 1 cup sifted confectioners' sugar. Add a few drops more water, if necessary, to make spreading consistency.

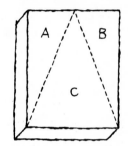 

CHRISTMAS TREE CAKE

Prepare Betty Crocker Yellow Cake Mix as directed on package. Pour batter into greased and floured oblong pan, 13x9x2 inches. Sprinkle with 2 tablespoons green decorators' sugar and 2 tablespoons multicolored nonpareils. Swirl through batter with spatula. Bake as directed on package. Remove from pan and cool.

Cover large tray or cardboard with aluminum foil or foil wrapping paper. Cut cake as shown in diagram.

Prepare Betty Crocker Fluffy White Frosting Mix as directed on package. Tint frosting light green with one or two drops green food coloring. Arrange cake pieces A and B on tray to make tree shape. Frost. Place piece C on top; frost top and sides, making strokes through frosting to resemble branches.

Sprinkle entire cake with green decorators' sugar. Insert 3 candy canes in the bottom of the cake to make trunk. Place 9 red candles on outer edges of cake.

> **Betty Crocker Note:** For a different effect, frosting may be left white and decorated with red candied cherries and silver dragées.

MYSTERY FRUITCAKE

Pictured opposite.

1 package Betty Crocker Yellow Cake Mix*
4 cups mixed candied fruit (two 1-pound jars)
½ cup <u>each</u> whole red and green candied cherries
    (¼ pound each)
1½ cups seedless raisins (½ pound)
1 cup dates, cut up (6½ ounces)
4¼ cups pecan halves (1 pound)
1 package Betty Crocker Fluffy White Frosting Mix

Bake cake as directed on package. Cool. Crumble cooled cake into large bowl and add remaining ingredients except frosting mix.

Prepare frosting mix as directed on package; add to fruit-nut-cake mixture. Stir with spoon or toss together with hands until mixture is damp and blended thoroughly.

Pack tightly into aluminum foil-lined tube pan, 10x4 inches, or two aluminum foil-lined loaf pans, 8½x4½x2½ inches or 9x5x3 inches. With buttered hands, pat down until smooth. Cover cake with aluminum foil and chill in refrigerator *at least* 24 hours; it improves if stored longer. Cake should be kept refrigerated. Slice with sharp knife and serve cold. *Makes one 6½-pound fruitcake.*

*Our Honey Spice, White or Devils Food Cake Mix may be used in place of Yellow.

For a Smaller Fruitcake: Follow recipe (above) except —use only one layer of cake and half of fruits, nuts and frosting. *Pack tightly* into one aluminum foil-lined loaf pan. Frost other cake layer with remaining frosting.

Fruitcake Balls: Follow recipe for Smaller Fruitcake (above) except—chop cherries and nuts. Shape into 1-inch balls. Chill. Roll balls in confectioners' sugar. Serve on wooden picks stuck into an apple or orange; use as a centerpiece on a platter of Christmas cookies.

Fruitcake Squares: Follow recipe for Smaller Fruitcake (above) except—pat fruitcake mixture into an oblong pan, 13x9x2 inches, to make a layer about ½ inch thick. Chill. Prepare Betty Crocker Creamy White Frosting Mix as directed on package except—blend in 1½ teaspoons rum flavoring. Frost cake. Cut into 1-inch squares.

Steamed Pudding: Follow recipe for Smaller Fruitcake (above) except—pack mixture into well-greased individual gelatin molds. Cover with aluminum foil. Steam 30 minutes (see page 107). Let stand 5 minutes before removing pudding from molds. To remove pudding, tap mold lightly against table surface, allowing pudding to slide out onto serving plate. Serve warm topped with Hard Sauce (page 105). Hard Sauce may be tinted with food coloring.

OLD-FASHIONED FRUITCAKE

¾ cup plus 2 tablespoons boiling water
1 package Betty Crocker Spice 'n Apple Cake Mix
⅓ cup butter
4 eggs
1 tablespoon brandy flavoring or vanilla
½ cup Gold Medal Flour (regular or Wondra)
1 cup candied cherries (6 to 7 ounces)
2½ cups chopped mixed candied fruit (1 pound)
1½ cups golden raisins (½ pound)
2 cups chopped walnuts (about ½ pound)
1 cup chopped blanched almonds (5 ounces)
1 can (3½ ounces) flaked coconut

Add water to cake mix (dry mix) in large mixer bowl. Blend well; let stand 30 minutes. *Heat oven to 300°.* Grease and line with aluminum foil or brown paper two shiny loaf pans, 8½x4½x2½ inches or 9x5x3 inches. Add butter, eggs and flavoring to cake mix; beat 4 minutes medium speed on mixer. Mix flour, fruit, nuts and coconut; blend fruit mixture into cake batter. Pour batter into prepared pans. Place on lowest rack in oven. Bake 8½-inch loaf *2¼ to 2½ hours,* 9-inch loaf *1¾ hours,* or until wooden pick inserted in center comes out clean. Remove from pan and cool 3 hours. Wrap tightly in aluminum foil and store in refrigerator. If desired, pour Fruitcake Glaze (below) over cake.

Fruitcake Glaze: Combine ¼ cup light corn syrup and 2 tablespoons water; bring just to a rolling boil. Remove from heat. Cool to lukewarm. Pour over cool cake before or after storing.

CHRISTMAS CENTERPIECE CAKES

Bake your favorite flavor Betty Crocker Layer Cake Mix in two round layer pans, 8 or 9x1½ inches, as directed on package. Cool.

Prepare Betty Crocker Fluffy White Frosting Mix as directed on package. Decorate cake in one of the following ways:

Christmas Tree: Fill and frost cake, reserving ½ cup of frosting. With a knife, draw outline of a Christmas tree on top of cake. Tint the ½ cup frosting green and fill in outline of tree. Sprinkle multicolored nonpareils on tree.

Holiday Wreath: Fill and frost cake. Decorate top of cake in wreath shape with walnut halves and red and green candied cherries.

Candlelight 'n Snow Cake: Sprinkle entire cake with shredded coconut. Place 20 to 25 tiny red or green candles on top of cake. Light candles just before serving.

Pictured clockwise from top: Bûche de Noël, Butter Mix Cookies, Flaming Poinsettia Cake, Santa's Sled, Christmas Holly Wreaths, Mystery Fruitcake; in center: Santa Lucia Crown

ONCE IN A BLUE MOON

Lights, camera, action—for the exciting, picturesque cakes which you see in home movies and photo albums, recording life's important milestones.

First, the classic beauties—regal and traditional cakes for serious moments like weddings and anniversaries. Then come the dramatic cakes—colorful and imaginative for the once-in-a-lifetime excitement of graduation and bridal showers. Or those for fun times, like an election or bon voyage party.

Remember, make these pretty as a picture, because that's how once-in-a-blue-moon cakes are likely to end—pictured for posterity.

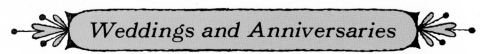

Weddings and Anniversaries

SMALL TIERED WEDDING CAKE

Perfect for an anniversary celebration, shower, graduation or reunion—simply vary the colors and decorations.

You will need 3 packages Betty Crocker White Cake Mix and 2 packages Betty Crocker Fluffy White Frosting Mix.

Bake 1 package of cake mix in an oblong pan, 13x9x2 inches, as directed. Cool. Repeat for second cake. Prepare third package of cake mix as directed on package. Bake half the batter in a square pan, 9x9x2 inches, for *25 to 30 minutes at 350°*. Cool. Use remaining batter to bake 15 to 18 cupcakes as directed on package. (Use cupcakes as desired.)

Prepare frosting mix as directed on package, mixing one package at a time. Tint a pastel color, if desired. (Tint both at same time in large mixing bowl so all icing will be same color.)

Place one oblong layer upside down on mirror, tray or large serving plate. Frost top; place second oblong layer on top; frost sides and top.

Cut square cake in half to make two rectangles, each 9x4½ inches. Place one on center of iced oblong cake. Frost top; place last layer on top; frost sides and top. Make fancy swirls in icing and decorate with silver dragées, if desired. The traditional bride and groom, wedding bells or tiny spray of flowers can top the cake. *About 50 servings.*

Cutting: Top tier—about 18 pieces
(cut two slices lengthwise by nine crosswise)
Bottom tier—about 48 pieces
(cut four slices lengthwise by twelve crosswise)

SMALL ANNIVERSARY CAKE

This is ideal for any anniversary celebration—just vary the decorations.

Heat oven to 350°. Grease and flour 4 tier pans. (Pan sizes must be 9 inches, 7 inches, 5 inches and 3 inches.) Prepare Betty Crocker Lemon Velvet Cake Mix as directed on package. Pour batter into prepared pans, filling each about half full. Bake *25 to 30 minutes*, or until wooden pick inserted in center comes out clean. Cool 10 minutes; remove from pans. When thoroughly cool, trim slightly rounded tops to make level.

Prepare Betty Crocker Fluffy White Frosting Mix as directed on package. Reserve 1 cup for Decorator Icing. Frost one layer at a time, sides first, then top.

Make Decorator Icing (page 24). Using decorating cone with writing tip (see page 25), make diamond lattice design on sides of cake. Place silver dragées at points of diamonds. Top with bells, flowers or other appropriate decorations. *16 to 20 servings.*

TIERED WEDDING CAKE

You will need 7 packages Betty Crocker White Cake Mix and 6 packages Betty Crocker Creamy White Frosting Mix. Bake cakes the day before they are to be assembled (or they may be baked earlier and frozen).

Heat oven to 350°. Generously grease an oblong pan, 13x9x2 inches (do not use glass). Line bottom of pan with heavy brown paper; grease paper and dust with flour. Bake Betty Crocker White Cake Mix as directed. Cool. When cake is cool, slice off rounded top for ease in stacking. Repeat for remaining 6 cake mixes.

Prepare Betty Crocker Creamy White Frosting Mix as directed on package, mixing 2 packages at a time, as needed. Additional packages of frosting mix may be needed for more elaborate decoration. (As a guide, 1 package contains enough frosting to make scroll design for border around top of each tier.) Select a special decoration for top of cake, such as flowers or wedding bells.

Place layers upside down, removing brown paper from each layer after it is in place. Place two 13x9x2-inch layers together lengthwise on mirror, tray or large serving plate; frost top. Place 2 more layers directly on top of the frosted layers. Frost sides and top; let set. Cover a 12x8-inch piece of cardboard with aluminum foil; place it in center of first tier with the 12-inch edge parallel to 18-inch edge of cake. Place the fifth layer on top of the cardboard; frost top. Place the sixth layer directly on top of the fifth; frost sides and top; let set. Cover an 8x6-inch piece of cardboard with aluminum foil; place it in center of second tier with the 8-inch edge parallel to 18-inch edge of cake. Cut seventh layer in half. Place half of the layer on top of cardboard; frost top. Place last half layer directly on top; frost sides and top. *Makes about 160 2x1-inch pieces.*

Cutting: Top tier—about 24 pieces
    (cut four slices lengthwise by six crosswise)
    Middle tier—about 48 pieces
    (cut four slices lengthwise by twelve crosswise)
    Bottom tier—about 96 pieces
    (cut four slices lengthwise by twenty-four crosswise)

For wedding anniversaries, bake the same beautiful cake, changing the colors and decorations to suit the year. For the triumphant tenth, decorate with pretty tin can flowers. For the festive fifteenth, trim with rock candy and serve on a crystal platter. And for the fiftieth, lavish with golden leaves and dragées and display on a golden tray.

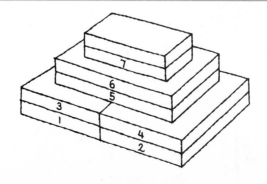

BRIDAL WREATH WEDDING CAKE

7 packages Betty Crocker White Cake Mix
6 packages Betty Crocker Fluffy White Frosting Mix
4 pounds confectioners' sugar
Silver dragées, sugar wedding bells or flowers and bride
**   and groom, if desired**

Two days before wedding:
Bake 6 packages of cake mix in round layer pans, 9x1½ inches, as directed, preparing 1 package at a time. Cool.

Grease and flour two 3-pound shortening cans (about 4¾ inches in diameter). Prepare seventh package of cake mix. Pour 2 cups batter into each shortening can. Bake *40 to 45 minutes at 350°.* Use remaining **batter** to bake about 6 cupcakes as directed on package. (Freeze for later use.) Remove layers from cans. Cool and trim off rounded top crusts.

One day before wedding:
Assemble cake as follows on a mirror, tray or large serving plate. Use 9 layers to make base. Trim slightly rounded tops to make layers level. Use 3 layers for each section of cloverleaf.

Prepare Wedding Cake Icing (page 115) as needed, one recipe at a time.

Assemble one set of 3 layers, using one recipe of icing—⅓ cup between each layer and the remaining icing on sides and top.

Prepare second recipe of icing, adding 1 to 2 cups more sifted confectioners' sugar to make stiff enough to hold its shape; flute bottom and top edge of frosted layers with icing in decorating cone (see page 24). Repeat for second and third "set of layers" (using third and fourth recipe of icing); place second set of layers beside first set; place third set to form cloverleaf (see diagram), leaving small space in center for a support.

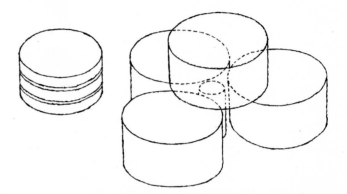

To form a support for remaining layers, place a glass or aluminum foil-covered container of the same height as frosted layers in center of cloverleaf.

Place fourth set of 3 layers on aluminum foil-covered cardboard circle, about 8 inches in diameter; fill and frost, using fifth recipe of icing. Place on top of support. Set small set of layers on aluminum foil-covered cardboard circle, about 4 inches in diameter; fill and frost, using sixth recipe of icing. Center on top of cake.

Decorate with remaining icing, fluting bottom and top edges of last two tiers; make scallops and flowers as desired. Decorate with dragées, bells, flowers and bride and groom.

After frosting sets (½ to 1 hour), wrap entire cake in plastic wrap by draping long pieces loosely over cake. Each cake makes twenty-eight slices (each about 4x2x1 inch). If desired, slices may be cut in half crosswise to make twice as many servings.

Cake cut into 4x2x1-inch slices yields *112 servings.*

Wedding Cake Icing: In small mixer bowl, prepare 1 package of frosting mix as directed except—add ½ teaspoon almond extract, if desired. Transfer to large bowl and blend in 2 cups sifted confectioners' sugar, 1 cup at a time, using low speed on mixer.

Cutting the Cake:

Set aside the top tier (to be frozen for the couple's first anniversary) and begin cutting the second tier. For uniform servings first cut the cake into quarters. Then cut each quarter into slices as shown. When tier of cake is completely served, remove cardboard and cut cakes of cloverleaf in the same manner.

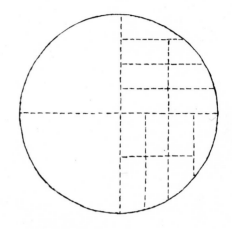

PETITS FOURS WEDDING CAKE

An easy way of serving a wedding cake—as individual petits fours. The tiered effect is unusual and the little cakes eliminate any cutting problem. Any color scheme or motif may be used to harmonize with desired theme.

Heat oven to 350°. Prepare Betty Crocker White Cake Mix as directed on package. Pour into greased and floured jelly roll pan, 15½x10½x1 inch; bake *25 to 30 minutes.* Cool. Cut into 3x1½-inch rectangles or 1¾-inch squares. Repeat, using another package of cake mix. Glaze cakes, following directions for Petits Fours (page 116). Decorate as desired.

Arrange on tiered cake stands or cake plates with support sets (now available commercially). Place a bride and groom, wedding bells or spray of flowers on top tier. *Makes sixty 3x1½-inch or eighty 1¾-inch petits fours.*

Betty Crocker Note: For larger Petits Fours Wedding Cake, make a third sheet cake and add additional plate as base.

Showers

PETITS FOURS

Pictured on page 87.

Heat oven to 350°. Prepare Betty Crocker White Cake Mix as directed on package. Pour batter into greased and floured jelly roll pan, 15½x10½x1 inch; bake *25 to 30 minutes.* Cool. Cut cake into small squares, rounds, diamonds, hearts or other fancy shapes.

Glaze cut cakes by placing upside down, one at a time, on cooling rack over large bowl. With a small measuring cup, pour Petits Fours Icing (below) over top, so entire cake is covered at one time. (Glaze which drips off cakes into bowl can be reheated and used again.) Decorate tops with silver dragées, candy flowers or Icing: Blend 1 cup sifted confectioners' sugar with 2 to 4 teaspoons water—use in decorating cone. *Makes about thirty-five 2-inch squares or about fifty-four 1½-inch squares.*

Betty Crocker Note: Cakes may also be glazed by placing each on a fork over icing in double boiler and spooning glaze over each. With a spatula or another fork, push off cake onto cooling rack to set.

Petits Fours Icing:
9 cups sifted confectioners' sugar (about 2 pounds)
½ cup water
½ cup light corn syrup
1 teaspoon vanilla
½ teaspoon almond extract

Combine ingredients in top of double boiler and heat just to lukewarm. (Do not overheat icing or it will become dull.) Remove from heat, leaving icing over hot water to keep it thin. If desired, tint part of icing delicate pastel colors with food coloring. If necessary, add hot water, a few drops at a time, for proper consistency.

Apricot-glazed Petits Fours: Follow recipe (above) except—before glazing Petits Fours with Icing, glaze each with apricot preserves: In saucepan, heat 1 jar (12 ounces) apricot preserves with 3 tablespoons water; strain. Place each Petit Four on fork over saucepan; spoon warm apricot glaze over each. Place on cooling racks; let set about 1 hour. Glaze with Petits Fours Icing as directed above.

Other little cakes appropriate for a shower may be found on pages 85 and 86.

MINIATURE BOUQUETS

Bake any flavor Betty Crocker Layer Cake Mix in paper baking cups as directed on package. Cool.

Prepare Betty Crocker Fluffy White Frosting Mix as directed on package. Frost cupcakes, reserving 1½ cups frosting.

Decorate with Flowers (below). Center each cupcake on a 6-inch doily; lace ribbons through doilies and tie around cupcakes.

Flowers: Make Decorator Icing (page 24) with 1½ cups reserved frosting. Follow directions for decorating (see page 25). Tint ½ cup pink and use with petal tip to make roses; tint ½ cup light blue or yellow and use with star tip to make drop flowers; tint 3 tablespoons light green and use with leaf tip to make leaves; make a border around each cupcake with white frosting and star tip.

BRIDAL BOUQUET CAKE

Pictured on cover.

Bake Betty Crocker White Cake Mix in two round layer pans, 8 or 9x1½ inches, as directed on package. Cool.

Prepare Bridal Bouquet Icing (below). Reserve 1 cup; cover with plastic wrap and set aside. Tint half of remaining icing pale pink. With large petal tip, make about 10 white roses and 10 pink roses, forming each rose on waxed paper as directed (see page 25).

When roses are set, fill and frost cake with Wedding Cake Icing (page 115). Arrange roses on frosted cake in desired pattern. Using the reserved frosting and a decorating cone, make fluted border around base of cake and fill in spaces around roses as desired with lattice design, lily of the valley, rosettes or leaves (see page 25).

Bridal Bouquet Icing: Prepare Betty Crocker Fluffy White Frosting Mix as directed on package. Transfer to large bowl. Fold in 1 pound (about 4½ cups) sifted confectioners' sugar, 1 cup at a time. Frosting should be stiff enough to hold its shape. If necessary, blend in more sifted confectioners' sugar.

BRIDE'S CAKE

Rich yet delicate—an elegant cake that tastes as good as it looks.

You'll need 2 packages Betty Crocker White Cake Mix and 4 packages Betty Crocker Creamy White Frosting Mix.

Heat oven to 350°. Prepare one package of cake mix as directed. Pour batter into greased and floured jelly roll pan, 15½x10½x1 inch. Bake *25 to 30 minutes.* Remove from pan and cool. Repeat for second cake.

Blend 2 packages frosting mix (dry mix), ½ cup hot water and ¼ cup light corn syrup. Beat until smooth. Cut both cakes into fourths crosswise. Frost tops of 4 cake strips; stack unfrosted strips over frosted ones. This will give four double-layer cakes. Add 1 to 2 tablespoons hot water to remaining frosting to thin; cover sides of the four cakes with this frosting. Let set about ½ hour.

Prepare 2 packages frosting mix as directed, using ⅓ cup white shortening, ½ cup hot water and 1 to 1½ teaspoons almond extract. Frost tops and sides of cakes, reserving some frosting for decorating. Tint pale pink. Using cake decorating cone with star tip (see page 25), pipe frosting around top edges of cakes or decorate as desired. (More frosting for making flowers, leaves, etc., may be made with another package of frosting mix.)

Arrange cakes on large tray, mirror or large pieces of doily-covered cardboard arranged in a square with inside corners touching. Fill center with white and pink flowers and tall white candles. Tuck greens, such as boxwood, around edge of cake.

To serve, cut each cake in half lengthwise, then into about 12 slices. *Makes 96 small servings.* (For large servings, do not slice cake lengthwise.)

Betty Crocker Note: For large receptions, extra cakes may be decorated and used to replace original ones as they are cut and served. If carefully stored, cakes may be baked the day before they are decorated.

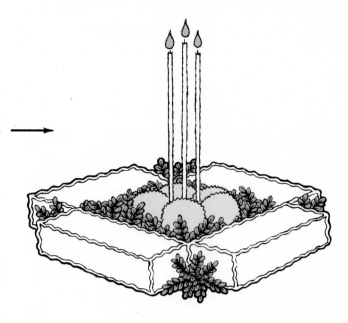

SUN SHOWER CAKE

Bake your favorite flavor Betty Crocker Layer Cake Mix in two round layer pans, 8 or 9x1½ inches, as directed on package. Cool.

Prepare Betty Crocker Lemon Fluff Frosting Mix as directed on package. Fill and frost cake. Decorate top or sides with "umbrellas" made from lemon, lime and orange candy slices.

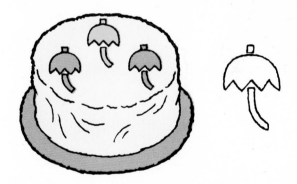

To make umbrellas: With scissors, cut 3 small V's from bottom of candy slice to make umbrella top. Cut out center of another candy slice (same color) and use "rind" for handle. Cut a small piece off handle to make tip of umbrella. Assemble as shown. Repeat to make more umbrellas.

Another good cake for a shower is the Sweet Sixteen Cake (page 71); decorate as desired for the occasion.

TWIN HEART BRIDAL SHOWER CAKE

Pictured on page 5.

Heat oven to 350°. Grease and flour two heart-shaped pans, 9 inches wide at the widest part and 1½ inches deep. Prepare Betty Crocker White Cake Mix as directed on package. Pour batter into prepared pans. Bake *30 to 35 minutes.* Cool.

Repeat, using another package of cake mix.

Prepare 2 packages Betty Crocker Fluffy White Frosting Mix, one at a time, as directed on package. Tint a delicate pastel, if desired. Fill and frost sides and tops of cakes. *25 to 30 servings.*

SWEETHEART FLOWER CAKE

Follow recipe for Have A Heart Cake (page 97) using Betty Crocker White Cake Mix. Tint batter a delicate pink.

Prepare Betty Crocker Fluffy White Frosting Mix as directed on package; tint pink. Frost cake. Decorate top and base of cake with Frosted Flowers (below).

Frosted Flowers: Use small roses, carnations, bachelor buttons, violets or chrysanthemums. Beat 1 egg white slightly and add 1 tablespoon water. With a small soft brush, brush on egg white, coating the flower petals. Sprinkle with granulated or colored decorators' sugar. Place on rack to dry.

BRIDAL SHOWER CAKE

Prepare Betty Crocker Yellow Cake Mix as directed on package. Pour batter into one greased and floured square pan, 9x9x2 inches, and one round layer pan, 9x1½ inches. (Batter should be the same depth in both pans.) Bake as directed on package. Cool.

Place square layer upside down on cake platter. Placing round layer right side up on cutting board, cut umbrella as shown in diagram.

Prepare Betty Crocker Fluffy White Frosting Mix as directed on package. Reserve 1 cup. Use 1 to 1¼ cups to frost sides and top of square base. Tint remaining frosting pink with red food coloring. Place umbrella, handle and knob on base and frost with pink frosting.

Make Decorator Icing (page 24) with reserved 1 cup frosting. Fill decorating cone with frosting and, using different tips (see page 25), decorate ribs of umbrella, knob and handle. Make small flowers on cake and borders on the edges of umbrella and cake. Decorate with silver dragées.

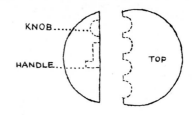

Pictured from top to bottom: Bridal Shower Cake, Miniature Bride's Cakes, Sweetheart Flower Cake

MINIATURE BRIDE'S CAKES

Pictured on page 118.

Heat oven to 350°. Prepare Betty Crocker White Cake Mix as directed on package. Pour batter into greased and floured jelly roll pan, 15½x10½x1 inch; bake *25 to 30 minutes.* Cool.

With cookie cutters or paper patterns and sharp knife, cut cake into sixteen 2¼-inch circles and sixteen 1½-inch circles. Prepare Petits Fours Icing (page 116). Place small amount of icing on top of large circles; place small circles on top to form miniature cakes. Glaze cakes by placing on cooling rack, one at a time, over large bowl. Pour icing over top with a small measuring cup so entire cake is covered at one time. If necessary, tilt rack to cover lower sides. (Glaze which drips off cakes into bowl can be reheated and used again.) Decorate cakes with silver dragées or candy flowers. Place each cake on a small paper doily. *Makes 16 miniature cakes.*

DOUBLE RING BRIDE'S CAKE

Heat oven to 350°. Grease and flour a 3-quart ring mold. Prepare Betty Crocker White Cake Mix as directed on package. Pour batter into prepared pan. Bake *35 to 40 minutes.* Cool slightly. Remove from pan.

Repeat, using another package of cake mix.

When cakes are thoroughly cool, place side by side, edges touching, on a large plate or tray. Frost with Icing (below), reserving 1½ cups for decorating. Fold in about 1 cup more sifted confectioners' sugar to reserved frosting, so it will be stiff enough to hold its shape. Using decorating cone, make fluted border along bottom and top edge of rings or other designs as desired (see page 24). Place wedding bells or flowers with streamers at center of double ring.

Icing: Prepare 2 packages Betty Crocker Fluffy White Frosting Mix as directed except—use 1 cup boiling water. In large mixer bowl, beat 5 to 7 minutes or until soft peaks form. Add 1 teaspoon almond extract, if desired. Blend in 4 cups sifted confectioners' sugar, 1 cup at a time, at low speed on mixer.

Betty Crocker Note: Cover the frosted cake loosely with plastic wrap to keep frosting soft.

CRADLE CAKE

Pictured above.

Bake any flavor Betty Crocker Layer Cake Mix in two round layer pans, 8x1½ inches, as directed on package. Cool.

Cut 1½-inch slice from two sides of each layer; cut each 1½-inch slice in half lengthwise (see diagram). Place 4 larger strips under ends of each oblong (oblong is bed section) to make rockers. Place smallest pieces crust side up on ends of each oblong for head and foot.

Prepare Betty Crocker Fluffy White Frosting Mix as directed on package. Tint a pastel shade. Frost and decorate for a baby shower. *Makes 2 cradles.*

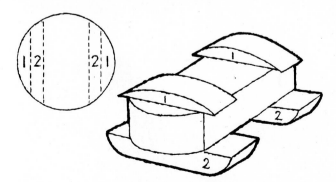

BABY'S BOOTIES

Pictured on page 119.

Bake Betty Crocker White Cake Mix in paper baking cups as directed on package. Cool. Remove papers.

Place one cupcake upside down on plate. Form toe of bootie from second cupcake by cutting off small portion of side to form a flat surface. Cut cupcake horizontally in half. Place top half right side up with flat cut edge next to cupcake on plate (see diagram). For other booties, use bottom halves of cupcakes. (Each bootie is formed with 1½ cupcakes.) *Makes 20 to 24 booties.*

Girls' Booties: Prepare Betty Crocker Fluffy White Frosting Mix as directed on package except—tint pink. Frost each cupcake bootie, joining cut "toe" to cupcake with frosting. Decorate booties with bows made from rolled gumdrops or with miniature marshmallows.

Boys' Booties: Prepare Betty Crocker Creamy White Frosting Mix as directed on package. Reserve ½ cup frosting and tint blue or green; use to pipe design on white frosted booties (see page 24). Decorate with bows made from rolled gumdrops or with miniature marshmallows.

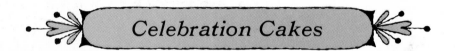

Celebration Cakes

CHRISTENING CAKE

A sweet tradition! Almost as rich as English fruitcake— yet you make it with a mix. Serve with pride as the godparents toast the honored infant's future.

Prepare Old-fashioned Fruitcake (page 110) except— use Betty Crocker Honey Spice Cake Mix. Cut two pieces of aluminum foil, each 18x14 inches; fold each piece in half lengthwise and place in greased 9x5x3-inch loaf pan. (Foil should line bottom and form a 3- to 4-inch collar above edge of pan.) Bake *3 to 3½ hours.* Cool.

When ready to frost, cut 3-inch piece from one end of loaf. Place 3-inch piece cut side down on serving plate and trim to make square. With hands, shape contents of 1 can (8 ounces) almond paste to fit top of square; place on top. Frost cake with Wedding Cake Icing (page 115), reserving 1 cup. Blend ½ cup sifted confectioners' sugar into reserved icing; tint ⅓ cup pink or blue. Use white icing in decorating cone to make fluted border, scrolls and swags on cake (see page 25). With tinted icing, write name of child and christening date on top. Decorate as desired with remaining icing. To serve, cut into ½-inch slices. Save remaining fruit loaf for later use.

MORTARBOARD CAKE

Bake any flavor Betty Crocker Layer Cake Mix in one greased and floured square pan, 9x9x2 inches, *25 to 30 minutes,* and one round layer pan, 8x1½ inches, as directed on package. Cool.

Place square layer on piece of cardboard cut to size. Round layer may be placed on large cake plate or breadboard. Prepare any flavor Betty Crocker Frosting Mix as directed on package. Frost top and sides of both layers, using square layer on top to resemble a mortarboard. For tie and tassel, use contrasting ribbon with a marshmallow attached to end. (Square layer may be lifted off for easy cutting.)

PARTY DIPLOMAS

Bake Betty Crocker Lemon Chiffon Cake Mix in two shiny ungreased loaf pans, 9x5x3 inches, as directed on inner packet. Cool. Remove from pans.

Slice cooled cake into ¼-inch slices. Spread each with Betty Crocker Lemon Satin ready-to-spread Frosting, roll like a jelly roll and tie with ribbons in school colors. *Each loaf makes about 30 diplomas.*

REUNION CAKE

Bake Betty Crocker Lemon Velvet Cake Mix in an oblong pan, 13x9x2 inches, as directed on package. Remove from pan. Cool.

Prepare Betty Crocker Creamy White Frosting Mix as directed on package. Reserve ¼ cup. Frost cake with remaining frosting. Add 4 to 6 drops food coloring to reserved frosting. With decorating cone and writing tip (see page 25), print on cake:

WELCOME BACK
CLASS OF 19—— (year you graduated)

Cut triangles of paper and paste on wooden picks to make pennants. On pennants, write the number of the reunion. Insert in cake.

Also good for a reunion are the Twin Pennant Cakes (page 104). Or, for a larger group, make the Small Tiered Wedding Cake (page 112) and decorate in an appropriate manner.

ELECTION RETURNS PARTY CAKE

Prepare any flavor Betty Crocker Layer Cake Mix as directed on package. Pour batter into one greased and floured square pan, 8x8x2 inches, and one round layer pan, 9x1½ inches. Batter should be the same depth in both pans (check level with a wooden pick). Bake as directed on package for 9-inch layers. Cool.

Donkey: Cut ears and head from the square cake (diagram A); trim the triangular pieces to resemble ears and large piece to resemble head. Assemble cake as shown in sketch. Frost with Betty Crocker Chocolate Satin ready-to-spread Frosting, attaching ears to donkey head. Make nostrils with reserved vanilla frosting from elephant.

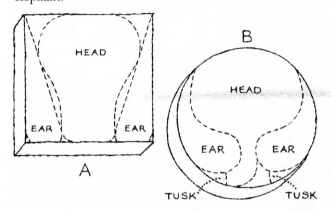

Elephant: Cut head and trunk in one piece from round layer; trim leftover pieces for ears and tusks (diagram B). Assemble cake as shown in sketch. Reserve ¼ cup Betty Crocker Vanilla Satin ready-to-spread Frosting for decorating donkey and frosting tusks white. Tint remaining frosting pink and use to frost head and ears. Make eyes on both animal heads from marshmallows and small black gumdrops; attach to cakes with frosting so that the elephant and donkey are looking at each other. Attach a black gumdrop to the tip of the elephant's trunk.

"KING FOR A DAY" CAKE

Bake Betty Crocker Dark Chocolate Fudge Cake Mix in two round layer pans, 8 or 9x1½ inches, as directed on package. Cool.

Prepare Betty Crocker Fluffy White Frosting Mix as directed on package. Fill and frost cake, making top smooth. Soften 1 packet (1 ounce) premelted chocolate in hot water and snip off tiny corner or use Chocolate Decorator Icing (page 69) to outline a crown on top of cake and write man's name below. Place colorful candies or silver dragées at points of crown.

For a "Queen for a Day" cake, make the Fairy Crown Cake (page 66).

"YOU'RE A SMART COOKIE" CAKE

Bake any flavor Betty Crocker Layer Cake Mix in two round layer pans, 8 or 9x1½ inches, as directed on package. Cool. Prepare Betty Crocker Fluffy White Frosting Mix as directed on package. Fill and frost cake, reserving 1 cup for decorating. Fold 1 to 1½ cups sifted confectioners' sugar into reserved frosting; tint as desired. Using decorating cone (see page 24), decorate 9 Gingerbread Boy Cookies (below) and press into sides of frosted cake. Make fluted border around edge of cake and write "You're a Smart Cookie" on top.

Gingerbread Boy Cookies: Add ⅓ cup lukewarm water to 1 package Betty Crocker Gingerbread Mix (dry mix). Blend until smooth. Chill 1 to 2 hours. Heat oven to 375°. Roll dough ⅛ inch thick on floured cloth-covered board. (Use a small amount of dough at a time; keep remainder chilled.) Cut with floured gingerbread boy cookie cutter and place on lightly greased baking sheet. Repeat. Bake 8 to 10 minutes. Cool.

Other cakes suitable for promotion, special awards or victory celebrations are the Feather in Your Hat Cake (page 72) and the Baseball Mitt Cake (page 67).

To make an unusual cake for a housewarming, follow directions for Hansel and Gretel's Cake (page 63) and decorate as desired.

BON VOYAGE CAKE

Pictured above.

Bake any flavor Betty Crocker Layer Cake Mix in two round layer pans, 8 or 9x1½ inches, as directed on package. Cool.

Using a geography book or world atlas, make a tracing of the continent or country which the honored guest will be visiting. (Just be certain the tracing does not extend beyond measurement of the top of the cake.)

Next, place tracing on baking sheet or flat plate; cover with waxed paper. Soften 1 packet (1 ounce) premelted chocolate in hot water and snip off tiny corner. Squeeze small amount of chocolate onto center of waxed paper over the tracing. Use small spatula or knife to spread chocolate within lines of tracing. Reserve about 2 teaspoons chocolate in packet for lettering.

Place chocolate "map" in freezer until firm. Fill and frost cake with Betty Crocker Fluffy White Frosting Mix prepared as directed on package. Keep top of cake smooth. Remove chocolate "map" from waxed paper by peeling paper away; work quickly and transfer map to top of cake.

Write "Bon Voyage!" across top of cake with reserved melted chocolate. If desired, place small flags of foreign countries around outside edge of cake.

CAKES FOR THE CONNOISSEUR

Soft candlelight, romantic music, a bouquet of flowers—the ideal setting for the cakes in this chapter. Any one of these deserves such a carefully planned background; each is a masterpiece worthy of star billing for your most elaborate entertaining.

First in this group are the spectaculars, for which you are producer and director —performer, too, at serving time. Next, a splendid around-the-world collection, based on recipes or flavors from afar. Last, a selection of "originals" called work-of-art cakes—inspired by fine paintings, the theatre and the dance.

You'll be an artist in your own right, once you have created a connoisseur's cake. And your reputation as a hostess will soar!

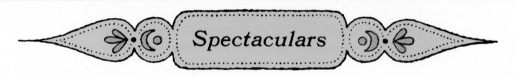

Spectaculars

PISTACHIO CRÈME CAKE

Prepare Betty Crocker White Cake Mix as directed on package except—add 1 teaspoon nutmeg to dry mix before mixing. Pour batter into two greased and floured round layer pans, 9x1½ inches. Bake as directed. Cool.

Split cake to make 4 layers (see page 20). Spread about ⅔ cup Frosting à la Crème (below) between first and second layers; spread Green Grape and Pistachio Nut Filling (below) between second and third layers; spread ⅔ cup more Frosting à la Crème between third and fourth layers. Frost top and sides of cake with remaining Frosting à la Crème.

Garnish with pistachio nuts and several clusters of green grapes. Chill at least 2 hours before serving. Store leftover cake in refrigerator.

Frosting à la Crème: Add 2 cups whipping cream to Betty Crocker Lemon Fluff Frosting Mix (dry mix) in mixer bowl. Chill 1 hour. Blend; beat until stiff.

Green Grape and Pistachio Nut Filling:

⅔ cup sugar
2 egg yolks
⅔ cup light cream
½ teaspoon vanilla
½ cup fresh seedless green grapes, halved
½ cup chopped pistachio nuts

Mix sugar, egg yolks and cream thoroughly in saucepan. Cook over low heat 5 to 10 minutes, stirring constantly, until thickened. Remove from heat. Add vanilla, grapes and nuts. Cool thoroughly.

FLUFF ELEGANTÉ ANGEL

Prepare Betty Crocker Angel Food Cake Mix as directed on package except—substitute strong cold coffee for water. Pour batter into ungreased tube pan, 10x4 inches. Bake as directed on package. Cool. Remove from pan.

Prepare Betty Crocker Fluffy White Frosting Mix as directed on package. Fold in ½ cup dairy sour cream. Frost sides and top of cake. Garnish with sliced toasted almonds. Refrigerate.

COINTREAU-GLAZED CHIFFON

Prepare Betty Crocker Lemon Chiffon Cake Mix as directed on package except—fold 2 tablespoons grated orange peel into prepared batter. Pour batter into ungreased tube pan, 10x4 inches. Bake as directed. Cool. Remove from pan.

Pour and spread with Cointreau Glaze (below).

Cointreau Glaze:

4¾ cups sifted confectioners' sugar
1 tablespoon grated orange peel
¼ cup orange juice
2 tablespoons Cointreau
1 or 2 drops yellow food coloring

Blend all ingredients thoroughly. If necessary, add 1 or 2 teaspoons more orange juice.

BAKED ALASKA

Pictured above.

1 package Betty Crocker Yellow Cake Mix
1 quart brick strawberry ice cream
1 package Betty Crocker Fluffy White Frosting Mix or
   Meringue (below)
Strawberries Jubilee (page 126)

Bake cake mix in one round layer pan, 9x1½ inches, and one square pan, 9x9x2 inches, as directed on package. Cool.

Place square cake on aluminum foil-covered baking sheet. Place the hard brick of ice cream on cake. Trim cake, leaving a 1-inch edge around ice cream. Freeze cake and ice cream.

At serving time, heat oven to 500°. Prepare frosting mix as directed on package or make Meringue. Cover frozen cake and ice cream completely with frosting, sealing it to the foil. Bake *3 to 5 minutes*, or until lightly browned. Trim foil to edge of frosting; transfer cake to serving plate. Serve at once topped with Strawberries Jubilee. *12 servings.*

Freeze round layer for later use.

Meringue: Beat 4 egg whites with ½ teaspoon cream of tartar until frothy. Gradually beat in ⅔ cup sugar. Continue beating until meringue is stiff and glossy.

> *Betty Crocker Note:* The complete sealing of ice cream and cake with frosting or meringue is the secret of a successful Baked Alaska.

BAKED ALASKA SANDWICH

1 package Betty Crocker Devils Food Cake Mix
2 pints brick peppermint ice cream
2 packages Betty Crocker Fluffy White Frosting Mix or
   Meringue (left)
Slivered almonds, if desired
Chocolate Sauce (page 55)

Heat oven to 350°. Prepare cake mix as directed on package. Pour batter into greased and floured jelly roll pan, 15½x10½x1 inch. Bake *25 to 30 minutes*. Cool.

Cut cake into 3 lengthwise strips; cut strips crosswise in half to make 6 pieces. For *each* sandwich alternate layers of cake and sliced brick ice cream, using 3 layers of cake and 2 of ice cream (1 pint). Repeat to make second sandwich. Wrap and freeze.

At serving time, heat oven to 500°. Prepare 1 package frosting mix as directed or make Meringue. Remove one sandwich from freezer; place on aluminum foil-covered baking sheet and immediately cover frozen sandwich with frosting, sealing it to the foil. Garnish with slivered almonds. Bake *3 to 5 minutes*, or until lightly browned. Trim foil to edge of frosting; transfer cake to small serving plate. Serve at once topped with Chocolate Sauce. *6 to 8 servings from each sandwich.*

ANGEL ALEXANDER

Bake Betty Crocker Angel Food Cake Mix in ungreased tube pan, 10x4 inches, as directed on package. Cool.

About 2½ hours before serving, combine 2 tablespoons light cream with ½ cup white crème de cacao. With a 5-inch wooden skewer, make many holes of varying depths in cake. Pour half of crème de cacao mixture into holes; let cake stand in pan 2 hours.

Just before serving, invert cake onto serving plate. Make more holes in top and pour in remaining crème de cacao mixture. Whip 1½ cups whipping cream with ⅓ cup confectioners' sugar until stiff. Frost cake. Decorate top with shaved chocolate. Refrigerate.

VERSAILLES CHOCOLATE TORTE

Very European—thin-as-thin cake rounds stacked and filled with nuts and chocolate cream.

1 package Betty Crocker Yellow Cake Mix
⅓ cup soft butter
1 egg, slightly beaten
1 package Betty Crocker Chocolate Fudge Frosting Mix
2 cups whipping cream
1 teaspoon vanilla
1 cup chopped nuts

Heat oven to 350°. Combine cake mix (dry mix), butter and egg thoroughly with fork or pastry blender. Shape dough into ball and cut into 6 equal parts. With a well-floured rolling pin, roll each part onto bottom of an inverted 9-inch round layer pan.

Bake *8 to 10 minutes,* or until edges brown slightly. While warm, carefully loosen rounds with a spatula and ease off onto dish towel. Cool.

Add frosting mix (dry mix) to whipping cream and vanilla in small mixer bowl. Chill thoroughly. Blend; beat until stiff. Fold in nuts. Fill layers (about 1 cup between each), spreading mixture evenly. Allow torte to mellow in refrigerator 5 hours or overnight.

To serve, sprinkle top with sifted confectioners' sugar. Garnish with bananas or other fresh fruits in season. Refrigerate. *14 to 16 servings.*

Sour Cream Torte: Follow recipe (above) except—substitute 1½ cups dairy sour cream for the whipping cream and vanilla. When preparing filling, sift dry frosting mix; then fold in sour cream and nuts. Fill layers, using ½ to ⅔ cup filling between each.

Dark Chocolate Torte: Follow recipe (above) except—use Betty Crocker Dark Chocolate Fudge Cake Mix and Betty Crocker Dark Chocolate Fudge Frosting Mix.

Betty Crocker Notes:

1. Place wet towel under cake pan to prevent pan from slipping while rolling dough.
2. Roll round almost to edge, but not past, to get attractive rounds. If dough droops slightly over edge of pan during baking, it may be trimmed with scissors.
3. If you have only two 9-inch round layer pans, roll pastry rounds two at a time and bake two at a time. (Cover remaining dough with plastic wrap.)
4. Loosen layers from pan immediately after removing from oven. Allow to set a minute or two; then slip off onto towel.
5. Place a little frosting on plate to keep bottom layer from slipping.

CRISP MERINGUE SHELLS

Pictured on page 127.

Heat oven to 275°. In small mixer bowl, blend ⅓ cup boiling water, 1 package Betty Crocker Fluffy White Frosting Mix (dry mix) and ⅓ cup sifted confectioners' sugar. Beat 3 to 5 minutes high speed on mixer, until mixture is thick and holds very stiff peaks. Scrape sides and bottom of bowl occasionally. Drop about ⅓ cup mixture for each meringue shell onto baking sheet covered with aluminum foil or brown paper. Shape centers with back of spoon. Bake *45 minutes*. Turn off oven; do not open door; leave meringues in for 45 minutes longer to dry out completely.

Fill with ice cream or your favorite filling. Top with fruit or one of the sauces on this page. *Makes 8 shells.*

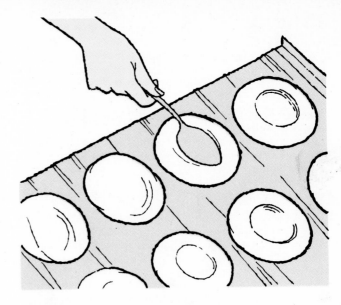

Betty Crocker Note: If meringues are slightly warm, allow them to remain on the brown paper 2 or 3 minutes more. Store meringues lightly covered with waxed paper.

Meringue Chantilly Dessert: Follow recipe (above) except—drop mixture by rounded teaspoonfuls onto prepared baking sheet.

Whip 1 cup whipping cream with 1½ cups confectioners' sugar and 1½ teaspoons vanilla until stiff. Place flat sides of two cooled meringues together with about 2 heaping tablespoonfuls of whipped cream mixture. Repeat with remaining meringues. Serve immediately or chill 1 hour. Pour frozen raspberries, partially thawed, over chilled meringues. *8 to 10 servings.*

Cherries Jubilee: Melt ¾ cup currant jelly in chafing dish over direct heat. Add 1 can (1 pound) pitted Bing cherries and 1 tablespoon grated orange peel. Heat slowly to simmering, stirring occasionally. Remove from heat.

For a glamorous touch, add ½ cup warmed brandy just before serving. Without stirring, light it with a match; spoon the flaming cherries over each serving. *8 to 10 servings.*

Strawberries Jubilee: Thaw and drain 1 package (16 ounces) frozen strawberries, reserving syrup. Blend 2 teaspoons cornstarch into syrup; cook over medium heat until thick and clear. Remove from heat; stir in strawberries. Pour sauce into chafing dish; serve warm.

Flame as directed for Cherries Jubilee (above) except—use only 2 to 3 tablespoons brandy.

Mincemeat-Wine Sauce: Thin 1 cup prepared mincemeat with ½ cup port wine. Heat and serve warm. *Makes 1½ cups.*

Vanilla, Lemon or Nutmeg Sauce:

1 cup sugar
2 tablespoons cornstarch
2 cups water
¼ cup butter or margarine
2 teaspoons vanilla or 2 tablespoons lemon juice with 2 tablespoons grated lemon peel or 2 teaspoons nutmeg

Mix sugar and cornstarch in saucepan. Gradually stir in water. Boil 1 minute, stirring constantly. Remove from heat. Stir in butter and flavoring. *Makes 2 cups.*

Cinnamon-Blueberry Sauce:

1 package (16 ounces) frozen blueberries (2 cups)
¼ cup water
¼ cup sugar
2 tablespoons lemon juice
2 teaspoons cornstarch
½ teaspoon cinnamon

Blend all ingredients in saucepan. Bring to boil; simmer 5 minutes, stirring occasionally. Remove from heat and serve warm. *Makes about 1⅓ cups.*

Amber Sauce:

1 cup granulated or brown sugar (packed)
½ cup light corn syrup
¼ cup butter or margarine
½ cup light cream

Mix all ingredients. Cook over *low* heat for 5 minutes. Remove from heat and serve warm. *Makes 2 cups.*

Any of these sauces may also be used:

Chocolate Sauce (page 55).
Golden Caramel Sauce (page 56).
Celestial Sauce (page 107).
Orange Sauce (page 106).

NEAPOLITAN ANGEL

Bake Betty Crocker Angel Food Cake Mix in ungreased tube pan, 10x4 inches, as directed on package. Cool; remove from pan.

Cut out 1 inch of cake from center to enlarge center hole. Fill with 1 quart softened chocolate ice cream. Wrap in aluminum foil or plastic wrap. Freeze until firm. Before serving, whip 1 cup whipping cream with ¼ cup confectioners' sugar until stiff. Tint light pink; frost sides and top of cake but do not cover ice cream.

Betty Crocker Note: Ice cream bought in a 1-quart round container will slip easily into enlarged center hole.

Confetti Ice Cream Angel: Follow recipe (above) except—use Betty Crocker Confetti Angel Food Cake Mix; fill cake with strawberry ice cream and leave whipping cream untinted.

Lemon-Lime Chiffon: Follow recipe (above) except—use Betty Crocker Lemon Chiffon Cake Mix; fill cake with lime sherbet and frost with whipped cream tinted yellow.

ICE CREAM SUNDAE CAKE

1 package Betty Crocker Devils Food Cake Mix
3 pints brick strawberry ice cream
1 package Betty Crocker Fluffy White Frosting Mix
½ cup Chocolate Sauce (page 55)
Chopped nuts

Bake cake in two round layer pans, 9x1½ inches, as directed on package. Cool.

Split cake to make 4 layers (see page 20). Working quickly, slice and spread 1 pint slightly softened ice cream between each layer, not quite to edge. Wrap sides of cake in double thickness of aluminum foil and freeze several hours or overnight.

Just before serving, prepare frosting mix as directed on package. Frost cake. Drizzle Chocolate Sauce from center down sides of cake. Sprinkle entire top lightly with chopped nuts. Refrigerate about ½ hour or serve immediately.

Delicious variations:
Our Yellow Cake Mix, chocolate ice cream, Chocolate Sauce (page 55).
Our Lemon Velvet Cake Mix, pistachio ice cream, Lemon Sauce (page 126).
Our Dark Chocolate Fudge Cake Mix, coffee ice cream, Chocolate Sauce (page 55).
Our Honey Spice Cake Mix, Butter Brickle ice cream, Golden Caramel Sauce (page 56).

GÂTEAU PARISIENNE

Pictured on page 5.

Prepare Betty Crocker Angel Food Cake Mix as directed on package except—add 1 teaspoon pumpkin pie spice during last ½ minute of mixing. Bake in ungreased tube pan, 10x4 inches, as directed. Cool. Remove from pan.

Whip 1½ cups whipping cream with ⅓ cup confectioners' sugar until stiff peaks form. Fold in ¼ cup dark crème de cacao. Frost cake. Decorate with Frosted Grapes (page 23). Refrigerate.

LEMON MERINGUE CHIFFON CAKE

Pictured at left.

Bake Betty Crocker Lemon Chiffon Cake Mix in ungreased tube pan, 10x4 inches, as directed on package. Cool. Remove from pan.

Heat oven to 400°. Split cake to make 3 layers (see page 20). Place on aluminum foil-covered baking sheet. Spread Lemon Filling (page 89) between layers, reserving a small amount to garnish the top. Frost sides and top with Betty Crocker Fluffy White Frosting Mix prepared as directed on package.

Bake 8 *to 10 minutes*, or until delicately browned. Thin the reserved filling with a little hot water and spoon over frosting, letting some run down the sides.

> *Betty Crocker Note:* For easy transfer of cake to serving plate, cut foil around bottom of cake; slip spatulas under foil and lift cake.

Lemon Velvet Meringue Cake: Bake Betty Crocker Lemon Velvet Cake Mix in two round layer pans, 9x1½ inches, as directed on package. Cool. Split cake to make 4 layers (see page 20). Fill cake with Lemon Filling (page 89). Frost with Betty Crocker Fluffy White Frosting Mix prepared as directed on package. Brown as directed above.

GRASSHOPPER PIE

Pictured at left.

1 package Betty Crocker Fluffy White Frosting Mix
¼ cup white crème de cacao
¼ cup crème de menthe
1½ cups whipping cream
2 teaspoons unflavored gelatin
¼ cup cold water
1 cup crushed chocolate wafers
3 tablespoons butter or margarine, melted

Chill frosting mix (dry mix), crème de cacao, crème de menthe and whipping cream 1 hour in small mixer bowl.

Soften gelatin in cold water; dissolve over hot water. Cool to room temperature.

Mix chocolate wafer crumbs and butter; press evenly and firmly into an 8-inch pie pan.

Beat chilled frosting mixture just until it starts to thicken. Gradually add gelatin. Beat until stiff. Mound mixture into pie crust. Freeze until firm, about 5 hours or overnight. Remove from freezer and serve immediately. If desired, garnish pie with 2 tablespoons crushed chocolate wafers sprinkled over the top.

Cherry Variation(Pictured at left): Follow recipe (above) except—use Betty Crocker Cherry Fluff Frosting Mix and substitute ½ cup cherry liqueur for the crème de cacao and crème de menthe.

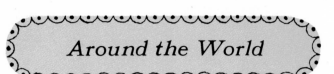

Around the World

CHOCOLATE FRENCH SILK CAKE

Bake Betty Crocker Devils Food Cake Mix in two round layer pans, 9x1½ inches, as directed on package. Cool.

Split cake to make 4 layers (see page 20). Fill and frost cake with French Silk Frosting (below). Press ¾ to 1 cup chopped walnuts onto sides of cake. Chill several hours before serving. Refrigerate leftover cake. *12 to 16 servings.*

French Silk Frosting: In small mixer bowl, combine Betty Crocker Chocolate Fudge Frosting Mix (dry mix), 1 cup soft butter or margarine, 1 egg and 2 teaspoons vanilla. Beat low speed on mixer until blended. Beat high speed until light and fluffy.

Betty Crocker Notes:
1. Use waxed paper strips around edge of cake while frosting and pressing nuts onto sides. Remove waxed paper before chilling cake.
2. Remove cake from refrigerator 10 to 15 minutes before serving. This will allow frosting to soften slightly.

Lemon French Silk Cake: Use Betty Crocker Lemon Velvet Cake Mix and Lemon Velvet Frosting Mix. Omit vanilla from frosting. Garnish with candy lemon slices.

Caramel French Silk Cake: Use Betty Crocker Yellow Cake Mix and Golden Caramel Frosting Mix. Garnish with chopped pecans; omit walnuts.

Pastel French Silk Cake: Use Betty Crocker White Cake Mix and Creamy White Frosting Mix. Substitute 1½ teaspoons vanilla, ¼ teaspoon almond extract and a few drops red, yellow or green food coloring for flavoring in the frosting. Garnish with flaked coconut; omit walnuts.

CARAWAY POUND CAKE

Heat oven to 350°. Grease and flour a tube pan, 10x4 inches, bundt pan or 2-quart anodized aluminum mold. Prepare Betty Crocker Yellow Cake Mix as directed on package except—use 2 tablespoons less water and add ⅓ cup caraway seeds to batter. Pour into prepared pan. Bake *50 to 55 minutes*, or until wooden pick inserted in center comes out clean. Cool 10 minutes; remove from pan. Sprinkle top with confectioners' sugar. *16 to 20 servings.*

EASY ENGLISH TRIFLE

Bake Betty Crocker Yellow Cake Mix* in an oblong pan, 13x9x2 inches, as directed on package. Cool.

Cook 1 package (about 3½ ounces) vanilla pudding and pie filling as directed on package except—use 2½ cups milk. Stir in 1 tablespoon sherry flavoring. Cool.

Cut cake in half. Cut one half of cake into ¾-inch strips. Arrange strips in bottom of loaf pan, 9x5x3 inches. Spread cake with apricot, strawberry or raspberry jam. Cover with pudding. Repeat layers. Chill 4 hours or until set. Garnish top with toasted slivered almonds. To serve, spoon into dessert dishes. *8 to 10 servings.*

Serve other half of cake as desired.

Other good mixes for this recipe include our Devils Food, Honey Spice, Lemon Velvet or Lemon Chiffon.

IRISH COFFEE TORTE

Prepare Betty Crocker Yellow Cake Mix as directed on package except—substitute cold double-strength coffee for water. Pour batter into two round layer pans, 9x1½ inches. Bake as directed on package. Cool.

Split cake to make 4 layers (see page 20). Sprinkle each layer with 1 tablespoon Irish whiskey.

Whip 1½ cups whipping cream with ⅓ cup confectioners' sugar until stiff. Spread between layers and on top of cake (leave sides unfrosted). Chill.

DANISH AEBLESKIVER

Rich little pancake balls add a foreign touch at a party brunch. In Denmark, they're baked in special cast iron pans and turned with steel knitting needles to brown.

Prepare batter for Kaffeeklatsch Pancakes (page 79). Place small amount of butter in each cup of Danish aebleskiver pan. Heat pan slightly; fill cups ⅔ full of batter. Cook until bubbly; turn carefully with metal skewers; finish baking on other side. Remove from pan; place on paper towels. Sprinkle confectioners' sugar over top. Serve with sweetened lingonberries or cranberries, if desired.

NORWEGIAN RAINBOW DESSERT (Blöte Kage)

Bake Betty Crocker Lemon Chiffon Cake Mix in ungreased tube pan, 10x4 inches, as directed on package. Cool. Remove from pan.

Split cake to make 4 layers (see page 20). Whip 3 cups whipping cream with 6 tablespoons confectioners' sugar until stiff. Reassemble cake with fillings (below). Cover top and sides with the remaining whipped cream (3 cups). Sprinkle with blanched and finely chopped green pistachio nuts. Chill 3 hours before serving. Arrange apricot halves, rounded side out, around base of cake. Add a few green leaves.

Pineapple Filling: Soften 2 teaspoons unflavored gelatin in 1 tablespoon pineapple juice. Dissolve over hot water. Stir into 1 cup drained crushed pineapple. Tint with few drops green food coloring. Chill. When partially set, fold in 1 cup of the whipped cream. Spread between first and second layers.

Apricot Filling: Soften 2 teaspoons unflavored gelatin in 1 tablespoon pineapple juice. Dissolve over hot water. Stir into 1 cup mashed cooked apricot. Chill. When partially set, fold in 1 cup of the whipped cream. Spread between second and third layers.

Raspberry Filling: Soften 2 teaspoons unflavored gelatin in 1 tablespoon pineapple juice. Dissolve over hot water. Stir into 1 cup thick raspberry jam. Chill. When partially set, fold in 1 cup of the whipped cream. Spread between third and fourth layers.

HAZELNUT TORTE

1 package Betty Crocker Yellow Cake Mix
1 cup finely chopped hazelnuts or filberts
1½ cups whipping cream
⅓ cup confectioners' sugar
1 package Betty Crocker Chocolate Fudge Frosting Mix

Prepare cake mix as directed on package except—fold nuts into batter. Pour batter into two greased and floured round layer pans, 8 or 9x1½ inches. Bake as directed. Cool.

Split cake to make 4 layers (see page 20). Whip cream with confectioners' sugar until stiff. Fill layers. Frost sides and top of cake with frosting mix prepared as directed on package.

FINNISH APPLE PIE

1 package Betty Crocker Yellow Cake Mix
1 egg, beaten
⅓ cup shortening
2 cans (1 pound each) applesauce (4 cups)
¼ cup cornstarch
1 tablespoon lemon juice
2 teaspoons cinnamon
1 teaspoon nutmeg
1 package Betty Crocker Fluffy White Frosting Mix
½ cup flaked coconut

Heat oven to 350°. Mix cake mix (dry mix), egg and shortening. Press into two greased 9-inch pie pans or one greased oblong pan, 13x9x2 inches. Bake *20 to 25 minutes.* Cool.

Mix applesauce, cornstarch, lemon juice, cinnamon and nutmeg in saucepan. Bring to boil. Cook until thickened and clear, 2 to 3 minutes. Pour over crust.

Heat oven to 500°. Prepare frosting mix as directed on package. Stir in coconut. Spread over applesauce mixture. Brown lightly *5 to 8 minutes.* Serve warm. *8 servings from each pie or 15 to 20 servings from oblong.*

ICELANDIC TERTA

Prepare Betty Crocker Yellow Cake Mix as directed on package except—if desired, add ½ teaspoon freshly ground cardamom seed to dry mix. Pour batter into two greased and floured round layer pans, 9x1½ inches. Bake as directed. Cool.

Split cake to make 4 layers (see page 20). Fill with Date-Fig Filling (below). Sprinkle top of cake with sifted confectioners' sugar.

Date-Fig Filling:
2 packages (6½ ounces each) dates, chopped
½ cup finely chopped figs
1 cup sugar
1½ cups water

Cook all ingredients together until thick. Cool.

Betty Crocker Note: Cardamom seed in the shell has a truer, better flavor than the already-ground variety. Therefore, shell your own and crush it.

MODERN MARZIPAN

Mix version of a famed old-world candy, flavored with almond, shaped and tinted like tiny fruits and vegetables. A work of art for cookie plate, candy dish or a Christmas box of goodies.

With fork, mix Betty Crocker Creamy White Frosting Mix (dry mix), ½ cup soft butter or margarine and ½ teaspoon almond extract or vanilla. Work with hands to form a ball. Knead 20 to 30 times on board lightly dusted with confectioners' sugar. Divide fondant into 4 portions; tint each as indicated on page. Mix food coloring into fondant, a drop at a time; knead for thorough distribution. Allow candies to set a short time before painting blush on them. Use wooden pick with small swab of cotton on end for painting blush on rounded sides of fruit. For most fruits, use one teaspoonful of fondant. *Makes 4 to 5 dozen.*

> *Betty Crocker Note:* Work with each portion of fondant individually so it will not dry out. Candies store nicely when wrapped carefully in plastic wrap. They freeze beautifully, too.

Yellow Fondant: Add 2 to 3 drops yellow food coloring.
Bananas—Roll fondant into banana shape, tapering ends. Flatten top slightly to show planes on fruit and bend slightly for curve. Mix 3 drops red food coloring, 2 drops yellow food coloring, 1 drop blue food coloring and ½ teaspoon water; use to paint on characteristic markings.

Pears—Roll fondant into a ball, then into cone shape. Bend top slightly. Insert piece of stick cinnamon or colored wooden pick for stem. For red blush, mix ⅛ teaspoon red food coloring with 1 teaspoon water and paint rounded sides.

Peaches—Roll fondant into a ball. Make crease down one side with wooden pick. Stick a whole clove in blossom end. For red blush, mix ⅛ teaspoon red food coloring with 1 teaspoon water.

Red Fondant: Add 3 to 5 drops red food coloring.
Apples—Roll fondant into a ball. Stick small piece of stick cinnamon or colored wooden pick in stem top and whole clove in blossom end. For red blush, mix ⅛ teaspoon red food coloring with 1 teaspoon water.

Strawberries—Roll fondant into a ball; form a heart shape. Roll in red decorators' sugar. Press sugar into candy by rolling between palms of hands. For texture, punch candy with blunt end of wooden pick. Place small piece of green colored wooden pick or green dough into top for stem.

Plums—Roll fondant into a ball. Make crease down one side with wooden pick. Stick a whole clove in blossom end. For blush, mix ⅛ teaspoon blue food coloring and 2 drops red food coloring with 1 teaspoon water.

Orange Fondant: Add 3 drops red food coloring and 2 drops yellow food coloring.
Oranges—Roll fondant into a ball. Roll in orange decorators' sugar. Press sugar into candy by rolling between palms of hands. Insert a whole clove in blossom end.

Apricots—Roll fondant into a ball. Make crease down one side with wooden pick. Stick a whole clove in blossom end. For red blush, mix ⅛ teaspoon red food coloring with 1 teaspoon water.

Pumpkins—Roll fondant into a ball. Make several creases down sides with wooden pick to resemble pumpkin grooves. Press top a little to give flat look. Place small pieces of green colored wooden pick or green dough into top for stem.

Green Fondant: Add 4 to 5 drops green food coloring.
Green apples—Roll fondant into a ball. Press small piece of stick cinnamon or colored wooden pick in stem top and whole clove in blossom end. For red blush, mix ⅛ teaspoon red food coloring with 1 teaspoon water.

VIENNESE WALNUT TORTE

Pictured above.

1 package Betty Crocker Devils Food Cake Mix
2 egg whites
1 cup brown sugar (packed)
2 teaspoons lemon juice
½ cup chopped walnuts
1 teaspoon granulated sugar
½ teaspoon cinnamon
1 package (about 3½ ounces) vanilla pudding and pie filling

Bake cake in two square pans, 8x8x2 inches, or two round layer pans, 9x1½ inches, as directed on package. Cool. Remove from pans and place one layer upside down on baking sheet and one layer top side up on baking sheet.

Heat oven to 400°. Beat egg whites until frothy. Gradually beat in brown sugar and lemon juice. Continue beating until stiff. Spread meringue over top of each layer on baking sheet. Mix nuts, granulated sugar and cinnamon; sprinkle over meringue. Bake *6 to 8 minutes*, or until delicately browned. Cool.

Cook pudding as directed on package. Cool. Carefully split cake to make 4 layers (see page 20). Put layers together with pudding. (Keep one meringue-topped layer for top; do not spread with pudding.) Chill. *14 to 16 servings.*

Delightful variations include:

Betty Crocker Yellow Cake Mix with chocolate pudding and pie filling.
Betty Crocker White Cake Mix with lemon pudding and pie filling.
Betty Crocker Honey Spice Cake Mix with butterscotch or caramel pudding and pie filling.

EASY SACHER TORTE

Very much like the classic Viennese dessert. Moist and fudgy rich, spread with apricot jam and an elegant chocolate glaze.

1 package (about 4 ounces) chocolate pudding and pie filling
1 package Betty Crocker Devils Food Cake Mix
½ to ¾ cup apricot jam
2 tablespoons butter or margarine
¼ cup water
1 package Betty Crocker Chocolate Fudge Frosting Mix

Heat oven to 350°. Grease and flour a 9-inch spring-form pan. Cook pudding as directed on package. Stir cake mix (dry mix) into hot pudding. Pour into prepared pan. Bake *45 to 50 minutes.* Remove from pan. Cool.

Simmer apricot jam over low heat, stirring constantly, about 5 minutes. Spread over top and sides of cake.

Melt butter with water in top of double boiler. Stir in frosting mix (dry mix) until smooth. Heat over rapidly boiling water about 5 minutes, stirring occasionally. Pour and spread over apricot glaze on top and sides of cake. Work quickly, for this will set up to a smooth firm glaze.

Betty Crocker Note: If a 9-inch springform pan is not available, shape a collar of double thickness aluminum foil and place in 9-inch round layer pan.

PEACH KUCHEN

½ cup soft butter or margarine
1 package Betty Crocker Yellow Cake Mix
½ cup flaked coconut
1 can (1 pound 13 ounces) cling peach slices, well drained
½ cup sugar
1 teaspoon cinnamon
1 cup dairy sour cream
2 egg yolks or 1 egg

Heat oven to 350°. Cut butter into cake mix (dry mix) until mixture resembles coarse cornmeal. Mix in coconut. Lightly press an even layer of mixture over bottom and halfway up sides of ungreased oblong pan, 13x9x2 inches. Bake *10 minutes.*

Remove from oven and arrange peach slices over pastry. Sprinkle peaches with mixture of sugar and cinnamon. Mix sour cream and egg yolks; pour over peaches. Return to oven and bake *30 minutes longer.* (Do not overbake.) Serve warm. *12 to 15 servings.*

CALCUTTA CURRY CAKE

Pictured at right.

Prepare Betty Crocker Yellow Cake Mix as directed on package except—add 1 teaspoon curry powder to dry mix before adding liquid. Pour batter into two greased and floured round layer pans, 9x1½ inches. Bake as directed. Cool.

Split cake to make 4 layers (see page 20). Fill and frost cake with Fluffy Topping (below), using ½ cup between each layer and the remaining topping on sides and top. Refrigerate. Serve with 3 or more side dishes of any of the following:

    Slivered toasted almonds
    Salted peanuts
    Toasted coconut
    Raisins
    Mandarin orange segments
    Pineapple tidbits
    Chopped kumquats

Fluffy Topping: Add 1 package Betty Crocker Fluffy White Frosting Mix (dry mix) to 2 cups whipping cream in small mixer bowl. Chill 1 hour. Blend; beat until stiff.

HAWAIIAN CHIFFON CAKE

Bake Betty Crocker Lemon Chiffon Cake Mix in ungreased tube pan, 10x4 inches, as directed on package. Cool. Remove from pan.

Split cake to make 3 layers (see page 20). Whip 3½ cups whipping cream with 1 cup confectioners' sugar until it forms soft peaks. Reassemble cake with fillings (below). Frost cake with remaining whipped cream, to which 2 teaspoons rum flavoring has been added. Cover entire cake with 1½ cups crushed peanut brittle (about ½ pound). Chill or freeze cake before serving. If frozen, thaw in refrigerator 2 to 3 hours before serving.

Pineapple Filling: To 2 cups whipped cream, add a few drops green food coloring, 1½ teaspoons vanilla and 1 can (8¾ ounces) crushed pineapple, well drained. Spread between first and second layers of cake.

Coconut Filling: To 2 cups whipped cream, add a few drops red food coloring, 1½ teaspoons vanilla and ½ cup flaked coconut. Spread between second and third layers of cake.

PIZZA FRUIT PLATTER

Pictured on cover.

1 package Betty Crocker Yellow Cake Mix
¼ cup water
2 eggs
¼ cup butter or margarine
¼ cup brown sugar (packed)
½ cup chopped nuts
1 envelope (2 ounces) dessert topping mix
1 pint strawberries, halved (reserve 7 whole strawberries for center)
1 can (1 pound 4½ ounces) pineapple spears
2 dozen seedless green grapes
1 banana, peeled and sliced
Apricot Glaze (below)

Heat oven to 350°. Line bottom of 12-inch round pizza pan with aluminum foil. Grease and flour square pan, 9x9x2 inches. Combine half the cake mix (dry mix), the water, eggs, butter and brown sugar in mixing bowl; mix thoroughly. Blend in remaining cake mix. Fold in nuts. Divide batter evenly between prepared pans. Bake 12-inch cake *15 to 20 minutes* and 9-inch cake *20 to 25 minutes*. Cool and remove round cake from pan.

Prepare topping mix as directed on package and spread over round cake. Arrange fruits in circular pattern over topping. Start with halved strawberries on outer edge, then arrange pineapple spears, grapes, banana slices and end with reserved whole strawberries in center. Brush with Apricot Glaze. Refrigerate until serving time. Cut into pie-shaped wedges to serve. (The square cake may be frosted and cut into bars for future use.) *12 servings.*

Apricot Glaze: Heat ½ cup apricot preserves with 2 tablespoons water until preserves are melted. Remove from heat. Strain and cool.

MANDARIN TOWER CAKE

Inspired by the decorative and popular Oriental dessert of Chinese fruits served in a pyramid of crushed ice.

Prepare Betty Crocker White Cake Mix as directed on package except—add 1 teaspoon almond extract. Pour batter into one round layer pan, 8x1½ inches, and one round layer pan, 9x1½ inches. (Batter should be the same depth in both pans—check level with a wooden pick.) Bake as directed on package. Cool.

From 9-inch layer cut a circle about 5½ inches in diameter (1¼ inches in from sides of cake); cut another circle about 1½ inches in diameter (2 inches in from edge of first circle). From 8-inch layer cut a circle about 3½ inches in diameter (2 inches in from sides of cake).

Whip 2 cups whipping cream with ½ cup confectioners' sugar and 1 teaspoon almond extract. Spread a thin coating of whipped cream on sides and tops of circles, stacking circles in decreasing size. Frost with whipped cream, making cake resemble a smooth-sided cone.

Place date slivers, apricots, pineapple tidbits, almonds, lichee nuts and mandarin orange segments in spiral design around cake, working from bottom to top (see sketch). Make a Kumquat Flower for top of cake (page 23).

BRASILIA MOCHA CAKE

Prepare Betty Crocker Devils Food Cake Mix as directed on package except—add ¼ cup regular-grind coffee before mixing. Fold 1 cup chopped toasted almonds into prepared batter. Pour batter into two greased and floured round layer pans, 9x1½ inches. Bake as directed on package. Cool.

Prepare Betty Crocker Creamy White Frosting Mix as directed on package except—add 1½ teaspoons instant coffee before mixing. Fill layers and frost top of cake. Decorate with candied coffee beans or Chocolate Curls (page 23) arranged in an attractive design on top of cake.

JAMAICAN RUM PIE

1 package Betty Crocker Fluffy White Frosting Mix
¼ cup light rum
1½ cups whipping cream
2 teaspoons unflavored gelatin
¼ cup cold water
1 cup graham cracker crumbs
2 tablespoons sugar
¼ cup butter or margarine, melted

Chill frosting mix (dry mix), rum and whipping cream 1 hour in small mixer bowl.

Soften gelatin in cold water; dissolve over hot water. Cool to room temperature.

Heat oven to 350°. Mix crumbs, sugar and melted butter; press mixture firmly and evenly against bottom and sides of an 8-inch pie pan. Bake *10 minutes.* Cool.

Beat chilled frosting mixture just until it starts to thicken. Gradually add gelatin. Beat until stiff. Mound into graham cracker crust. Freeze until firm, about 5 hours or overnight. Remove from freezer and serve immediately.

RAVINI (Greek Syrup Cake)

Prepare Betty Crocker Yellow Cake Mix as directed on package except—add 1 teaspoon lemon extract to the batter. Pour batter into greased and floured oblong pan, 13x9x2 inches. Bake as directed. Cool about 5 minutes; cut into squares.

While cake is baking, dissolve 1 cup sugar in 1 cup water. Add 2 cinnamon sticks. Bring mixture to boiling and allow to boil about 15 minutes. Cool. Remove cinnamon sticks from syrup and pour syrup over cake. Cool. Serve plain or sprinkle with confectioners' sugar. *15 servings.*

RIO-REVEL CAKE

1 package Betty Crocker Angel Food Cake Mix
1 package (3¾ ounces) chocolate-flavored whipped dessert mix
¼ cup light rum
1½ cups whipping cream
⅓ cup confectioners' sugar

Bake cake in ungreased tube pan, 10x4 inches, as directed on package. Cool. Remove from pan.

Split cake to make 3 layers (see page 20). Prepare whipped dessert mix as directed on package except—substitute rum for ¼ cup of the chilled water. Spread 2 cake layers with chocolate mixture. Refrigerate layers separately until chocolate mixture is firm, about 1 hour. Reassemble cake.

Whip cream with confectioners' sugar until stiff; frost sides and top of cake. Decorate top of cake with Allegretti Design (page 22) and Brazil Nut Curls (page 23). Chill until serving time.

BAVARIAN POPPY SEED CAKE

Measure amount of water called for on Betty Crocker White Cake Mix package; soak ½ cup rinsed poppy seeds in this water for 1 hour.

Prepare cake mix as directed on package except—use poppy seed-water mixture instead of water. Pour batter into two greased and floured round layer pans, 8 or 9x1½ inches. Bake as directed on package. Cool.

Make Custard Cream Filling (below) and spread between layers. Frost sides and top with Betty Crocker Fluffy White Frosting Mix prepared as directed on package. (Refrigerate cake if not used immediately.)

Custard Cream Filling:

½ cup sugar
¼ cup Gold Medal Flour (regular or Wondra)
¼ teaspoon salt
1¼ cups milk
1 egg or 2 egg yolks, slightly beaten
1½ tablespoons butter or margarine
1 teaspoon vanilla

Mix sugar, flour and salt in saucepan. Stir in milk. Cook over low heat, stirring until mixture boils. Boil 1 minute. Remove from heat. Slowly stir at least half of hot mixture into egg. Blend into remaining hot mixture in saucepan. Bring to boil. Remove from heat. Stir in butter and vanilla. Chill thoroughly.

CONTINENTAL APRICOT-ALMOND TORTE

Prepare Betty Crocker White Cake Mix as directed on package except—stir in 1 teaspoon almond extract. Pour batter into two greased and floured round layer pans, 8 or 9x1½ inches. Sprinkle ½ cup thinly sliced un-blanched almonds over batter in one pan. Press gently into batter. Bake both layers as directed on package. Cool.

Split cake to make 4 layers (see page 20). Use layer with almonds as top layer. Spread ⅓ to ½ cup apricot jam between first and second layers. Spread Betty Crocker Vanilla Satin ready-to-spread Frosting between second and third layers. Spread ⅓ to ½ cup apricot jam between third and fourth layers. Frost sides with remaining frosting. Leave top unfrosted.

Betty Crocker Note: For an authentic European touch, sprinkle split layers with sherry before spreading with jam.

Other Betty Crocker Cake Mixes suitable for this recipe:

German Chocolate
Yellow
Dark Chocolate Fudge

Work-of-Art

PICASSO HARLEQUIN CAKE

Pictured on cover.

Bake Betty Crocker Devils Food Cake Mix in two square pans, 8x8x2 inches, as directed on package for 9-inch layers. Cool.

Split cake to make 4 layers (see page 20). Fill with Harlequin Fillings (below). Frost top of cake with half can of Betty Crocker Chocolate Satin ready-to-spread Frosting. On top of cake, outline a harlequin design of 6 diamonds; fill each with a different color decorators' sugar or chopped nuts.

Harlequin Fillings: Whip 1½ cups whipping cream with ⅓ cup confectioners' sugar until it forms soft peaks. (Do not whip stiff.) Divide into 3 parts. Tint one part green and fold in ¼ cup chopped pistachio nuts or toasted almonds. Spread between first and second layers. Tint one part pink and fold in ¼ cup crushed peppermint candy or ¼ teaspoon peppermint extract. Spread between second and third layers. Tint remaining part yellow and fold in ½ to 1 teaspoon rum flavoring. Spread between third and fourth layers.

VAN GOGH SUNFLOWER CAKE

Bake Betty Crocker Yellow Cake Mix in two round layer pans, 9x1½ inches, as directed on package. Cool. Prepare Betty Crocker Lemon Velvet Frosting Mix as directed on package. Fill and frost cake.

On top of cake, outline a large sunflower with 8 to 10 big petals. Make grooves in each petal with two strokes of spatula, bringing point of petal to edge of cake. With a small brush and yellow food coloring, "paint" shading in each petal. Decorate center of flower with chopped pistachio nuts.

MADAME BUTTERFLY CAKE

Bake any flavor Betty Crocker Layer Cake Mix in two round layer pans, 8 or 9x1½ inches, as directed on package. Cool.

Prepare Betty Crocker Fluffy White Frosting Mix as directed on package. Tint orange, using red and yellow food coloring. Fill layers. Cut cake in half. Place rounded sides back to back. Frost sides and top of cake. Coat with shredded coconut. With melted chocolate, outline butterfly on top of cake. Use candles for antennae.

Betty Crocker Note: For melted chocolate, soften 1 envelope (1 ounce) premelted chocolate in hot water. Snip a tiny corner to make outlines.

FRUIT GLAZE CÉZANNE

Pictured above.

Bake Betty Crocker Yellow Cake Mix in two round layer pans, 8 or 9x1½ inches, as directed on package. Cool.

For glaze, thaw and drain 1 package (12 ounces) frozen sliced peaches, reserving syrup. Mix syrup with 2 teaspoons cornstarch and cook over medium heat, stirring constantly, until mixture comes to a boil and is thickened and clear, about 1 minute. Cool.

Arrange half of drained peach slices and other fruits, such as grape or cherry halves, banana slices, pieces of pineapple, in an attractive design on top of one cake layer. Brush glaze on top of fruit with small brush, or spoon over fruit carefully (add a few drops water if glaze is too thick).

Whip 1½ cups whipping cream with ⅓ cup confectioners' sugar until stiff. Chop remainder of peach slices coarsely and fold into 1 cup of the whipped cream. Use to fill layers; place glazed fruit layer on top. Frost sides of cake with remaining whipped cream. Chill.

Betty Crocker Note: To serve, slice cake with a very sharp thin knife.

SUGAR PLUM FAIRY CAKE

⅔ cup dairy sour cream
1 package Betty Crocker Creamy White Frosting Mix
1 package Betty Crocker White Cake Mix
¼ cup soft butter
Sugar Plums (below)

Add sour cream to frosting mix (dry mix) in small mixer bowl; chill.

Bake cake in two round layer pans, 8 or 9x1½ inches, as directed on package. Cool.

Blend butter into sour cream and frosting mix; beat 1 minute low speed on mixer. *Do not overbeat.* Fill and frost cake. Garnish top and sides with several clusters (4 or 5) Sugar Plums (cut Plums in half for side); arrange artificial holly leaves around Sugar Plums. Chill.

Sugar Plums:
1 package Betty Crocker Creamy White Frosting Mix
½ cup soft butter or margarine
½ teaspoon almond extract
Few drops each red and blue food coloring
Cube sugar, crushed

Combine frosting mix (dry mix), butter and almond extract with fork. Work with hands to form a ball. Place a few drops food coloring inside ball. Knead 20 to 30 times on board lightly dusted with confectioners' sugar. Roll into 1-inch balls. Roll these in crushed cube sugar. Refrigerate until ready to use.

TOP

SWAN LAKE CREAM PUFFS

1 cup water
½ cup butter
1 cup Gold Medal Flour (regular or Wondra)
4 eggs
Strawberry Chantilly Fluff Topping (page 94)

Heat oven to 400°. Heat water and butter to a rolling boil in saucepan. Stir in flour. Stir vigorously over low heat until mixture forms a ball (about 1 minute). Remove from heat. Beat in eggs thoroughly, one at a time. Continue beating until smooth. Pipe about ½ cup of dough through a pastry tube into a neck and head, 2½ inches high (see diagram); repeat to make 12. Bake *20 minutes.*

Drop remaining dough from spoon onto ungreased baking sheet. Make 12 mounds, 3 inches apart. Bake *40 to 45 minutes,* or until puffed, golden brown and dry. Allow to cool slowly, away from drafts. Cut off tops with sharp knife. Scoop out soft dough. Fill with Strawberry Chantilly Fluff Topping.

Insert a neck and head in each swan, cutting a hole if necessary. Cut each top in half and insert for lifted wings. Sprinkle with confectioners' sugar. Serve immediately. *Makes 12 "swans."*

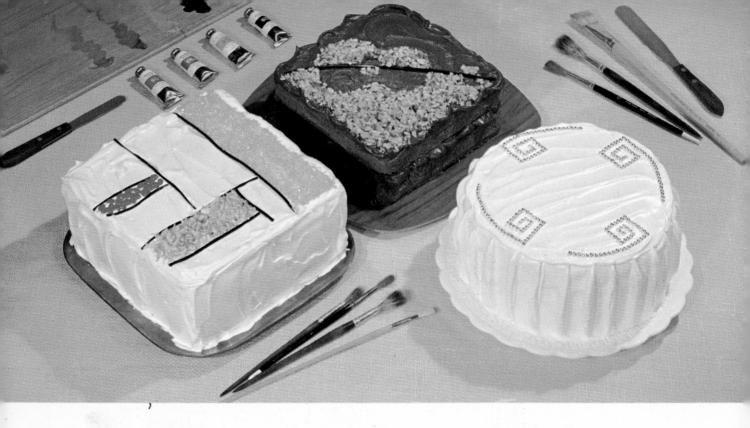

BRAQUE GUITAR CAKE

Combine ⅔ cup dairy sour cream and Betty Crocker Dark Chocolate Fudge Frosting Mix (dry mix) in small mixer bowl. Chill.

Bake Betty Crocker Dark Chocolate Fudge Cake Mix in two square pans, 8x8x2 inches or 9x9x2 inches, as directed on package for 9-inch round layers. Cool.

Add ¼ cup soft butter to chilled frosting mixture. Blend; beat 1 minute low speed on mixer. *Do not overbeat.* Fill layers and frost top of cake, leaving sides unfrosted.

Place 9-inch piece of shoestring licorice diagonally across top of cake. Outline guitar on one side; fill in with chopped walnuts. Refrigerate.

Chocolate Gourmet's Delight Cake: Follow recipe (above) except—split cake to make 4 layers (see page 20). Fill and frost with Brown Satin Frosting: sift 1 package Betty Crocker Chocolate Fudge Frosting Mix. Fold in 1½ cups dairy sour cream.

GREEK KEY CAKE

Prepare Betty Crocker White Cake Mix as directed on package except—stir 1 teaspoon almond extract into batter. Pour batter into two greased and floured round layer pans, 8 or 9x1½ inches. Bake as directed. Cool.

Split cake to make 4 layers (see page 20). Fill layers with Lemon Filling (page 89). Frost cake with Betty Crocker Fluffy White Frosting Mix prepared as directed on package. Spread frosting smoothly on sides and top.

For Greek column effect, make ridges around side of frosted cake by drawing tip of ¾-inch spatula through frosting from base of cake to top. With about 20 gold or silver dragées for each, form 4 Greek key shapes on top of cake, keeping dragées close together and backs of keys on edge of cake.

MONDRIAN CAKE

Heat oven to 350°. Prepare Betty Crocker White Cake Mix as directed on package except—add 1 or 2 drops anise oil or 1 tablespoon crushed anise seed to batter. Pour batter into two greased and floured square pans, 9x9x2 inches. Bake *25 to 30 minutes.* Remove from pans. Cool.

Prepare Betty Crocker Fluffy White Frosting Mix as directed on package. Fill and frost, squaring edges of cake as much as possible. Make a Mondrian design on top of cake, using pieces of black shoestring licorice as dividers and filling spaces with red cinnamon candies, yellow decorators' sugar and coconut tinted blue (see page 19).